Website Law

Website Law

The Legal Guide for Website Owners and Bloggers

by Tom James, J.D.

Echion Books ❖ Plymouth, Minn.

Echion, LLC
P.O. Box 46162
Plymouth, MN 55446

www.EchionBooks.com

First printing.

Published in Plymouth, Minnesota
Printed in the United States of America

ISBN-13: 978-1-946397-00-3
Library of Congress Control Number: 2016919938

10 9 8 7 6 5 4 3 2 1

NOTE TO READER

This book grew out of my work with people with a presence on the Web, people wanting to establish one, and people facing serious legal problems as a result of having one. Most have been ordinary people with real jobs who never dreamed they might one day receive a cease-and-desist letter or find themselves facing copyright infringement settlement demands in the 4- to 6-digit range. Nowadays, auto mechanics, store clerks, teachers, college students, retirees – even children -- are grappling with intellectual property issues. Not that long ago, these kinds of issues were rarely a topic of discussion outside of Beverly Hills and Madison Avenue. Today you can find people talking about them nearly everywhere you go.

The new millennium has ushered in a tidal wave of Internet-related litigation of unprecedented proportion. And much of it ultimately can be traced to the popular misconceptions that people have about whether and how laws apply to online activity. I've found that very few people who operate a website or blog deliberately set out to do illegal things. To the contrary, the vast majority of the people I've come across would gladly have complied with the law if they only had a better understanding of what it requires. Hence this book.

The book is organized into three parts. Part 1 begins with an explanation of what the basic rules of copyright are. It then identifies and explains the kinds of legal issues (copyright and others) that can arise with respect to each kind of material a website owner or blogger might use – text; drawings; photographs, music/audio; video; computer programs; trademarks; information. Part 2 identifies and describes the contours of fair use, the public domain, and other potential copyright defenses. Part 3 describes steps you can take to acquire a right -- or to remove doubt about your right -- to publish something you've either found on another website or had created for you by a web designer or other content provider.

"Key Points" are listed at the end of each chapter. These are only intended to make the information presented in a chapter easier to digest. You should not rely exclusively on them. If you do, you may overlook important exceptions, qualifications and clarifications.

The book has been written for readers of average intelligence and education. An advanced degree in law is neither assumed nor required.

The information provided applies to both commercial and noncommercial websites. Commercial websites, however, are required to comply with an additional array of regulations that cannot be adequately covered in a volume of this size. Owners of commercial sites should use one or more of several available treatises on e-commerce as a companion to this one.

This book provides general information and commentary about the law, not legal advice. While I am an attorney, I am not your attorney. Neither your acquisition of this book nor your reading of it creates an attorney-client relationship between us. You should hire a licensed attorney if you need legal advice regarding your website or blog.

Laws are always changing, especially those that relate to the Internet. Consequently, no assurance can be made that the information in this book will still be current by the time you acquire it. It is a good idea to keep informed about new developments in this area of the law. If you have a question or need specific legal advice about your website or blog, you should consult an attorney.

The liabilities, defenses and immunities discussed in this book relate to U.S. law. The laws of other countries are different. Website hosts, owners, and bloggers should be careful about traveling to other countries. Before entering a country, you should review the Internet content regulations of that country very carefully, with a view to determining whether you may have transmitted prohibited content into it via your website or blog.

A reference to the laws of a particular country does not imply anything about the laws of other countries. By the same token, the omission of a reference to a difference between U.S. and foreign laws should not be taken to mean that U.S. and foreign laws on a particular subject are identical, or even similar.

All of the examples in this book are hypothetical. Any similarity to any person, whether living or dead, or to any past, present or future legal entity, is purely coincidental.

This book employs both masculine and feminine pronouns. In all events, and unless the context clearly indicates otherwise, the masculine includes the feminine; the feminine includes the masculine; and the use of either pronoun includes transsexuals, bisexuals, asexuals, and every other variant that has been or may in the future be used in the taxonomy of human beings.

CONTENTS

Appendices 339

PART ONE

Limitations on Content

INTRODUCTION

In countless ways the Internet is radically enhancing our access to information and empowering us to share ideas and connect with the entire world. Speech thrives online freed of limitations inherent in traditional print or broadcast media that are created by corporate gatekeepers. Preserving the Internet's open architecture is critical to sustaining free speech.[1]

The Internet is infused with a spirit of freedom. The fight for Net neutrality -- the idea that the Internet should be available for anyone to use, free from efforts to control it – reflects that spirit. The right to freedom of speech is enshrined in the First Amendment of the American constitution. The United States Supreme Court has declared it to be such a fundamental right that it is protected by both the First and the Fourteenth Amendments.

It is not an absolute right, however. The same constitution that protects it also empowers Congress to pass laws protecting copyrights and to regulate interstate commerce. In addition, the Supreme Court has created a few exceptions of its own.

The Court has interpreted the First Amendment as establishing an implied hierarchy of categories of speech, with some categories receiving lower levels of protection than others. Political speech receives a very high amount of constitutional protection. Obscenity receives none at all. Other kinds of speech receive a level of protection somewhere between these two extremes. Commercial speech is an example. It receives some constitutional protection, but the Court has held that federal and state governments have much greater room to regulate in this area than they have to regulate political or religious speech.

Further complicating matters is the fact that the Constitution only imposes limits on governmental power. Its prohibitions against infringement

---

[1]Electronic Frontier Foundation, "Free Speech," https://www.eff.org/issues/free-speech (retrieved on October 6, 2016.)

on freedom of speech apply only to state and federal governmental actions, not to the actions of private individuals or businesses. Thus, for example, web hosts and social media networks, in the absence of any agreement otherwise, may freely censor the speech of those who use their services.

The Internet is not quite the Wild Frontier of free expression we imagine it to be. There are many restrictions, emanating from many different sources, on what may be published online. Failing to recognize them puts website owners and bloggers at serious risk of being sued, or worse, going to jail. Copyright infringement filings in federal court, for example, have skyrocketed since the advent of the Internet. Untold numbers of people – estimated to be in the thousands – have received cease-and-desist letters or have been sued for large sums of money for publishing things to their websites or blogs. Sadly, many of these people honestly believed their activities were protected by the First Amendment, or they erroneously believed the material was in the public domain or that their publication of it was fair use.

Bloggers and website owners are increasingly coming under attack for trademark infringement or dilution, as well. And defamation and invasion of privacy lawsuits also are on the rise.

Does this mean you should abandon all hope and leave the Internet to those who are better positioned to fight legal battles than you are? Absolutely not. It just means you need to know what your rights and liabilities as an online publisher are. The Digital Millennium Copyright Act, the Communications Decency Act, compulsory and statutory licenses, fair use, the public domain, and other laws and judicially-created defenses offer some strong protections for those website owners and bloggers who know what they are and how to use them. Each is subject to exceptions, qualifications and conditions, however. It is important to know what these are, too.

Will the increasingly complex matrix of laws regulating online publishing ultimately destroy freedom speech? The answer, as with many things, is maybe, but it doesn't have to. There are many things that legislators, regulators and judges could do to better protect and promote speech rights. Several organizations are working hard to get them to do those things. In the meantime, knowledge of the currently applicable laws is your best strategy for reducing legal risks while still getting your message across.

CHAPTER 1

Copyright basics

The Internet is probably the greatest innovation for the exchange of information and ideas there has ever been. Anyone with an Internet connection has quick and easy access to literally millions of books, stories, articles, photographs, drawings, software programs, music and video clips, most of which are very easy to download or copy and paste. This is a real boon for science, education and the arts. Unfortunately, it is also a great setup for copyright infringement. In fact, it would be difficult to imagine a better one.

Over 300 million unique Internet users seek or access infringing content each month. So much infringing content has been uploaded to the Internet that some businesses actually generate significant revenue streams simply by issuing and settling claims of online copyright infringement against website owners and bloggers. And copyright litigation has skyrocketed. Infringement filings in federal court tripled between 2010 and 2015 alone.

If you are a website owner or blogger, you need to have at least a basic understanding of copyright law. Otherwise, you may find yourself facing threats of costly copyright litigation if you or a visitor to your site posts infringing content, even if you mistakenly believed the material was in the public domain or that having no profit motive made it "fair use."

SCOPE OF PROTECTION

The federal Copyright Act gives the owner of the copyright in a created work the exclusive right to reproduce, distribute, publicly display, publicly perform, and make derivative works based on the work. (Ownership of the copyright originally belongs to the author, but any or all of these rights may be transferred to others. In the case of a work made for hire, the employer is treated as the author.)

Copyright protection exists for any kind of work of authorship that is fixed in a tangible medium of expression. This can include nonfiction as well as fiction and poetry; plays, screenplays, and other dramatic works; drawings; paintings; graphic art; photographs; architectural designs; music; sound recordings; motion pictures; audiovisual works; computer programs; pantomimes; and choreography.

Computer files that are stored on a server or a digital storage device (such as a computer) are fixed in a tangible medium. Therefore, website content and email messages are protected by copyright. Copyright law affords the same basic protections to material appearing on a website page, an online blog, or in an email message as it gives to materials that are fixed in print.

The purpose of a work, or its intended use, is not relevant. Nor are artistic merit and aesthetic value.

Copyright protection exists for both commercial and noncommercial works. Business logos, although generally known to be protected by trademark law, may also be protected by copyright law in some cases.

One popular myth that never seems to die is that anything the public can view online is "in the public domain" and therefore may be freely copied. Sometimes this is qualified by the assertion that anything you can download for free from the Internet is in the public domain. Neither statement is true. Generally, you may not copy content from another web page and paste it to your own without permission, even if it's a free site and even if you came across it as the result of a Google search. The author of content appearing on a web page may have a protected copyright interest in what he creates irrespective of the fact that he has chosen to make it available on his website. The fact that an author has chosen to make his work available for free on one website does not mean that he has consented to making it available on others.

Another popular myth is that the act of posting something to the Internet creates an "implied license" for anyone who finds it to freely copy it. Publishing a work on the Internet does not operate as a wavier of copyright protection. Again, the fact that an author has chosen to make his creation available for viewing on one website does not mean that he has chosen to make it available on others.

The same is true of email messages. Many people seem to think that sending a person a letter or an email message amounts to an "implied gift" of the contents of the letter or email message. This is not true. The contents of a letter or an email message are protected by copyright law to the same extent as any other expressive work is. Just as a novelist does not part with his copyright when he sends his manuscript to a critic for review, so the writer of an email message does not part with his copyright in the message when he sends it to someone.

It also is not true that material may be freely copied if there is no copyright notice on it. At one time, publishing something without a copyright notice could cause the author to lose his copyright protection, but that is no longer the law. Works published on or after March 1, 1989 are protected by copyright whether copyright notices appear on them or not.

Affixing the words, "All rights reserved" is not necessary to protect the copyright in a work. Copyright protection is not lost as a result of failing to include that statement. Including these words on your website or blog might possibly be useful in terms of bolstering a denial of an allegation of a grant of a license to use, but failing to include the notice neither creates a license nor causes copyright protection to be lost.

Registration is not essential to the existence of a copyright, either. A copyright may exist even if it is not registered with the Copyright Office. A copyright automatically comes into existence when an original work is first fixed in a tangible medium of expression, even if no application for registration is ever filed. Of course, there are substantial benefits to registering a copyright, and it can have a very significant impact on the amount of damages that may be recovered in the event of infringement. Moreover, registration is required in order to file a claim in court. The copyright itself exists before then, though. Liability for infringement may be incurred before the copyright in the work is registered.

As a general rule, then, you should assume that everything on the Internet -- and all text, photographs and artwork you find elsewhere, such as in a book, magazine, art gallery, etc. -- is protected by copyright. The fact that someone has published something to a public website does not mean the material is in the public domain, or that the copyright owner has given an "implied license" for anyone to copy it. Material may be protected by copyright even if there is no copyright notice on it; and it may be protected even if the copyright has not been registered. If you come across something on the Internet, or in an email message, you should assume that someone has a protected copyright interest in it.

For this reason, you should make it your general policy to avoid copying things from other websites (or scanning other people's artwork or text into your computer for use on your website.) Create your own original material for your website or blog. If you want to communicate factual, nonproprietary information that you found on another website, that's fine, insofar as copyright law is concerned; but choose your own words to do it. (Note that republishing information from another website may expose you to liability for misappropriation of information, under some circumstances. See Chapter 8.)

If you determine that you really want or need to copy something you found on another site to your own website or blog, then you should investigate to determine whether it is indeed protected by copyright. If it's not, then go ahead and copy it, provided that doing so does not violate any of the other laws described elsewhere in this book. If it is protected by copyright, then you should investigate further to determine who owns the copyright so you may seek a license or permission to use the material. In some cases, it may be possible to use copyright-protected material without permission by invoking the fair use doctrine. As we shall see, however, you should proceed with extreme caution when relying on "fair use" as a defense to copyright infringement.

There are only five limited circumstances in which you may use another person's work without violating copyright law:

- material of a kind that is never protected by copyright law
- formerly protected works that have entered the public domain
- fair use of copyright protected works
- license or assignment of rights from the copyright owner
- it was created for you as a work made for hire.

Before delving into these subjects, though, it will be helpful to know about two kinds of creative work that can receive copyright protection even though their creation involves some copying of pre-existing copyrighted works – compilations and derivative works.

COMPILATIONS

A compilation is a collection of data and/or authored works. Anthologies (of short stories, poems, etc.), photograph or artwork collections, catalogs, almanacs, directories and computer databases are examples of compilations.

The selection and arrangement of things to include in a compilation can take some thought and creativity. For that reason, a compilation is considered a work of authorship on the part of the compiler. This means that the editor of a collection of stories may have a protected copyright interest in the collection – specifically, in the selection and arrangement of the elements in a collection – even if he did not actually write any of them.

A copyright in a compilation may be protected by copyright even if the individual elements included in it are not. Even though factual information may not be protected by copyright, the selection of facts, and the choice of how to arrange and present them may be. By the same token, the selection and arrangement of a compilation of public domain works may be protected by copyright even though none of the works included in it is.

Since a compilation may be protected by copyright even if its individual components are not, it is risky to copy and paste a data compilation (or a portion of it) from another website. Suppose, for example, that you come across an article about the "ten worst criminals in 19th century America" that states facts about selected 19th century American criminals. Since facts are not protected by copyright, you might think you are safe in republishing the article to your website without having to worry about getting permission from the copyright owner. You would be wrong. The author's decisions to select the particular criminals he did, to include the particular information about them that he did, and to arrange the information in the manner that he did, may be protected by copyright.

In the case of a compilation of authored works, it is important to keep in mind that the copyright in the compilation and the copyright(s) in the individual works within it are separate things. The copyright in a compilation exists independently of any copyright in the elements. An editor may own a copyright in the selection and arrangement aspects of a compilation of short stories. An author of a story in the collection, however, continues to own the copyright in the story notwithstanding its inclusion in the collection (unless, of course, he has transferred it, in which case it is owned by the transferee.)

Getting permission from the owner of the compilation copyright does not give you permission to copy an individual work within the collection unless the compilation copyright owner happens to own the copyright in the individual work, too.

The owner of the copyright in a compilation is presumed to possess the right to reproduce and distribute the works contributed to it only as part of that compilation or a revision of that compilation. Merely owning the copyright in a compilation does not give rise to a right to copy, display or distribute -- or to authorize others to copy, display or distribute -- an individual story or article that is included in the collection.

The owner of the copyright in a compilation has an exclusive right to make revisions to the compilation, such as by rearranging the order, adding new stories or information to the compilation, removing a story or fact from the compilation, and so on. The author of a copyrighted work appearing in the compilation, however, has the exclusive right to make derivative works of his copyrighted work. Accordingly, the owner of the copyright in the compilation does not have the right to alter or modify the content of a copyrighted work that appears in the compilation.

Copyright protection for a compilation does not confer copyright protection on portions of it that would not otherwise receive copyright protection. Owning the copyright in a data compilation does not mean that you own the data. If something would not be protected by copyright before it was compiled, then it will remain unprotected by copyright after the compilation. Only the manner in which the data is selected, arranged, presented or expressed in a compilation is protected by a copyright in the compilation.

DERIVATIVE WORKS

A derivative work is one that contains elements of a pre-existing work but in modified form. Examples of derivative works include: translations, dramatizations, fictionalizations, musical arrangements, screenplays, movie versions of novels, sound recordings of musical compositions, lithographs based on paintings, sculptures based on drawings, drawings based on photographs, abridgements, condensations, adaptations, annotations, revisions, and updated websites.

A derivative work does not receive copyright protection unless the modifications or additions involve at least a modicum of creativity and originality. De minimis contributions or variations from the original do not suffice.

A copyright in a derivative work arises only if the person creating it has the right to use the pre-existing work. The author initially has an exclusive right to make derivative works from his work. No one else may do so without either a license or an assignment of the copyright from the author.

Ownership of a copyright in a derivative work only confers rights in the newly-created aspects, not the original work itself. No matter how brilliant and creative your Star Wars sequel is, you will not own a copyright in it unless the owner of the copyright in the original Star Wars has assigned the copyright to you, or at least granted you a derivative works license.

Because anyone can freely use works that are in the public domain, a person creating a derivative work from a public domain work gets copyright protection for the derivative work so created. The copyright in the derivative work, however, does not confer ownership of the copyright in the original work on the author of the derivative work. Other people can make their own derivative works based on the same public domain work. The copyright in a derivative work only protects rights in material that is newly created for the derivative work.

UNPROTECTED MATTER

Not everything receives copyright protection. Only the expressive elements of a work that are fixed in a tangible medium of expression receive copyright protection, and then only if they are original, creative, and produced by a human.

IDEAS AND INFORMATION

Copyright only protects the expression of ideas and information; it does not protect the ideas and information themselves.

Facts and theories cannot be owned by anyone, but the words used to express them, and the selection and arrangement of facts and theories in a book or other presentation may be protected by copyright.

For the same reason, the plot or theme of a novel cannot be owned by anyone. A copyright can exist in the choice of words used to flesh out a plot, but not the plot or theme itself.

Scientific and technical drawings and diagrams receive copyright protection only for the original artwork and text in them. The ideas or discoveries illustrated in them are not protected by copyright.

A new game, or an idea for a new game, is not protected by copyright. The artwork and/or audiovisual works that are displayed in the course of the game, and any textual matter describing the game, may be copyrighted, but the game itself (the method and procedure involved, and the rules for playing it) is not.

Algorithms, ingredient lists for recipes, blank forms, systems, methods, and processes are more examples of things that do not receive copyright protection because they are ideas. Again, though, the particular words or arrangement of symbols chosen to express those ideas may be protected by copyright.

Craft, stencil, pattern, and how-to works typically contain a mixture of expression, facts and ideas. A project, craft or design is an idea, as is the process for making a thing. The text, artwork and photographs included in a how-to book or article about the project, however, may be protected by copyright, to the extent they are not merged with the idea.

INVENTIONS, USEFUL ARTICLES AND UTILITARIAN ELEMENTS

Because an invention is an idea, it does not receive copyright protection no matter how creative or original it is. A person may have a copyright in the particular words he uses to describe an invention, but not in the idea or invention itself. For that kind of protection, a patent would be needed.

Copyright protection only extends to the non-utilitarian aspects of a work. Useful articles and the utilitarian aspects of designs, although possibly protected by patent law in some cases, are not protected by copyright law.

Sometimes it can be difficult to differentiate between a utilitarian idea and its expression. A good way to approach the problem is to analyze different aspects of a work individually. If the aspect under consideration serves a useful function, then it is most likely an idea rather than an expression, and therefore not protected by copyright. If it is non-utilitarian, then it is probably expressive, and therefore protected by copyright.

Architectural designs are an exception to the general rule that copyright does not protect utilitarian aspects of an expression. Some (but not all) utilitarian aspects of certain architectural works are protected by copyright. See Chapter 3 for more information.

MERGED EXPRESSIONS

To the extent a work of authorship does nothing more than communicate a fact or an idea, it is not protected by copyright. In these cases, the idea or fact is said to be merged with its expression.

MANUALS

The factual information, methods and procedures included in instructions and owner manuals are not protected by copyright. Any unmerged expressive content, such as stylized illustrations, may be protected by copyright, however. The selection and arrangement of information may be protected by copyright, too.

UNCREATIVE WORKS

Although copyright law, unlike patent law, does not require an author to demonstrate the creation of something novel and unique, a work must involve at least a modicum of creativity before it will receive copyright protection.

It is difficult to define exactly what is required in order to satisfy the creativity requirement. The quality, merit or value of the work is not relevant. What matters is that the author contributes something original and non-obvious that he came up with on his own.

At one time, courts applied a "sweat of the brow" doctrine, holding that the amount of effort an author put into a work determined whether it was creative or not. That doctrine has been abolished, however. Today, creativity is assessed by neither a qualitative nor a quantitative analysis.

Unfortunately, that has left us with no bright-line test for determining whether something is sufficiently creative to warrant copyright protection or not. It is possible, however, to identify certain kinds of things that have been deemed to be too uncreative to receive copyright protection. Examples of things that do not involve a sufficient level of creativity to warrant copyright protection include:

- titles
- names
- short phrases
- *scènes à faire*
- jokes and gags
- blank forms, charts and graphs
- fact-gathering
- alphabetization
- consecutive numbering
- page numbers
- colorization
- digitization
- fonts, typefaces, calligraphy and ornamentation
- geometric shapes
- familiar symbols
- uncreative compilation methods.

BLANK FORMS, CHARTS AND GRAPHS

Although the content of a form, graph or chart may receive copyright protection if it is sufficiently creative and original, the graph, chart or form itself does not.

UNORIGINAL WORKS

To receive copyright protection, a work must be original, meaning that an author must create the work independently, not by copying another work.

It is possible, in theory, for two different authors to have copyrights in identical works. Parallel independent creations of the same work both get copyright protection. If, on the other hand, the two creations were not independent – that is to say, if one author copied the other – then the one who copied would not receive copyright protection because his work would not meet the originality requirement.

COPY OF AN UNCOPYRIGHTED WORK

Copying another work does not result in a sufficiently original work to warrant copyright protection, and this is true regardless of whether the copied work is protected by copyright or not. Accordingly, a work that is created by copying a public domain work does not receive any greater copyright protection than a work that is created by copying a copyright-protected work does.

UNORIGINAL ELEMENTS OF DERIVATIVE WORKS

Because of the originality requirement, the creator of an authorized derivative work only acquires a copyright in the newly created aspects of the derivative work. The copyright in the copied aspects of the derivative work remains with the owner of the copyright in the original work.

This can be important when determining whose permission is needed to copy a work, or a portion of another work. In some cases, you may need the permission of both the original and the derivative author. In other cases, you may only need the permission of one of them. When in doubt, the safest course is to obtain permission from both.

The creator of an unauthorized derivative work does not acquire a copyright in any aspect of the derivative work. Illegal infringers do not acquire any copyright rights. As a result, copying from an unauthorized derivative work will not expose you to infringement liability to the author of the derivative work, but it may expose you to liability to the copyright owner.

NONHUMAN AUTHORSHIP

Copyright only protects works that are created by human beings. There is no copyright protection for materials that are created by natural forces, machines, or non-human animals.

A work, such as a painting, created by a non-human animal is not protected by copyright even if a human supplied the tools (paints, brush, etc)

Purely machine-generated output that is created without any human interaction is not protected by copyright. A human may use a machine to assist in the fixation of a work, and the result will be protected by copyright, but if the machine itself actually creates the work, then it is not.

Since copyright law only protects human authorship, the configurations, motions, etc. of natural objects that are caused by natural forces without human intervention – such as driftwood, or a cloud pattern in the sky – are not protected by copyright.

EXPRESSION THAT IS NOT FIXED IN A TANGIBLE MEDIUM

To receive copyright protection, a work must be fixed in a tangible medium of expression. This may be a traditional medium, such as paper and ink, or it may be something of more recent origin, such as a computer or other digital storage device.

A web page is considered a tangible medium of expression, as are email messages, computer disks and digital storage devices.

For a dramatic work, the fixation in tangible media might be the written screenplay or a filmed performance of it. Audiovisual works and sound recordings are usually fixed on either videotape or in digital media. Computer programs may be fixed on disk or other digital media, or the source code may be written on paper. The most common ways of fixing choreography in a tangible medium are by either written notation or a filmed performance of the dance. Architectural works are usually fixed in a blueprint, but can also be fixed in the building itself when it is actually constructed.

These are just examples. Any tangible medium of expression will suffice.

Although copyright protection does not arise until the expression is fixed in a tangible medium, it is important to remember that it is the expression itself, not the medium, that copyright law protects. Once it has been fixed in a tangible medium, copyright protection for the expression continues to exist even if all tangible copies of it are destroyed.

THOUGHTS

Thoughts are not protected by copyright unless and until they are fixed in a tangible medium of expression.

Although the act of fixing a work in a tangible medium is necessary to the establishment of a copyright interest, it is not sufficient. The person who performs the physical act of fixing a thought in a tangible medium of expression does not thereby become the owner of the copyright in the expression of the thought. The creator of expressive content may retain copyright ownership of the content even if he hires or directs another person to perform the act of fixation.

LIVE PERFORMANCES AND IMPROVISATION

Live musical performances and broadcasts receive copyright protection only if a tangible recording is made. The literary or musical work that is the subject of the performance (such as a play or the musical score) may be protected, however, if it has been fixed in print or other tangible medium.

Like live performances and broadcasts, an improvisation is not protected by copyright unless it is recorded.

FEDERAL EMBLEMS, NAMES, SLOGANS, AND INSIGNIA

Copyright protection cannot be claimed for certain federally protected emblems, names, slogans and insignia. And there are some symbols, slogans, etc. that only the federal government may use. See Chapter 3.

PUBLIC DOMAIN WORKS

When none of the exclusive rights associated with a copyright exist or continue to exist, a work is said to be in the public domain. Anyone may freely use material that is in the public domain without liability for copyright infringement.

You should never rely on someone else's assertion that a particular work is in the public domain. There is so much confusion and misinformation being spread about the meaning of "public domain" that people often come to the wrong conclusion. It is not unusual to hear a person who is being sued for copyright infringement say, "But the website said it was in the public domain!" Unfortunately, copyright infringement is a strict liability offense. A mistaken belief that a work is in the public domain is not a defense.

The best approach to take is to assume that any text or artwork you come across is not in the public domain. Assume you will need permission from the copyright owner before you copy text or artwork for use on your own website or blog. If you have reason to believe something may be in the public domain, investigate the copyright status of the work for yourself. Then analyze your findings with an accurate understanding of the rules for determining what is in the public domain and what is not.

For more information about the public domain, see Chapter 13

SUMMARY OF UNPROTECTED CONTENT

A quick reference list of copyright-free materials is set out in Appendix I.

FAIR USE

Even if a work is protected by copyright, there are some circumstances in which you are permitted to copy, distribute, display, perform or make derivative works from it without incurring liability for copyright infringement.

For various policy reasons, certain kinds of uses are considered "fair use," for which the permission of the copyright owner is not required.

As with the public domain concept, a considerable amount of confusion and misinformation is being spread about the meaning of "fair use." It would seem that hardly anybody really understands what it means or when it applies.

"Fair use" is a fluid concept with many gray areas. Unlike the "public domain" concept, there are very few bright-line rules. The safest strategy is to assume that your intended use of someone else's copyrighted material is not fair use. Then, either get permission from the copyright owner to copy and re-publish the material, or refrain from copying the expressive elements of the material. If you cannot or do not want to do that, then be very certain your intended use is "fair use" before copying the material. Litigation over the meaning and scope of fair use can be very expensive.

For more information about fair use, see Chapter 14.

MISAPPROPRIATION

"Misappropriation" simply means using somebody else's property without permission. The property may be either tangible or intangible. Misappropriation of a copyright or trademark is called *infringement*. Both monetary damages and injunctive relief are available to redress it.

There are some kinds of things that are not protected by copyright law, but which receive protection under state property laws. Information is an example. It is not protected by copyright law. There may be some situations, however, in which an information-gatherer has a proprietary interest in the information she has gathered. In these situations, using the information without permission may expose you to liability under a state's misappropriation laws.

Trade secrets are another example.

A person's name or likeness is another example. Copyright does not protect a person's name or physical appearance. Many states, however, recognize individual rights of privacy and publicity, so that unauthorized use of another person's name, voice or likeness may expose you to liability under state law.

Trade names and short phrases do not receive copyright protection, but they might receive protection under trademark or unfair competition laws.

Misappropriation of a trademark (trademark infringement) is addressed in Chapter 7. Misappropriations of information, personality (name, voice or likeness), and trade secrets are covered in Chapters 8 and 9.

OTHER LAWS

Copying or republishing material from other websites, or from print publications, can raise other legal issues besides copyright infringement. Depending on what you copy and how you use it, it may also expose you to liability for such things as defamation, invasion of privacy, trademark infringement, dilution, fraud, breach of contract, or in some cases, even criminal liability. A republisher of actionable or unlawful content that somebody else created may potentially be liable for the content, sometimes to the same extent as the original publisher of the content. These other potential sources of liability are discussed in Chapters 7 through 12.

KEY POINTS:

- ❖ Using content found online violates copyright law unless
  - It is subject matter that copyright law does not protect;
  - It is in the public domain;
  - You are making fair use of it; or
  - You are licensed to use it.
- ❖ Copyright protects expression, not facts and ideas.
- ❖ To the extent expression is merged with information or ideas, it is not protected by copyright
- ❖ Copyright protection exists only for creative, original, human expression.
- ❖ A work is protected when, and only when, it is fixed in a tangible medium of expression.
- ❖ A copyright may exist in the selection and arrangement of elements, whether or not those elements are protected by copyright.
- ❖ A compilation copyright is distinct from the copyrights in any individual works that are compiled in it.
- ❖ The owner of the copyright in a work has the exclusive right to create new works based on it ("derivative works.")
- ❖ Creating your own content is the best strategy for avoiding copyright problems.

CHAPTER 2

Text

COPYRIGHT

FACTS AND IDEAS VS. EXPRESSION

Literary works are generally protected by copyright. No one can claim copyright ownership of facts or ideas, however. Accordingly, republishing factual information or ideas from another website will not result in liability for copyright infringement.

Although facts and ideas are not protected by copyright, the choice of words used to express them may be. And the selection and arrangement of facts in a book or other presentation may be protected as a copyright interest in a compilation.

Publishing information may violate other laws, in some cases. See Chapter 8.

OWNER'S MANUALS AND INSTRUCTIONS

Some elements of owner's manuals and instructions may be protected by copyright, but the facts and ideas in them are not. Any unmerged expressive content (such as illustrations), may be protected. The selection and arrangement of the facts and ideas also may be protected.

INVENTIONS AND USEFUL ARTICLES

Because an invention is an idea, it does not receive copyright protection no matter how creative or original it is. A person may have a copyright in the particular words he uses to describe an invention, but not in the idea or invention itself. For that kind of protection, a patent would be needed.

STORY PLOTS

Although fiction and poetry receive copyright protection, the distinction between idea (no copyright protection) and the expression of an idea (copyright protection) applies here, too. Thus, the plot of a story (the idea expressed in the story) is not protected by copyright, but the words used to bring the plot to life may be.

ALGORITHMS, INGREDIENT LISTS, BLANK FORMS, PROCESSES

These are more examples of things that do not receive copyright protection because they are ideas. Again, though, the particular words or arrangement of symbols chosen to express those ideas, or their selection and arrangement in a compilation, may be protected by copyright.

MERGED EXPRESSIONS

To the extent a work of authorship does nothing more than communicate a fact or an idea, it is not protected by copyright. In these cases, the idea or fact is said to be merged with its expression.

> *Example:* Every part of the sentence, "The earth is moving through space" is essential to the idea or fact that the earth is moving through space. Since ideas and facts are not protected by copyright, no one can claim ownership of the idea or fact that the earth is moving through space. That being the case, no one can claim an exclusive right to say that the earth is moving through space.

Contest rules are another example. They do not receive copyright protection because the idea (the set of rules) is not separable from the expression of the idea.

On the other hand, any nonfunctional matter that is not essential to the expression of the idea does not merge, and may be protected by copyright. Illustrations, or examples inserted into a set of contest rules in order to help readers understand them better, are not necessary elements of the expression of the idea, so they do not merge, and therefore may be protected by copyright. The words, "like a bat out of hell," in the expression, "The earth is moving through space like a bat out of hell" are not necessary to the communication of the fact or idea that the earth is moving through space, so they do not merge, and therefore may be protected by copyright.

The statement, "The temperature in New York City today is 86°F" is another example of a fact that is merged with its expression. Nothing more is expressed in this sentence than the fact that the temperature in New York City today is 86°F. That being the case, the expression is "all fact," and therefore not protected by copyright. If the statement were, "Great Scott, the temperature in New York City today is a blistering 86°F," then only part of the expression would be merged with the idea, since it is possible to express the fact that it is 86°F in New York City today without using the words 'blistering' and 'Great Scott.'

The more "bare bones" an expression of an idea or information is, the more likely it is that the expression of the idea or information is merged with the idea or information itself, and therefore not protected by copyright.

THE CREATIVITY REQUIREMENT

SHORT PHRASES

Because it is believed that no significant amount of creativity goes into coming up with a short phrase, courts generally deny copyright protection to them. The greater risk in such cases is trademark infringement.

TITLES AND NAMES

For the same reason, titles and names are not protected by copyright. The content of a work that is identified by a particular title may be protected by copyright, but the title itself is not.

In some cases, a particular story character may receive copyright protection, if the character's description is sufficiently unique and descriptive. In these cases, the use of the character's name in conjunction with a character with the same description could be a copyright violation. The use of the same name for a completely different character, however, probably will not be. For example, if you were to write a story about a Vulcan named "Mr. Spock" who explores the universe aboard a starship, then you might be violating a *Star Trek* copyright. On the other hand, if you were to write a romance story in which one of the characters is a Philadelphia optometrist named Mr. Spock, you probably would not be violating a *Star Trek* copyright.

Although a name or the title of a work does not receive copyright protection, it may be protected as a trademark if it is used in connection with the marketing of goods or services. "Star Trek," for example, could be a trademark for science fiction books, so unauthorized use of it as the title of a book could subject you to liability for trademark infringement or dilution.

CHARACTERS

Determining whether the characters in a story are protected by copyright is a little more complicated.

The basic rule is that there is no copyright protection for the characters in a story unless the character's description is unique and distinctive.

It is a rule that is easy to state, but not always easy to apply.

Certainly if the character's description is the story, then the character itself may be protected by copyright. Tarzan of the Apes is an example of a character that is protected by copyright for this reason. The Tarzan character is a man who was raised by apes. That is also the story.

The amount of detail that is required in order for a character to be protected by copyright is difficult to gauge. The best that can be said is that the less unique and developed the character, the less likely it is to be protected by copyright. Conversely, the more unique and developed it is, the more likely it is to be protected by copyright.

An alien being who is stranded on earth is too general to receive copyright protection. As more distinctive features are added – e.g., powers of levitation and telepathy, a long neck and a big head, a penchant for saying, "Phone home" – the likelihood that unauthorized use of the character in a different story will be found to infringe a copyright increases.

The author or assignee of a copyright protected work has the exclusive right to make derivative works from it. A new story using unique and distinctive character(s) from a pre-existing story is an example of a derivative work. If you create such a story without permission, you may be liable for copyright infringement.

If the character is used in connection with the marketing of goods or services, it may also be protected as a trademark. Some fictional characters are protected under both copyright and trademark law.

SCÈNES À FAIRE

A *scène à faire* is a stock or standard literary device, typically in a play or other dramatic work. Basically, it is a scene or detail that is considered standard in works in a particular genre. The use of gadgetry in a spy novel or screenplay would be an example. A male serenading a lady outside her window would be an example of a *scène à faire* in the romance genre. *Scènes à faire* do not receive copyright protection.

Similarities between a scene in one work and a scene in another work do not infringe a copyright in the first work if they follow naturally from the situation. A couple seeking refuge in a church during a storm would be an example.

Stereotypical characters do not receive copyright protection, either. The description of a character as a drunken Irish policeman, for example, is not protected by copyright.

Details that are essential to the description of a particular scene are also considered *scènes à faire*. It has been held, for example, that a movie about the South Bronx featuring drunks, prostitutes, vermin, and junk cars does not infringe the copyright in a previous movie featuring those same things. The court ruled that any movie about the South Bronx would need to feature these things in order to be realistic.

Placing a list of variables at the beginning of the source code of a computer program is another example. The textual content of the list might be protected by copyright, but the practice of listing variables at the beginning is so standard that no one can claim a copyright in this kind of arrangement.

JOKES AND GAGS

Although a play, screenplay or other dramatic work receives copyright protection, a short joke or gag within it might not.

FACT-GATHERING

Gathering factual information is not considered a creative act. Selecting which facts to include in a work or a data compilation, however, may qualify as one. Deciding how to present and arrange the information may be a creative act, too, so long as it does not involve merely listing the information in some obvious way, such as alphabetical order.

The choice of words and/or images used to express facts may be protected, to the extent the expression is not merged with the idea expressed.

Although fact-gathering is not protected by copyright, there can be situations in which using information that someone else has gathered may subject you to liability. See Chapter 8.

ALPHABETIZATION AND CONSECUTIVE NUMBERING

Although the selection and arrangement of materials in a compilation generally receives copyright protection, courts have held that the arrangement cannot be an "obvious" one if it is to receive copyright protection. Thus, the mere act of arranging data entries in alphabetical or numerical order does not receive copyright protection.

A White Pages directory, or similar listing, generally is not protected by copyright because neither the text nor its arrangement qualifies for copyright protection. It may take a lot of work to gather and compile the information, but courts have abandoned the "sweat of the brow" test as a means of determining whether something is entitled to copyright protection or not. Instead, courts today focus on the nature of the material produced. Facts are not protected no matter how much work went into gathering them. The text in a White Pages directory is not protected because it is purely factual information that is merged with the expression of the information. The alphabetical and numerical arrangement of entries in the directory is not protected because it is not a sufficiently creative arrangement.

The arrangement of entries in a Yellow Pages directory, on the other hand, may be protected by copyright because at least a modicum of creativity goes into the formulation of categories into which to place directory listings.

PAGE NUMBERS

A page numbering system is not considered sufficiently creative to receive copyright protection.

NONHUMAN AUTHORSHIP

Works created by animals or machines are not protected by copyright. The fact that a machine is used to assist in the process of fixing a work in a tangible medium, however, does not mean that the work is not protected by copyright. A novel written by a human being using word processing software is a work of human authorship so it is protected by copyright, but a string of words generated entirely by a computer program is not.

FIXATION IN A TANGIBLE MEDIUM

THOUGHTS

Thoughts are not protected by copyright unless and until they are fixed in a tangible medium of expression. Thus, if A and B have a brainstorming session during which they flesh out a story, no copyright protection for the story details they've worked out exists until such time as it is written down or recorded in some other way. Until that happens, the story remains only an idea in which neither A nor B can claim copyright ownership.

Although a copyright interest does not arise until an expression of the thought is fixed in a tangible medium, the person who created the expression is the one who owns the copyright, even if somebody else does the actual fixation. An author who has a scrivener write down his words as he dictates them retains ownership of the copyright (assuming he can prove that he was indeed the author of the work.)

EXTEMPORANEOUS SPEECHES AND IMPROVISATION

Extemporaneous speech is not protected by copyright. It may become protected by copyright, though, if it is transcribed or recorded in a tangible medium of expression of some kind. The same is true of improvised comedy and unscripted dramatic performances.

MISAPPROPRIATION

Some things receive protection under state property laws irrespective of copyright law. Information is an example. It is not protected by copyright law. There may be some situations, however, in which an information-gatherer has a proprietary interest in the information she has gathered. When that is the case, using the information without permission may expose you to liability under a state's misappropriation laws.

Trade secrets are another example.

A person's name or likeness is another example. Copyright law does not protect a person's name or physical appearance. Many states, however, recognize individual rights of privacy and publicity, so that using another person's name, voice or likeness without permission may expose you to liability under state law.

Misappropriation is covered in Chapters 8 and 9.

BREACH OF CONTRACT

Many websites condition use of the site on the user's acceptance of "terms of service" or some other contractual agreement. These often impose restrictions, limitations and conditions on the user's right to copy, distribute, alter or use material from the site. If you fail to comply with these terms and conditions, copying material from the site may expose you to liability for breach of contract. If you use copyrighted material in an unauthorized manner, you may be liable for copyright infringement.

Review any terms of use, or other licensing agreement, and take care to ensure your compliance with them. When in doubt, contact the website owner for permission to use content from the site.

OTHER LEGAL ISSUES

Copying and republishing text from other websites or print publications doesn't just raise copyright issues. Depending on the content of the material you copy and how you use it, it may also expose you to other kinds of liability, such as defamation, invasion of privacy, trademark infringement, dilution, fraud, or other things. In some cases, a republisher of actionable or unlawful content may be held liable for the content, sometimes to the same extent as the original publisher of the content. These other potential sources of liability are discussed in Chapters 7 through 12.

REQUEST FOR PERMISSION

A sample request for permission to use copyrighted material is set out in Appendix IX.

KEY POINTS

- ❖ Copyright protects the particular words chosen to communicate a fact or idea, not the fact or idea itself.
- ❖ Copyright does not protect expression when it is merged with the fact or idea expressed.
- ❖ Uncreative or unoriginal written expressions, such as titles and short phrases, are not protected by copyright law, but are sometimes protected by trademark law.
- ❖ Story plots, thoughts and spoken words are not protected by copyright unless they are written down, recorded or fixed in a tangible medium in some other way.
- ❖ Ideas and factual information may be protected by laws other than copyright.
- ❖ Although republishing information found on another website may not put you at risk of copyright liability, under some circumstances it could put you at risk of liability for other reasons.

CHAPTER 3

Photographs & drawings

COPYRIGHT

Drawings, paintings, graphic art, photographs, and compilations of them generally qualify for copyright protection. Neither aesthetic nor commercial value is relevant. A student's doodle on a notepad is just as protected by copyright law as paintings, business logos and advertising art are.

The fact that a photograph or drawing has been published to the Internet does not mean it may be freely copied and republished.

A photograph or drawing may be protected by copyright even though it has no copyright notice on or near it.

SUBJECT VS. DEPICTION

Unless the scene or subject of a photograph or drawing is itself a copyrighted work, the subject or scene is not protected by copyright. Any number of people may take a photograph of the same tree, for example.

A scientific or technical drawing depicts facts and ideas, which are not protected by copyright. To the extent such drawings do nothing more than communicate information, the facts and ideas will be deemed to have merged with the expression of them, so there will be no copyright protection. If some expressive content that is not necessary for the communication of the fact or idea is added, though, then that aspect of the drawing may be protected by copyright.

Example 1. An illustration in a mathematics text consisting of nothing more than a line drawing of a sine function on a Cartesian coordinate graph expresses nothing more than the nature of the sine formula. As a result, a court would probably determine that the drawing and the idea are merged, so the drawing is entitled to no copyright protection.

Example 2. Now suppose the artist who created the illustration added ornamentation to the line to make it look like a rope or a snake. This ornamentation is not needed in order to convey facts and information about a sine formula. Since they are purely expressive aspects of the drawing, a court would probably rule that those aspects are protected by copyright law (assuming all other conditions for an enforceable copyright are satisfied.)

Stencils, patterns, and craft books and materials typically contain both copyrightable and non-copyrightable elements. A project, craft or design is a non-copyrightable idea, as is the process for making a thing. The text, artwork and photographs included in a how-to book or article about the project, however, may be protected by copyright, to the extent they are not merged with the idea

An idea for a new game is not protected by copyright. Artwork displayed in the course of the game, or in or on the packaging, may be copyrighted, but the game itself (the method and procedure involved; the rules for playing it) is not.

USEFUL ARTICLES AND UTILITARIAN FEATURES OF A WORK

Because legal protection for ideas is the province of patent law and not copyright law, copyright protection generally extends only to the non-utilitarian aspects of a work. Useful articles and the utilitarian aspects of creative works, although possibly protected by patent law in some cases, generally are not protected by copyright law.

For example, if an artist creates a sculpture of a chair, copyright protection only extends to the nonfunctional aspects of the sculpture. It does not extend to the functional aspects. Since the seat, back, and legs of a chair are functional aspects, creating another sculpture of an object with a seat, back and legs would not, in itself, infringe the copyright. Copying non-utilitarian aspects of the chair might, though. This would include any decorative ornamentation of the chair.

Similarly, the pattern pieces that are used to create a useful article, such as shapes that may be traced and used to make a sleeve for a dress, generally are not protected by copyright, because they have an intrinsic utilitarian function. Stencils or templates that contain a sufficient amount of original pictorial or graphic artwork or original compilations of such artwork, such as a stencil book that contains original, artistic images of animals, trees, and automobiles, may be protected by copyright, however.

Sometimes it can be difficult to differentiate between a utilitarian idea and its expression. A good way to approach the problem is to analyze different aspects of a work individually. If the aspect under consideration serves a useful function, then it is most likely an idea rather than an expression, and therefore not protected by copyright. If it is non-utilitarian, then it is probably expressive, and therefore protected by copyright.

Architectural designs are an exception to the general rule that copyright does not protect utilitarian aspects of an expression. See discussion, below.

PHOTOGRAPHS AND DRAWINGS OF DRAWINGS AND PHOTOGRAPHS

What if the scene captured in a photograph or painting is itself a work that is protected by copyright? Does a person who photographs or draws another person's painting, for example, have any protected copyright interest in the photograph or drawing so created? The answer, generally, is no.

Just as drawing or taking a photograph of a tree does not give a person a copyright protected interest in the tree, so drawing, digitizing or taking a photograph of a pre-existing work generally does not give a person a copyright in the underlying work. The copyright in the underlying work remains with the author of that work (or his assignee.)

Because the taking of a photograph is a means of copying the subject of the photograph, photographing a pre-existing work that is protected by copyright infringes the copyright owner's exclusive right of reproduction of the work. The maker of an infringing copy of a work acquires no copyright in the infringing copy.

Making drawings, lithographs or digitizations of existing photographs would infringe the exclusive rights of the copyright owner, as well. A modified version of a copyrighted work would be a derivative work. Only the copyright owner has the right to make derivative works from her work. An infringer acquires no copyright in an unauthorized derivative work, no matter how much effort and creativity went into making it.

A drawing of the same subject or scene depicted in a photograph is not a derivative work if it is independently created. For example, the fact that a photographer has taken a picture of the Grand Canyon as seen from a particular angle and distance, and in a particular lighting, does not mean that no one may thereafter make a drawing or painting of the Grand Canyon as seen from the same angle and distance and in the same lighting. What it means is that an artist cannot sit at his desk and try to draw or paint an image of the Grand Canyon using the photograph as a model. If the drawing is created in this manner, then it is a derivative work of the photograph. A copyright in a derivative work arises only if the person creating it has the authority (such as a license from the copyright owner) to use the pre-existing work.

DRAWINGS AND PHOTOGRAPHS OF PUBLIC DOMAIN MATERIAL

When a work is in the public domain, or when it is a kind of material that is not protected by copyright, it is not a violation of copyright law to copy it, distribute it, display it, or make derivative works from it. Since photographs and drawings of public domain works are not infringing, the person who creates the photograph or drawing acquires a copyright in the work so created (provided it is sufficiently creative. See the discussion of "slavish copying," below.) This means that if you wish to use a photograph or drawing of a public domain work on your website or blog, you only need concern yourself with the rights of the person who created the drawing or photograph of the work, not those of the author of the public domain work (or their assignees.).

The creator of a new work that incorporates elements of a public domain work does not thereby acquire copyright protection for the elements that are in the public domain. By photographing a painting of the Mona Lisa, for example, I do not thereby acquire the exclusive right to display an image of the Mona Lisa on the Internet.

The same is true of any material that receives no copyright protection. The basic shape of a triangle is not protected by copyright, so taking a photograph of one does not thereby give the photographer the right to prevent other people from displaying triangles on their websites.

ARCHITECTURAL DESIGNS

Architectural designs are an exception to the general rule that copyright does not protect ideas. Both the design for a building (form, arrangement and composition of spaces) and a depiction of it (blueprint, model or the actual building itself) may receive copyright protection if the building was constructed after November 30, 1990. The design must be fixed in a tangible medium, such as blueprints. The building itself, once constructed, also serves to fix the design in a tangible medium.

Architectural designs that were created before December 1, 1990 do not receive copyright protection if they were published before December 1, 1990, or if they are embodied in a building that was completed before December 1, 1990. An architectural design that was created before December 1, 1990 but was not published before December 1, 1990, and was not embodied in a completed building as of November 30, 1990 is protected by copyright only if a building embodying the design was completed by December 31, 2002. Copyright protection for architectural designs created before, and not published before December 1, 1990, terminated on December 31, 2002 if a building embodying the design had not been completed by then.

The building may be a house, office building, church, gazebo, etc. Designs for bridges, dams, roads and the like are not protected.

The blueprints or drawings of architectural designs may qualify for copyright protection even if the design does not. Unless a drawing qualifies for protection as an architectural work, however, only the expressive aspects of the drawing receive protection; the idea for the design of the building does not.

Architecture is also an exception to the general rule that copyright does not protect utilitarian aspects of an expression. Some utilitarian elements of an architectural design receive copyright protection. Standard functional features of buildings (doors, windows, etc.), however, do not. Standard configurations are not protected, either. A design consisting of a hallway with multiple rectangular rooms annexed to it is an example of a standard configuration for a motel which does not receive copyright protection.

PHOTOGRAPHS AND DRAWINGS OF BUILDINGS

Since a building is a medium for the expression of its architectural design, it would seem as if photographing or drawing a picture of a building without permission would infringe a copyright in the architectural design. Congress, however, has created an exemption from copyright infringement liability for photographs and drawings of buildings that are visible to the public. Copying someone else's photograph or drawing of a building might result in liability for infringement of the copyright in the photograph or drawing, but not for infringement of the copyright in the architecture.

The exemption does not extend to three-dimensional models or replicas. You can take a photograph or make a drawing of a copyright-protected building and post it to your website, but you cannot post other people's photographs or drawings of it without their permission, and you cannot make a replica or scale model of it.

INTERIOR DESIGN

Because interior design is not protected by copyright, photographing it should not expose you to liability for infringement. An individual work (such as a painting) does not lose copyright protection by virtue of being made an element of an interior design, though.

INDEPENDENT CREATION

Copyright infringement of a photograph or drawing occurs only when copying, distribution, public display, or the making of a derivative work of the photograph or drawing occurs. If two photographers, neither of whom is aware of the other's work, independently capture nearly identical photographs of the same scene, neither of them is guilty of infringement. Similarly, if two artists create nearly identical paintings, and neither one was aware of the other's painting at the time, then neither is guilty of infringement.

CREATIVITY

The creativity requirement for copyright protection is very easily satisfied in the case of photographs. The mere act of pushing a button on a camera to take a photograph suffices, even if the photographer played no part in designing, manufacturing or selecting the camera; gave no thought at all to angle, lighting, filters, etc.; had nothing to do with creating the scene depicted in the photograph; and whose only contribution to the creation of the photograph was to push a button on the camera.

ANGLE, DISTANCE AND LIGHTING

No copyright protection exists for the angle, distance or lighting employed in a photograph. Decisions about these matters are not deemed to be of a sufficiently creative nature to warrant copyright protection. The fact that one person has already taken a picture of the Eiffel Tower at a particular angle and distance, using a particular lighting, does not prevent another person from taking another photograph of the Eiffel Tower at exactly the same angle and distance, using exactly the same lighting.

RESTORED AND RETOUCHED PHOTOGRAPHS

Restoration of an aged or damaged photograph to its original condition is not considered a sufficiently creative act to warrant copyright protection.

Retouching a photograph, on the other hand, may qualify for copyright protection if a substantial amount of new content is added (such as using airbrushing to change the picture.)

COLORIZATION

Merely adding color(s) to a design, object or pre-existing work, or changing the color(s), generally is not a sufficiently creative act to warrant copyright protection. For example, merely changing the background color of a public domain photograph normally will not result in a copyright protected photograph. For the same reason, colorizing a copyrighted work will not yield a new derivative work.

On the other hand, altering colors in an unusual way (such as painting hair blue and painting the fingernails on a copy of the Mona Lisa) may result in a copyright protected work. Factors to be considered are: whether and how much creativity went into the selection of colors, how much human involvement there was, and the extent to which overall appearance is affected.

DIGITIZATION

Digitization is not a sufficiently creative act to warrant copyright protection. Merely digitizing an existing work does not result in the creation of a derivative work that is protected by copyright.

MEDICAL AND OTHER UTILITARIAN IMAGING

Certain kinds of images are not protected by copyright because they are intrinsically utilitarian. Examples include:

- X-rays
- magnetic resonance imaging (MRI's)
- echocardiography
- mammograms
- ultrasound
- iodinated ultra venous imaging
- angiography
- electrocardiography
- three-dimensional computed tomography
- positron emission tomography
- electroencephalography imaging
- computed axial tomography
- land and water surveys generated from data produced by echo-sounders.

Just as a copyright claim may be made in a compilation of data, though, so a copyright claim may be made in the selection, arrangement, and/or coordination of such images. For example, a claim may be made in the selection of particular X-rays to illustrate a medical text even though a claim cannot be made in the individual X-ray images themselves.

Also, a work created with one of these technologies may receive copyright protection if it is put to an expressive use, such as the creation of modern art.

"SLAVISH COPYING"

Although the act of pushing a button on a camera is generally considered a sufficiently creative act to warrant copyright protection, courts have held that it does not suffice when the subject of the photograph is another work of authorship, unless some significant additional content is added. Slavishly photographing, scanning or digitizing a pre-existing work will not result in the creation of a new copyrightable work if the copy is identical in visual appearance to the original, even if the work in question is in the public domain. An unretouched photograph of the Mona Lisa, for example, normally will not be protected by copyright.

Merely pushing a button on a camera to take a photograph of a lake is considered a sufficiently creative act to give rise to a copyright in the photograph, but merely pushing a button on a camera to take a photograph of a painting of a lake is not considered a sufficiently creative act to give rise to a copyright in the photograph.

Although a photographer has no copyright in a photograph she makes of another work of authorship, she may acquire rights in any significant creative modifications she makes to an image of the work, provided doing so does not infringe a copyright in the underlying work of authorship. A photographer who makes a significant modification of a public domain image (rather than simply creating a copy of it) acquires copyright protection for the modification. For example, if a photographer photoshops a mustache into her photograph of the Mona Lisa (which is in the public domain), she may acquire rights in the image she has created of the Mona Lisa with a mustache. A photograph depicting the Mona Lisa painting hanging in a gallery with visitors looking at it would probably be a sufficiently significant modification to earn copyright protection.

FONTS, TYPEFACES, CALLIGRAHY AND ORNAMENTATION

Fonts, typefaces, calligraphy and typographic ornamentation generally do not receive copyright protection, no matter how novel or creative they may be. This is because the creative aspect of the character cannot be separated from its utilitarian function.

On the other hand, if it is possible to separate the pictorial or graphic elements from the utilitarian aspects in a particular case, then the decorative elements may receive copyright protection. A letter drawn in the shape of another object would be an example. And typeface ornamentation that is separable from the typeface characters (such as flourishes, swirls, vector ornaments, scrollwork, borders and frames, wreaths, and the like) may be copyrightable. The ornamentation must involve something more than de minimis creativity, though. The mere use of text effects, such as chalk, neon lighting, beer glass, etc. will not suffice.

GEOMETRIC SHAPES

A drawing of an unadorned geometric shape, or an arrangement of geometric shapes in an obvious pattern, does not satisfy the creativity requirement. If they are arranged in a non-obvious way, however, the resulting arrangement may be protected by copyright.

FAMILIAR SYMBOLS

Common, well-known symbols and designs are not protected by copyright. The circle and slash (signifying "No") is just one example.

Federally owned emblems, insignias, symbols, slogans and characters

Some symbols, emblems, cartoon characters and insignia are not protected by copyright because Congress has reserved to the federal government the exclusive right to use them. These include such things as U.S. department or agency insignia; badges or ID cards; the Red Cross or Greek Cross symbol; the Red Crescent or Third Protocol Emblem; the 4-H emblem; the great seal of the United States; the official seal of the U.S. President, Vice President, Senate, House of Representatives or Congress; the Golden Eagle insignia; Smokey Bear; Woodsey Owl.

18 U.S.C. chapter 33 makes it a crime for any unauthorized person to make certain specified kinds of uses of these.

NONHUMAN AUTHORSHIP

Artwork created by animals, computers or natural forces is not protected by copyright.

There is a difference between the creation of a work and its fixation in a tangible medium, though. A human may use a machine to assist in the fixation of a work he has created, and the result will be protected by copyright. If, on the other hand, the machine itself actually creates the work, then it is not. Thus, a drawing created by using the Paint tool on a computer may be protected by copyright, but a computer-generated random array of patterns is not.

THE PUBLIC DOMAIN

The rules governing when photographs and drawings enter the public domain, including the duration of copyrights, are basically the same as the ones that apply to literary works. Except in the case of a work made for hire, the photographer is considered the author of a photograph, and the artist is considered the author of a drawing or painting.

The Internet is not "the public domain." Generally, you may not copy content from another web page and paste it to your own without permission, even if it's a free site and even if you came across it by doing a Google search. Some works that have been published to the Internet may be in the public domain, but it is not the appearance of them on the Internet that causes that to happen.

The rules for determining whether a work is in the public domain are set out in see Chapter 13.

OTHER CATEGORIES OF UNPROTECTED ARTWORK

For a more complete description of categories of works that do not receive copyright protection, see Chapter 1. A quick reference list is provided in Appendix I.

PUBLIC DISPLAY

The copyright owner has an exclusive right to publicly display the photograph or drawing in which he owns the copyright.

"Display" includes both direct displays (e.g., display of a photograph or painting on the wall of a gallery), and indirect ways of displaying things, such as transmitting an image to a television or movie screen. It also includes transmitting an image electronically via the Internet; emailing or uploading an image to a website; and showing an image on a screen. Posting to a social media website is another kind of "display."

The copyright owner has an exclusive right to publicly display the work, but anyone who has lawfully acquired a copy of it may display it privately.

A place is "public" only if either:

a)   it is open to the public; or
b)   a substantial number of people outside of family and social acquaintances gather to view the work.

An Internet website is "public" if it is accessible by the public, even if no one has actually visited it.

A display of images to Internet mailing list subscribers would qualify as a "public display" if the list comprises more than just a small group of family and friends.

An owner of a copy of a copyright-protected photograph or drawing may display it privately, but not publicly. Copyright law permits the lawful owner of a copy of a photograph or drawing to display it but only at the location where the copy is located. Uploading a photograph or drawing to an Internet website would not satisfy this requirement. Images displayed on a website are visible to more people than just those who are present in your home. They are visible to anyone with access to the Internet. Accordingly, it is a public display. As such, it may infringe the copyright.

FAIR USE

The "fair use" doctrine has become very difficult to apply in the case of photographs and drawings, as a result of court decisions declaring that the extent to which a modification of a photograph or drawing "transforms" it for a different use is of key importance in determining whether the modification is fair use or not. It can be difficult to reconcile this with the Copyright Act's explicit grant to authors (including photographers and artists) of an exclusive right to make derivative works using their copyright rights. The Copyright Act defines a derivative work as including a work that "transforms" the copyrighted work. This tension and the concept of fair use in general are discussed in Chapter 14.

LICENSING

Given the comparatively low level of certainty and predictability in the area of "fair use" jurisprudence relative to other areas of law, it is a good idea to get a license from the copyright owner if you plan to use an image that you do not own on your website or blog. A well-drafted license should remove any doubt about your right to use a particular photograph or drawing in the way that you want.

More information about image licensing may be found in Chapter 19.

"FREE" IMAGES AND IMAGE LICENSING WEBSITES

As a rule of thumb, you should always assume that any photograph or drawing you find online is protected by copyright, and that you will need to get permission or a license if you want to use it on your site. Of course, if, after analyzing it in the light of what you have learned in this book, you determine that it is in the public domain, then you will not need a license. And if it was created for you as a work made for hire, then you are the owner of the copyright and already have the right to use it. In all other cases, you should endeavor to secure a license.

When a website offers "free" or "royalty-free" images, specified uses may still be subject to conditions with which you must comply. If you fail to do so, you may be liable for copyright infringement, not just breach of contract.

For information about how to find royalty-free and/or public domain images and use them on your website or blog, see Chapter 19.

MORAL RIGHTS & THE VISUAL ARTISTS RIGHTS ACT

Moral rights are separate and distinct from copyright rights. While copyright protects an artist's exclusive right to use his creations (by reproducing, distributing or displaying them, or by making derivative works from them), it does not protect an artist's reputation. Moral rights legislation seeks to fill that gap, at least in part, by giving certain visual artists the right to have their works credited to them, and to prevent works not created by them from being attributed to them. They also seek to give these artists a right to prevent their artwork from being defaced or destroyed.

The laws of New York and several foreign countries have long sought to protect the moral rights of visual artists. Beginning December 1, 1990, United States federal law also protects the moral rights of visual artists.

The Visual Artists Rights Act ("VARA") strives to protect the reputation of certain visual artists in two ways: first, by requiring correct attribution of certain kinds of visual art to the artist; and second, by allowing certain visual artists to prevent the destruction or mutilation of their creations.

ATTRIBUTION

VARA gives certain visual artists the right to claim ownership of the works they create. A visual artist also has the right to prevent the use of his name as the author of any work of visual art that he did not create.

INTEGRITY

VARA gives certain visual artists the right to prevent the destruction, distortion, mutilation or other modification of their works.

Attributing a mutilated or modified version of a work of visual art to the original artist is also a violation of VARA.

INDEPENDENT OF COPYRIGHT

The "moral rights" protected by the VARA are independent of copyright. An artist continues to have moral rights even after he has assigned his copyright to someone else. Similarly, mere ownership of the copyright does not give a person standing to enforce VARA rights. Only the person who created the art has VARA rights.

LIMITATIONS ON VARA RIGHTS

VARA rights only exist for:

- paintings
- drawings
- prints
- sculptures
- still photographs produced solely for exhibition purposes that have been signed by the photographer.

The work must exist in only a single copy, or in a limited edition of no more than 200 copies that are signed and consecutively numbered by the author, or, in the case of a sculpture, in multiple cast, carved, or fabricated sculptures of 200 or fewer that are consecutively numbered by the author and bear the signature or other identifying mark of the author.

If a work does not meet these requirements, it is not protected by VARA. It might be protected by copyright, trademark or other law, though.

Although they may receive copyright protection, the following things are specifically excluded from VARA protection:

- posters (as distinguished from prints)
- maps and globes
- technical drawings, diagrams, and models
- applied art
- audiovisual works, such as motion pictures
- books, magazines, newspapers, and other periodicals
- electronic publications
- databases and electronic information services
- advertising, promotional or merchandising items, descriptive works, covering, or packaging materials or containers
- works that are not protected by copyright law
- works made for hire.

VARA does not protect public domain photographs or drawings, or any other material that is not protected by copyright.

For works created after December 1, 1990, VARA rights in a work terminate at the end of the calendar year in which the artist dies. In the case of collaborative works, they continue until the end of the calendar year in which the last surviving author dies. For works created before December 1, 1990, VARA rights last as long as copyright does, but only if the artist was still the owner of title to the work (i.e., had not sold or otherwise transferred title to it) as of December 1, 1990.

Artwork that is not protected by VARA may nevertheless be protected by other law, such as trademark or copyright law.

WAIVER AND TRANSFERABILITY

VARA rights are not transferrable, but the author may waive them. To be enforceable, the waiver must:

1) be written;
2) be signed by the artist;
3) expressly waive VARA rights;
4) identify the work; and
5) identify the uses of the work to which the wavier applies.

A waiver of VARA rights does not operate as a transfer of copyright in the work unless the agreement expressly so provides.

A waiver by one co-author waives VARA rights for all co-authors of a collaborative work.

A transfer of copyright, or a transfer of a copy in which a copyrighted work is embodied, does not operate as a waiver of VARA rights.

PRIVACY AND PUBLICITY RIGHTS

Invasion of an individual's right of privacy, such as by publishing a copy of a photograph of the person without permission, may expose you to liability even if you have a license from the copyright owner to republish the photograph. Similarly, exploiting a photograph of a person for commercial or other advantage may expose you to liability even if you have a license from the copyright owner to use the photograph in your advertising. Accordingly, you will want to ensure that you have appropriate authority from both the copyright owner and the subject of the photograph before you publish a copy of a photograph of a person to your website or blog.

Obtaining permission from both the photographer and the subject of the photograph is a very good idea even if you are not using a photograph for commercial purposes. Liability for copyright infringement can attach irrespective of your motive, as can liability for invasion of privacy in some cases. Ideally, the permission should be in writing and signed, inasmuch as that will make it easier to prove that consent was given.

Children are deemed incapable of giving a valid consent, so it is necessary for a parent or legal guardian to give consent on their behalf. Depending on state law, an incompetent, coerced, defrauded or traumatized person may be incapable of giving consent on her own behalf, too.

For more information about privacy and publicity rights, see Chapters 8 and 9. For more information about image licensing, see Chapter 19.

TRADEMARKS

PHOTOGRAPHS AND DRAWINGS AS TRADEMARKS

A photograph or drawing may be a trademark if it is used in connection with marketing goods or services. Using another person's trademark for commercial purposes or on a commercial website may expose you to liability for trademark infringement or dilution. For more information, see Chapter 7.

PHOTOGRAPHS AND DRAWINGS OF TRADEMARKS

Liability for trademark infringement arises only if a person uses another person's trademark, or something like it, in a way that is likely to cause consumers to become confused about the source, endorsement or sponsorship of goods or services. Publishing a photograph or drawing of a scene that only incidentally includes products or objects with trademarks displayed on them is not trademark infringement if it is not likely to confuse visitors to your website about the origin, sponsorship or endorsement of those goods or services.

LIKELIHOOD OF CONFUSION

If, instead of displaying photographs or drawings for purely artistic or aesthetic effect, you use them in connection with your marketing of goods or services, then you may be liable for trademark infringement if the way you use the photograph is likely to create confusion about the source, sponsorship or endorsement of the goods or services you are marketing.

For example, if you were to position a photograph of the Rolex logo in close proximity to non-Rolex watches that you offer for sale on your website, visitors would be very likely to mistakenly believe the watches you are selling are Rolex watches. This would put you at high risk of liability for trademark infringement.

A photograph of the Ford Motor Company logo on an auto repair service's website might put the service at risk of liability if it is likely to cause visitors to the site to believe his repair service is sponsored or endorsed by the Ford Company when it is not.

DILUTION OF FAMOUS TRADEMARKS

You may be liable for trademark dilution if you use a famous mark in such a way as to cause it to lose its distinctiveness as a brand ("dilution by blurring") or if you use it in such a way as to harm the reputation of the famous mark ("dilution by tarnishment.")

CONTRIBUTORY INFRINGEMENT

You may be liable for infringement even if you do not personally do things to cause confusion about the origin, endorsement or sponsorship of goods. If you provide a venue (such as a web site) for someone else's infringing acts, then you may be held liable as a contributor to the infringement.

COMMERCIAL VS. NONCOMMERCIAL USE

Generally speaking, trademark liability should not be a concern if you are merely depicting someone else's trademark for a noncommercial purpose on a purely noncommercial website, so long as your statements in connection with it are not false or misleading. It should become a concern if you use a photograph or drawing of someone else's mark to sell, lease, offer, advertise, market or endorse a product or service (which can include the website itself.)

If your website offers paid information, entertainment or other services – or if it displays advertisements or links to commercial web sites – then it may be classified as a commercial site. It may also be a commercial site if you receive revenue based on the number of clicks the site receives.

More information about trademark law may be found in Chapter 7.

COPYRIGHT-PROTECTED TRADEMARKS

If a trademark has sufficient creative content, then it may also be protected by copyright law. When that is the case, publishing a photograph or drawing of the trademark may be copyright infringement even if it is only used for a noncommercial purpose. See Chapters 13 and 14 for more information about possible fair-use and public domain defenses.

COMMERCIAL USE OF A PERSON'S IMAGE

Using a visual depiction of a person without that person's permission to falsely suggest or imply the person's manufacture, sponsorship or endorsement of a product or service may expose you to liability under various federal and state laws prohibiting unfair competition and false advertising.

PORNOGRAPHY & OTHER REGULATED CONTENT

Publishing or republishing certain kinds of photographs or drawings may have civil or criminal repercussions for other reasons. For example, if a photograph depicts obscenity or child pornography, then republishing it on your website would put you at risk of criminal prosecution. See Chapter 11.

SAMPLE RELEASE AND REQUEST FOR PERMISSION

For a sample model release, see Appendix V. A general purpose form for requesting permission to use copyrighted material appears in Appendix IX.

KEY POINTS:

❖ Photographs are protected by copyright, except when they:
  • depict another work that is protected by copyright
  • are slavish reproductions of public domain works; or
  • are in the public domain.
❖ Copyright protects the photograph, not the subject.
❖ Retouching gets copyright protection; restoration does not.
❖ Intrinsically utilitarian imaging is not protected by copyright.
❖ Photographs of buildings that are visible to the public do not infringe the copyright in the building's architecture.
❖ Using a photograph of a person may require permission from both the photographer and the subject.
❖ The incidental appearance of a trademark in a photograph is not infringement unless it is protected by copyright.
❖ Avoid making unauthorized modifications of artwork.
❖ Attribute artwork to the artist.
❖ Comply with all terms of service and licensing conditions.
❖ Non-copyright regulations of photographs and drawings exist in the areas of trademark, privacy, misappropriation and child pornography, among others.

CHAPTER 4

Music & Audio

MUSIC AND LYRICS

Copyright protection generally exists for musical compositions and lyrics, provided they are fixed in a tangible medium. Musical performances may receive copyright protection, too, if they are recorded. Copyrights in musical works and copyrights in recordings of musical performances are two different things.

In copyright law, a songwriter is called an "author of a musical work." If a musical work is created pursuant to a written work-for-hire agreement, then the employer or contractor who commissions the work, not the actual composer, is treated as the author.

COLLABORATIVE WORKS

As a general rule, if two or more people work together to create a musical work, then in the absence of an agreement otherwise, they own the copyright jointly.

The question whether a song is jointly owned, or whether an element of it (such as the lyrics) is owned separately by the creator of that element, is a question of intent. When a band, or a composer and a lyricist, create elements of a song with the intention that their respective contributions will be merged into inseparable or interdependent parts of a unitary whole, then they are joint owners of the song. Otherwise, each one is an individual owner of his or her individual contribution to the song.

Example 1. Bernie is a prolific poet. One day, Elton happens upon one of his poems and says, "Hey, I think I can put music to this." Bernie approves of the idea, so Elton proceeds to create a song using Bernie's poem as the lyric. Since Bernie did not have the intention of creating a song with Elton when he wrote the poem, the copyright in the song is not jointly owned. Instead, Bernie owns the copyright in the lyrics and Elton owns the copyright in the music.

Example 2. Elton asks Bernie to write lyrics for a song Elton is writing. Bernie proceeds to do so. Because they each intended their compositions to be parts of a unitary whole, Elton and Bernie would be joint owners of the copyright in the whole song (both the music and the lyrics) in this situation.

The determination whether the copyright(s) in a musical work is/are jointly or individually owned is helped greatly when there is a written agreement in place.

INDEPENDENT CREATION

If two different people independently create the same song, then they each own a separate copyright in it. A copyright gives a composer exclusive rights to make copies; distribute copies; publicly display it; publicly perform it; and make derivative works from it. None of these rights is violated when another person independently creates the same work without copying. Not being an infringing copy of another person's work, the work each author creates in such situations is sufficiently original to receive copyright protection.

Independent creation is a significant issue in the case of musical works because people create similar-sounding songs all the time. There are typically only a few standard chord progressions in a particular music genre; there are only a limited number of notes in a scale that will harmonize with a chord; and there is a shared pool of common musical techniques and devices (such as an incomplete cadence phrase followed by a complete cadence phrase) that every songwriter draws upon when composing a melody. Add to this the fact that a song may infringe the copyright in another song if the melodies are similar even if the lyrics are completely different, and the possibility that two composers might independently come up with the same or very similar musical compositions is not really all that far-fetched.

Be that as it may, courts tend to regard a high degree of similarity between two song melodies as strong circumstantial evidence of copying. If it can be proved that a composer had access to a song (e.g., it was broadcast on a radio station that he could have heard before he wrote his song), then a high degree of similarity between it and a song he later writes may suffice as circumstantial evidence of copying.

It is not necessary to prove intent to infringe in order to prevail on a copyright infringement claim. George Harrison was successfully sued on the basis that he subconsciously copied the melody of the Chiffons' song, "He's So Fine" for his song, "My Sweet Lord," although he was not consciously aware that he was doing it.

In those rare cases where two authors do independently create identical or very similar works without either one copying the other, they are not joint authors. They are each individual authors of the work.

THEMES, MOODS AND MESSAGES

As with any kind of work, copyright law only protects expression. The overall idea, theme, mood or message of a musical work is not protected by copyright. The fact that Grace Slick wrote an eerie song encouraging the use of psychedelic drugs, for example, would not give her the exclusive right to compose eerie songs that encourage the use of psychedelic drugs. For the same reason, Hank Williams does not have the exclusive right to write songs about people coming to regret their unfaithfulness.

THE CREATIVITY REQUIREMENT

In general, it may be said that the melody and lyrics of a song usually are protected by copyright, so long as they have not been copied from a previous copyrighted work. Other elements of a song -- such as the beat, rhythm, chord progression, and fills – generally are not protected by copyright. A musical work must involve at least a modicum of creativity in order to receive copyright protection.

It is difficult to define exactly what the creativity requirement means in the case of musical compositions and lyrics. The quality, merit or value of the work is not relevant. What matters is that the composer contributes something original and non-obvious that he came up with on his own.

At one time, courts applied a "sweat of the brow" doctrine, holding that the amount of effort an author put into a work determined whether it was creative or not. That doctrine has been abolished, however. Today, creativity is assessed by neither a qualitative nor a quantitative analysis.

Unfortunately, there are no clear tests for determining whether something is sufficiently creative to warrant copyright protection or not. It is possible, however, to identify certain kinds of things that have been deemed to be too uncreative to receive copyright protection.

SONG TITLES

Song titles are not protected by copyright. The content of a work that is identified by a particular title may be protected by copyright, but the title itself is not.

Although the title of a song does not receive copyright protection, it may be protected as a trademark if it is used in connection with the marketing of goods or services. "Ziggy Stardust" and "Yellow Submarine" are examples of song titles which, although not protected by copyright, are protected as trademarks. Taylor Swift and other popular recording artists have registered a number of their song titles as trademarks.

SHORT MUSICAL OR LYRICAL PHRASES

Because it is believed that no significant amount of creativity goes into coming up with a few words, phrases do not receive copyright protection.

The Copyright Office has taken the position that because a short phrase is not protected by copyright, a series of repetitions of it is not, either. In the Copyright Office's view, a song lyric consisting of multiple repetitions of the phrase, "I love you" would not be protected by copyright because the phrase "I love you" is too short to meet the creativity requirement.

It is not clear that the Copyright Office is correct about this. The band Devo's interminable, robotic repetition of the short phrase, "Are we not men? We are Devo" certainly seems to be a very creative way of expressing something that is much more artistically significant than what is conveyed by merely a single iteration of the phrase. Similarly, Andy Warhol's depiction of identical photographs of the exact same soup can in a pictorial series conveys an entirely different message than a single photograph of the soup can does. It makes an artistically creative statement about mass production that a single photograph of a can does not. There does not appear to be any sound doctrinal basis for declaring either Devo's or Warhol's work to be too "uncreative" to receive copyright protection.

The Copyright Office's opinions are not binding on courts, and it is not certain that all courts would take the Copyright Office's position on this point. Accordingly, it would be prudent to avoid copying song lyrics even if they consist of repetitions of a short phrase.

In any event, the greater risk, when copying a short phrase from a song, is that it might violate trademark rights. A growing number of popular recording stars are registering trademarks in short phrases from their songs. And a phrase from a song may be protected as a trademark even if it is not registered, if it is being used in connection with the marketing of a product or service.

CHORD PROGRESSIONS

Chord progressions (sometimes collectively called "harmony") are not protected by copyright. A particular combination of the chord progression with another musical element (such as the melody) may be protected, though.

RHYTHM

The beat or rhythm of a song is not protected by copyright.

ARRANGEMENT PARTS

As a general rule of thumb, it may be said that the melody and lyrics of a song may be protected by copyright, but arrangement parts usually are not. Thus, the rhythm, drum fills, and bass line generally are not protected by copyright.

An arrangement part may be protected by copyright, however, if it is incorporated into the melody. And a particular combination of arrangement parts, or an arrangement part with a chord progression, may be protected by copyright, if it is sufficiently creative and original.

That arrangement parts usually are not protected by copyright is only a rule of thumb. The ultimate question is whether the composer of the allegedly infringing composition copied (either consciously or subconsciously) a pre-existing song that is protected by copyright. To make that determination, courts compare each song, taken as a whole, against the other. The fact that the same rhythm or chord progression was used in both songs will not usually suffice as circumstantial evidence of copying, if the same rhythm or chord progression has been used in a lot of other songs, too. As the arrangement parts, and/or their use together, grow in distinctiveness and originality, however, it becomes less likely that a subsequent song's employment of them is merely coincidental. When the same rhythm accompaniment, chord progression, and arrangement parts are used together in a song with a similar melody or lyrics, the likelihood of a finding of copying, and therefore copyright infringement, increases considerably.

In short, even though the chord progression, harmonies, rhythm accompaniment, musical fill phrases and the like may not individually be protected by copyright, the arrangement, taken as a whole, may be -- provided it is not itself merely a copy of a pre-existing copyright-protected arrangement.

A copyright in an arrangement may exist independently of the copyright(s) in the melody and lyrics. For this reason, an original arrangement of a public domain song may be protected by copyright even though the song itself (melody and lyrics) is not. A new arrangement of a copyright-protected musical work, on the other hand, is protected by copyright only if it is either created or authorized by the owner of the copyright in the original musical work. Infringing derivative works are not protected by copyright.

DIGITIZATION

Digitization does not, by itself, receive copyright protection.

HUMAN AUTHORSHIP

There is no copyright protection for materials that are created by non-human animals, machines, or natural forces. For this reason, a recording of birds singing, or a musical notation of the melody being sung by a bird, is not protected by copyright. For the same reason, the sound of waves crashing is not protected by copyright, either.

Purely machine-generated output that is created without any human interaction is not protected by copyright. A human may use a machine to assist in the fixation of a work, and the result will be protected by copyright, but if the machine itself actually creates the work, then it is not. A song written by a human using musical notation software is a work of human authorship so it is protected by copyright. A sequence and arrangement of notes that is selected by a computer rather than by a human being is not.

Although musical works created by machines, animals or natural forces are not protected by copyright, a human being's exercise of judgment in the selection and arrangement of those sounds may be protected by copyright, provided it is sufficiently original and creative.

FIXATION IN A TANGIBLE MEDIUM

To receive copyright protection, a work must be fixed in some tangible medium of expression. This may be vinyl, recording tape, a digital storage device (including computers hosting websites), paper, piano roll, etc. Typically, musical works are fixed in sheet music, tablature, typewritten or handwritten lyrics, and/or a recording of a performance of the song.

Although a musical work must be fixed in a tangible medium to receive copyright protection, it is the expression, not the medium, that copyright law protects. Once a musical work has been fixed in a tangible medium, copyright protection for the expression continues to exist even if all tangible copies of it are destroyed.

SONG IDEAS

Almost everybody has had an idea for a new song at one time or another in their lives. Some may even have hummed, sung or picked it out on a guitar, piano or other musical instrument. Only those who have taken the further step of writing it out, or recording a performance of it, acquire a protected copyright interest in it, though. An expression of a musical idea, like any other kind of expression, must be fixed in a tangible medium of expression in order to receive copyright protection.

The creator of a work does not have to perform the act of fixation personally. A composer who hires a band and a recording studio to record a performance of a musical composition she communicates to them orally retains ownership of the copyright in the song.

In some cases, a person performing the fixation may acquire a copyright interest of his own, provided he adds at least a modicum of creative content. For example, a recording studio producer may acquire a copyright in the production component of the sound recording of a performance, while the recording artist retains a copyright in the performance component of a sound recording of the musical work and the composer retains the copyright in the musical work.

LIVE PERFORMANCES AND BROADCASTS

A live performance or broadcast of a song does not affect the copyright in the musical composition. If a song is protected by copyright at the time it is performed (that is to say, it has been written down or recorded before it is performed), then it will remain protected after it has been performed. If a song has not been fixed in some tangible medium of expression before it is performed, then a live performance or broadcast of it will not cause it to acquire copyright protection unless the performance is recorded.

IMPROVISATION

An improvisation is not protected by copyright unless and until it is recorded, transcribed or fixed in a tangible medium in some other way.

THE PUBLIC DOMAIN

Musical works that are in the public domain are not protected by copyright. See Chapter 13.

FAIR USE

In some situations, a limited amount of copying is permitted as "fair use." Contrary to popular belief, however, there is no rule to the effect that you are allowed to copy some specified number of bars of a song as "fair use." Courts evaluate fair use on a case-by-case basis, giving consideration to a number of factors. There have been cases in which copying less than six bars of a song has been held to be infringement.

For more information about fair use, see Chapter 14.

SOUND RECORDINGS

Sound recordings may be protected by copyright. A copyright in a sound recording of a musical composition is separate and distinct from the copyright in the musical composition.

Federal copyright protection for sound recordings came into existence on February 15, 1972. Before then, the performance and production elements of a sound recording were not protected by federal copyright law even if the owner of the copyright in the underlying work authorized the making of the recording.

That changed in 1972, when Congress established copyright protection for sound recordings. The result is that sound recordings made before February 15, 1972 do not receive federal copyright protection, but recordings made on or after February 15, 1972 do.

Although federal copyright protection for sound recordings did not exist before February 15, 1972, copyright protection for the underlying musical or literary works did. Unauthorized copying of a pre-1972 recording does not infringe a federal copyright in the sound recording, but it may be an infringement of the copyright in the musical composition and/or the lyrics.

Moreover, state law protection of rights in sound recordings did exist before February 15, 1972. Some states, such as California, continue to protect intellectual property rights in sound recordings that were made before February 15, 1972. Although Congress has enacted legislation preempting state copyright laws, Congress has not regulated with respect to sound recordings that were made before February 15, 1972. Consequently, sound recordings that were made before February 15, 1972 may still be subject to state intellectual property rights notwithstanding Congress's declaration of an intention to preempt state regulation of copyrights.

It is also important to note that although the U.S. Copyright Act does not protect pre-1972 sound recordings, sound recordings made in a foreign country may be protected by the copyright laws of that country. Several countries began protecting copyrights in sound recordings before the United States did.

DERIVATIVE WORKS

A sound recording is a derivative work of the work that is performed on it. A sound recording of a performance of a musical work is a derivative work of the musical work. A book-on-tape (audiobook) is a derivative work of a literary work.

Because the owner of the copyright in a work has the exclusive right to make derivative works of it, the owner of the copyright in a musical or literary work has the exclusive right to make sound recordings of it. A person who makes an unauthorized sound recording of a copyright protected work (such as a song or an oral reading of a book) is guilty of copyright infringement, and acquires no copyright rights in the recording so made.

A composer or author may grant another person a license to make a sound recording of a performance of his work. If that has been done, then copyright protection for the sound recording may come into existence.

A derivative work receives copyright protection only if the modifications and/or new material added involve enough creativity and originality to qualify for copyright protection. De minimis variations from the original do not suffice.

The copyright in a derivative work is distinct from the copyright in the underlying work. Ownership of the copyright in a derivative work only covers rights in the newly-created aspects, not the original work itself. It is for this reason that the producer and performers on an authorized sound recording of a musical work only acquire a copyright in the sound recording. The copyright in the musical composition remains with the owner of the copyright in the musical composition (usually it has been transferred to someone else.)

It should never be assumed that the owner of the copyright in a sound recording (such as a record company) also owns the copyright in the musical composition. Sometimes this is the case, but sometimes it is not. Singer-songwriters and bands that write their own songs frequently transfer the copyright in their musical works to a publisher, and recording companies then pursue rights to the song by negotiating with the publisher. This is not always the case, though. Some composers retain the copyrights to their music and work with recording companies directly. And even when a composer assigns rights to a publisher, a recording company that is interested in making and selling copies of a performance of a song may get either an outright transfer of the copyright in the musical work or, as sometimes happens, only a license to make a sound recording (derivative work) of it.

RECORDINGS OF PUBLIC DOMAIN WORKS

Because anyone can freely use works that are in the public domain, a person creating a derivative work from a public domain work gets copyright protection for the derivative work so created. The copyright in the derivative work, however, does not confer ownership of the copyright in the original work on the author of the derivative work. Other people can independently create their own derivative works based on the same public domain work.

The copyright in a derivative work only protects rights in material that is newly created for the derivative work. Thus, any number of recording companies can independently create recordings of performances of public domain songs, and none would be guilty of copyright infringement for doing so. An unauthorized recording of another sound recording, however, would be an infringement of the copyright in the sound recording, and this would be true even if the musical work that is performed on the sound recording is in the public domain.

DIGITIZATION

Digitization is not a sufficiently creative act to warrant copyright protection. Thus, digitizing a vinyl record album does not give rise to any new copyright rights.

UNORIGINAL ASPECTS OF A DERIVATIVE WORK

Because of the originality requirement, the creator of an authorized derivative work only acquires a copyright in the newly created aspects of the derivative work. The copyright in the copied aspects of the derivative work remains with the owner of the copyright in the original work.

This can be important when determining whose permission is needed to copy a work, or a portion of a work. In some cases, you may need the permission of both the original and the derivative work copyright owners. In other cases, you may only need the permission of one of them. In the case of a sound recording of a musical work, this means that in order to copy, distribute or live-stream it on your website, you may need to obtain licenses from both the owner of the copyright in the musical work and the owner of the copyright in the sound recording. If it is a compilation of sound recordings, such as a music album, that you want to copy, distribute, or live-stream, then you may also need a license from the owner of the copyright in the compilation.

BOOTLEG RECORDINGS

A bootleg recording is one that is created by recording a live performance without permission. If the performance is of a musical work that is protected by copyright, then the recording would be an infringement of the copyright in the musical work. It generally would not be an infringement of the copyright in the performance, however. Copyright protection for a performance generally only arises when the performance has been fixed in a tangible medium. Since a copyright does not exist at the time a performance is occurring, recording it generally cannot be infringement.

Under the Copyright Act's definition of "fixed," however, a work consisting of sounds and/or images that are simultaneously transmitted at the time an authorized recording of them is being made is considered "fixed" at the time of transmission. Thus, for example, if a band has hired someone to record their concert, then an unauthorized recording of the performance by another person would infringe the copyright in the performance.

Even if no authorized recording of a live performance is being made, an unauthorized recording would violate the Anti-Bootlegging Act, 17 U.S.C. § 1101. This statute provides that anyone who makes, transmits, distributes or makes copies of an unauthorized recording of a live musical performance is subject to the same penalties and liabilities as a copyright infringer.

COMPILATIONS

A compilation is a collection of authored works, unauthored items (such as data), or a combination of both. An album consisting of a collection of recordings of songs, or a compact disc containing recordings of thunder, rain and other natural sounds, are examples of compilations.

The selection and arrangement of things to include in a compilation can take some thought and creativity, so it is considered a work of authorship on the part of the compiler.

The copyright in a compilation exists independently from any copyright in the elements comprising the collection. A producer who selects and arranges the recordings to include on a "greatest hits" album may own the copyright in the compilation even though he does not own the copyrights in the individual recordings included on the album.

The owner of the copyright in a compilation is presumed to possess the right to reproduce and distribute the works contributed to it only as part of that compilation or a revision of that compilation. Merely owning the copyright in a compilation does not give rise to a right to copy, perform or distribute -- or to license others to copy, perform or distribute -- an individual work that is included in the collection.

The owner of the copyright in a compilation has an exclusive right to make revisions to the compilation, such as by rearranging the order, adding different recordings to the compilation, removing a particular recording from the compilation, and so on. The author of a copyrighted work appearing in the compilation, however, has the exclusive right to make derivative works of his copyrighted work. The owner of the copyright in the compilation does not have the right to alter or modify the content of a copyrighted song or sound recording that appears in the compilation.

Copyright protection for a compilation does not confer copyright protection on portions of it that would not otherwise receive copyright protection. Acquiring a compilation copyright in a collection of public domain songs or sound recordings does not thereby give the compiler any exclusive rights in the public domain songs or recordings themselves. Only the manner in which the songs and recordings are selected and arranged is protected by a copyright in the compilation.

PUBLIC DOMAIN SOUND RECORDINGS

See Chapter 13

FAIR USE OF SOUND RECORDINGS

See Chapter 14.

TRADEMARKS

Musical works and sound recordings, or portions of them, may be protected trademarks if they are used in connection with the marketing of a product or service. Called "sound marks," these are typically jingles or combinations of sounds, such as the familiar set of three chime tones used by NBC.

A work may be protected by trademark law even though it is not protected by copyright law. A short musical phrase or the title of a song, for example, might not be protected by copyright, but it could be protected as a trademark. Conversely, a work may be protected by copyright law even though it is not protected by trademark law. Any copyright-protected song that is not used in connection with the marketing of a product or service would be an example of that.

SONG TITLES AND PORTIONS OF LYRICS

Although titles and short phrases do not receive copyright protection, it is not uncommon for them to be used as trademarks, and many are legally protected as such. Trademark registrations of song titles and phrases from lyrics have increased significantly in this millennium.

COMMERCIAL USE

Potential trademark infringement liability should be a concern to you if you are using someone else's mark, or something similar to it, to sell, lease, offer, promote or advertise goods or services, or if you operate a commercial website or blog. A commercial site is one from which you receive revenue, even if it is only a small amount of revenue from a Google AdSense advertisement that is placed on your website, or payment or free product given to you with the expectation that you will provide a product review. Linking to a commercial site may also cause your site to be considered a commercial website.

Even a commercial website or blog, however, is allowed to make certain kinds of "fair use" of music and sound recordings.

For more information about trademark fair use, see Chapter 7.

MISAPPROPRIATION OF VOICE

Although privacy and publicity rights are most commonly associated with photographs and videotapes, the same general kinds of considerations can apply to sound recordings, too. For example, using a recording of another person's voice, or of an impersonation of the person's voice, for commercial or political advantage (such as to state or imply endorsement or sponsorship of a product, service or candidate) could expose you to liability for misappropriation of personality.

PRIVACY

Making or publishing an unauthorized recording of another person's conversation or private activities could expose you to liability for invasion of privacy in some states.

DEFAMATION AND OTHER LAWS

Although it doesn't happen very happen, there have been cases where people have been held liable for defamation or violation of other laws on the basis of the publication of an audio recording. The analysis in these cases is not significantly different. For example, just as liability may arise from photoshopping a picture in order to present a person in a false light, so liability may arise from splicing, deleting portions of, or making other edits to an audio recording to present a person in a false light.

LICENSING

See Chapter 20.

KEY POINTS:

- ❖ Music and lyrics receive copyright protection only if they are creative, original, and fixed in a tangible medium.
- ❖ Arrangements and recordings of musical works receive copyright protection only if created by or pursuant to a valid license from the copyright owner.
- ❖ Copyrights in sound recordings and in the works recorded in them are separate things.
- ❖ Unrecorded improvisation is not protected by copyright.
- ❖ Some song titles and short phrases may be protected trademarks.

CHAPTER 5

Video

COPYRIGHT

The Copyright Act defines an audiovisual work as "a series of related images which are intrinsically intended to be shown by the use of machines, or devices such as projectors, viewers, or electronic equipment, together with accompanying sounds, if any...." (17 U.S.C. § 101.) Movies, soundtracks, webinar presentations, slide shows, and videogames are examples.

An audiovisual work may or may not have an audio element. If it does, then the sound receives protection as part of the audiovisual work.

Because an audiovisual work is defined as a series of images, a single image accompanied by music, narration, etc. is not an "audiovisual work." The image may be separately protected by copyright as a photograph or visual artwork, but not as an audiovisual work.

The production, recording and performances in an audiovisual work may be protected by copyright.

PLOTS, THEMES AND MOVIE IDEAS

The plot or theme of a movie is not protected by copyright. An idea for a movie or other audiovisual work also is not protected by copyright. The words, sounds, images and effects used to express these things might be protected if they have been fixed in a tangible medium, such as film.

VIDEOGAMES

An idea for a videogame, or the system or method by which a game is played, is not protected by copyright. Audiovisual works, musical works, sound recordings, visual artwork and text that are incorporated into a game may be protected by copyright, but the game itself (the method and procedure involved, algorithm, and the rules for playing it) are not.

DOCUMENTARIES

Gathering factual information is not considered a creative act. Therefore, neither the factual information presented in a documentary nor the research that went into it is protected by copyright.

Although factual information is not itself protected by copyright, the exercise of judgment about which facts to include, and how to arrange and present them, in a documentary may be sufficiently creative acts to be protected by copyright, provided the selection and arrangement is not obvious. A documentary that merely states all known facts about an event, in chronological order, would be an example of a selection and arrangement that is too obvious to be protected by copyright. Copyright only protects creative acts; compiling facts in a way that requires no exercise of judgment at all is not a creative act.

The choice of words and/or images used to present facts and information may be protected, to the extent the expression is not merged with the information.

Although fact-gathering is not protected by copyright, there can be situations in which using information that someone else has gathered may subject you to liability for misappropriation of information. See Chapter 8.

TITLES, SHORT PHRASES, JOKES AND GAGS

The titles of audiovisual works are not protected by copyright. Generally speaking, neither are short phrases, jokes, gags, and the names of fictional characters.

CHARACTERS

A character in an audiovisual work may receive copyright protection if the character's description is sufficiently unique and detailed. In these cases, the use of the character's name in conjunction with a character with the same description could be a copyright violation. The use of the same name for a completely different character, however, probably will not be. For example, if you were to produce a film about a Vulcan named "Mr. Spock" who explores the universe aboard a starship, then you might be violating a *Star Trek* copyright. On the other hand, if you were to produce a romantic comedy in which one of the characters is a Philadelphia optometrist named Mr. Spock, you probably would not be.

The amount of detail that is required in order for a character to be protected by copyright is difficult to gauge. An alien being who is stranded on earth is too general to receive copyright protection. As more distinctive features are added – e.g., powers of levitation and telepathy, a long neck and a big head, perhaps a penchant for uttering the phrase, "Phone home" – the likelihood that unauthorized use of the character in a different movie will be found to be copyright infringement increases.

Although names, characters and short phrases are not protected by copyright, they may be protected as trademarks if they are used in connection with the marketing of goods or services. "Star Trek," for example, could be a trademark for a series of science fiction books, so unauthorized use of it as the title of a movie could violate trademark law.

Some characters are protected under both copyright and trademark law.

The copyright in an audiovisual work and the copyright in a character within it may be owned by different persons.

SCÈNES À FAIRE

A *scène à faire* is a stock or standard literary device in a screenplay or other dramatic work. It is a scene or detail that is considered standard in works in a particular genre. The use of gadgetry in a spy movie would be an example. A male serenading a lady outside her window would be an example of a *scène à faire* in a romance. *Scènes à faire* do not receive copyright protection.

Similarities between a scene in one work and a scene in another work do not infringe a copyright in the first work if the events that unfold in the scene follow naturally from the situation. A couple seeking refuge in a church during a storm would be an example.

Stereotypical characters do not receive copyright protection, either. A drunken Irish policeman, for example, is not protected by copyright.

Details that are essential to the depiction of a particular scene are also considered *scènes à faire*. It has been held, for example, that a movie about the South Bronx featuring drunks, prostitutes, vermin, and junk cars does not infringe the copyright in a previous movie featuring those same things. Any movie about the South Bronx would need to feature those things in order to be realistic.

COLORIZATION

Merely adding color(s) to a movie is not a sufficiently creative act to get copyright protection, so colorizing a black-and-white movie will not yield a new derivative work. Altering colors in an unusual way, on the other hand, may result in a copyrightable work. Factors to be considered are: whether and how much creativity went into the selection of colors, how much human involvement there was, and the extent to which overall appearance is affected. An unauthorized derivative work, however, does not get copyright protection.

DIGITIZATION

Digitization of a pre-existing work is not a sufficiently creative human act to warrant copyright protection.

COMPUTER- OR NATURE-GENERATED FOOTAGE

Purely machine-generated output that is created without any human interaction is not protected by copyright. A human may use a machine (such as a video camera) to assist in the fixation of a work, and the result will be protected by copyright, but if the machine itself actually creates the work, then it is not. Thus, a motion picture created by a human being using a camera is a work of human authorship so it is protected by copyright, but a computer-generated random array of sounds and moving images is not.

Because human authorship is required, scenes created by natural forces are not protected by copyright. The swirling motion of a tornado, for instance, is not protected by copyright. The manner in which a human being presents it on film might be protected by copyright, but the tornado itself is not.

FIXATION IN A TANGIBLE MEDIUM

Copyright protection does not arise until a work is fixed in a tangible medium. For this reason, even a well-thought-out idea for a movie is not protected by copyright until it is written down or recorded in some way. Unrecorded improvisations are not protected by copyright, either.

Once a work is fixed in a tangible medium, though, it is the expression that receives copyright protection; the medium itself does not. If copyright protection for an audiovisual work has come into existence at any point, then it continues to exist even if all tangible copies of it are destroyed.

COPIED WORKS

The act of copying another work is not sufficiently creative to receive copyright protection. Slavishly copying a video that is in the public domain will not yield a work that is protected by copyright.

Copying a video that is protected by copyright without the copyright owner's permission is infringement. Infringing works are not protected by copyright.

DERIVATIVE WORKS

A derivative work is one that contains elements of a pre-existing work but in modified form. A presentation that includes a movie clip is an example of a derivative work of an audiovisual work. A movie based on a novel is also an example of a derivative work.

The owner of the copyright has an exclusive right to make derivative works based on her work, unless she grants another person permission to do so.

The maker of an authorized derivative work acquires a copyright in the derivative work, but not in the underlying work. The maker of an unauthorized derivative work of a copyright-protected work acquires no rights.

A person creating a derivative work from a public domain work gets copyright protection for the derivative work so created, but does not thereby acquire a copyright in the original work.

De minimis contributions or variations from the original do not suffice as derivative works.

VIDEOS THAT HAVE BEEN PUBLISHED TO THE INTERNET

Many people believe that anything the public can view online for free is in the public domain and therefore may be freely copied. This is not true. Generally, you may not copy content from another web page and paste it to your own without permission, even if it's a free site. The author of content appearing on a web page has a protected copyright interest in what he creates. The fact that he has chosen to make it available on his website for free does not mean that he has chosen to make it available on yours. And the fact that someone else has chosen to upload an audiovisual work to YouTube or another video-sharing service does not mean that the work is now in the public domain or that you have an "implied license" to copy and distribute it.

To the contrary, much of the uploading to sites like YouTube is done in violation of copyright laws. Copying an illegally distributed copy is infringement to the same extent that copying the original is.

Moreover, because audiovisual works may contain within them several individual copyrights in things like musical compositions, choreography, the screenplay and/or the novel on which it is based, etc., unauthorized copying and pasting of an audiovisual work to your website could subject you to multiple claims of copyright infringement.

PUBLIC DOMAIN WORKS

Audiovisual works that are in the public domain do not receive copyright protection. A separately copyrighted element of an audiovisual work may be protected by copyright even if the audiovisual work is in the public domain, though. For example, the fact that a filmmaker has dedicated the film to the public domain does not necessarily mean that the screenplay is in the public domain, too. And the fact that a film is in the public domain does not necessarily mean that musical works performed in it are.

For more information about the public domain, see Chapter 13

FAIR USE

See Chapter 14.

SOUNDTRACKS

A soundtrack accompanying a motion picture does not get copyright protection as a sound recording. Instead, it receives copyright protection as an element of the audiovisual work.

A pre-existing sound recording that is incorporated into the soundtrack of a movie does not thereby lose its copyright protection as a sound recording, however. Use of a pre-existing sound recording without the permission of the copyright owner is an infringement of the copyright in the sound recording. This is why movie-makers must obtain licenses to use previously made sound recordings in their movies.

OTHER ELEMENTS OF AUDIOVISUAL WORKS

An audiovisual work may contain within it several different kinds of works in addition to the soundtrack. Typical elements of an audiovisual work include a screenplay (which, in turn, may be a derivative work of a novel); musical works; sound recordings; artwork; choreography; production; direction; and possibly others. Some of these things may be protected by copyright independently of the audiovisual work, if they were created independently of the creation of the audiovisual work, and were not created pursuant to a work-for-hire agreement for use in the audiovisual work.

CHOREOGRAPHY AND PANTOMIME

Choreography and pantomime receive copyright protection if they are fixed in a tangible medium. Videotaping a dance or pantomime performance is one way to fix choreography or pantomime in a tangible medium. A written notation or description of it is another way, but this is not required if a video recording of a performance of it is made.

TRADEMARKS

Trademark law provides protection for motion marks, that is, motions or sequences of motions that are used in connection with the marketing of a product or service. The Peabody Duck March is an example of a motion mark. The registration describes the elements of the "Peabody Duck March as performed at The Peabody Hotels" as a "red carpet being rolled out, the appearance of the ducks and uniformed Duckmaster at the elevator door, and the march of the ducks down the red carpet, up the steps, and into the fountain where they begin swimming. The mark also includes the fanfare in reverse sequence."

MOVIE TITLES, SHORT PHRASES AND CHARACTERS

Movie titles, characters and short phrases do not often receive copyright protection, but they are often protected trademarks. *Star Wars*, for example, is a registered trademark.

See Chapter 7 for more information about trademarks.

PRIVACY

Publishing video recordings can raise significant privacy and publicity rights issues. See Chapters 8 and 9.

OBSCENITY AND CHILD PORNOGRAPHY

Publishing, sharing, storing, promoting or viewing video clips depicting obscenity or child pornography, or facilitating any of these activities, puts you at risk of a criminal conviction for which some of the harshest sentences provided for in American law may be imposed. It may include a multiple-year prison sentence and hundreds of thousands of dollars in fines, among other things. For more information about these things, see Chapter 11.

PRODUCT LIABILITY

A manufacturer or distributor of a product may be liable to a consumer if the consumer suffers harm as a result of a defect in the product.

Digital media containing an audiovisual work can be a product, but the expressive content stored on it is not. In *James v. Meow Media, Inc.*, 300 F.3d 683, 688 (6th Cir. 2002) a court rejected an attempt to hold the creator of violent videogames and movies liable for allegedly desensitizing viewers to violence. The court differentiated between a container of content, which may be a product, and the communicative expression contained within it, which is not.

KEY POINTS:

* ❖ Audiovisual works may be protected by copyright.
* ❖ Individual elements of an audiovisual work may be protected by separate copyrights.
* ❖ An audiovisual work, or a portion of it, may be protected by trademark law as a motion mark.
* ❖ The expressive content of an audiovisual work is not a "product" for purposes of product liability law.
* ❖ Do not become involved in any way with publishing, promoting, viewing or sharing videos depicting obscenity or child pornography.

CHAPTER 6

Computer Programs

COPYRIGHT PROTECTION

Computer programs may be protected by copyright. Because ideas are not protected by copyright, though, only the literal components of a program receive copyright protection. The nonliteral aspects (the algorithm, the functions performed, the systems and methods used) do not. The sequence, structure and organization of a program are not protected by copyright.

The written expression of a program receives copyright protection. This includes both source code and object code.

In general, an aspect of a computer program is not protected by copyright if it is something that is necessary to make the program perform its function. Elements of the program, including the user interface, are protected by copyright only to the extent they are not necessary to operate the program.

The menu command hierarchy is a functional aspect of a program, and therefore is not protected by copyright.

Although using the same algorithm, system or method to perform the same functions as another computer program does not expose you to liability for copyright infringement, it may expose you to liability for patent infringement if the software is patented.

Source code receives copyright protection as a literary work, and the same general rules apply. This includes the rule that when an idea is merged with the expression of it, the expression is not protected by copyright. In these situations, the thing is treated as an idea rather than an expression, and therefore is not protected by copyright. The more "bare bones" an expression of an idea or information is, the more likely it is that the expression of the idea or information is merged with the idea or information itself, and therefore not protected by copyright.

CREATIVITY

Uncreative elements of a computer program are not protected by copyright. The appearance of a variable listing at the beginning of the source code is an example. This practice is so common and uncreative that it is considered a *scène à faire*. Therefore, it is not protected by copyright.

FIXATION IN A TANGIBLE MEDIUM

Like the copyright in any other kind of work, a copyright in a computer program arises when, and only when, it is fixed in a tangible medium of expression. The medium may be print, digital, or something else. Examples include a compact disc, a digital storage device, or a website. (A website is stored on a server, which is a tangible medium.)

Copyright in a computer program arises automatically upon fixation. Registration is not required, although doing so can be beneficial in terms of protecting against infringement.

PUBLIC DOMAIN PROGRAMS

Public domain programs are not protected by copyright. See Chapter 13

FAIR USE

For more information about fair use, see Chapter 14.

DERIVATIVE WORKS

A derivative work is one that contains elements of a pre-existing work but in modified form. An updated version of a computer program is one example. A program that is incorporated into another computer program, or into a website, is another example.

Only the copyright owner has a right to make derivative works, unless he has expressly transferred that right to another person.

The maker of an unauthorized derivative work of a copyright-protected work acquires no copyright in the derivative work so made. A copyright in a derivative work arises only if the person creating it has the right to do so.

The creator of an authorized derivative work does get copyright protection, but only for the newly-created elements of the derivative work.

The owner of the copyright in the original program retains ownership of the copyright in the original program.

Because anyone can freely use public domain works, any number of people may create derivative works from public domain software. Each such author only receives copyright protection for the new elements he or she creates, however, not the original public domain work itself.

No rights arise by virtue of the creation of a derivative work unless the modifications involve some originality and creativity. Neither slavish copying nor making only trivial variations to the original give rise to a copyright in a derivative work.

COMPUTER DATABASES

A computer database is a compilation. A person may own a copyright in a compilation even if he does not own a copyright in its individual components, and even if the database consists of items that are not protected by copyright (such as factual information.)

The compilation of a computerized database is not protected by copyright, however, unless some creativity goes into the selection or arrangement of the items in the database. An exercise of judgment as to the words and/or images that are used to communicate information contained in a database, and the manner in which the information is arranged and displayed, may receive copyright protection, to the extent the information is not merged with the expression of it, and provided the arrangement is not random or an obvious one (such as an alphabetical list.) Creating categories for the organization of the data is a sufficiently creative act to warrant copyright protection.

The individual components of a compilation may also be protected by copyright. The fact that an author's copyrighted work is included in a compilation does not, in itself, have the effect of transferring the author's copyright to the owner of the copyright in the compilation.

The owner of the copyright in a compilation has an exclusive right to make revisions to the compilation, such as by rearranging the order, adding new information to the compilation, removing a fact from the compilation, and so on. The author of a copyrighted work appearing in the compilation, however, has the exclusive right to make derivative works of his copyrighted work. The owner of the copyright in the compilation does not automatically have the right to alter or modify the content of a copyrighted work that appears in the compilation.

MISAPPROPRIATION OF INFORMATION

The owner of a copyright in a computer database does not have a copyright in the data that is compiled within it. Copyright protection for a compilation does not confer copyright protection on portions of it that would not otherwise be protected. Only the manner in which the data is selected, arranged, presented or expressed in a compilation may be protected by a copyright in the compilation.

Although information is not protected by copyright, there may be circumstances in which republishing it may expose you to liability for misappropriation. See Chapter 8.

PATENT PROTECTION

Although the systems, methods and processes in a computer are not protected by copyright, they may be protected by patent law, provided they are sufficiently novel and original to qualify the program as a new invention.

Unlike copyrights, which automatically arise upon the fixation of a work in a tangible medium, a patent does not exist until an appropriate governmental agency issues one. In the United States, that would be the U.S. Patent Office.

A provisional patent is a temporary patent that may be issued while an application for a patent is pending. If a patent is granted, then some protection for infringement occurring between the time the U.S. Patent Office published the application and the time the patent was issued may exist under 35 U.S.C. § 154, provided the alleged infringer had notice of the publication.

The law with respect to software patents is in a state of flux. Nevertheless, it is important to be aware that copying a software program may potentially expose you to liability not only for copyright infringement, but also for patent infringement.

PATENT INFRINGEMENT

Patent infringement occurs when a person makes, uses or sells a patented invention in the United States without the permission of the patent owner. Since the patentable claim in a computer software program involves some original process or method, infringement does not occur unless you actually implement or sell that process or method. If, for example, you deploy someone else's payment processing software on your website, and a patent has been issued for the method or process embodied in it, and that patent is still active, then you might be liable for patent infringement.

Selling embodiments of another person's patented software program, or selling access to it from your website, may subject you to liability for patent infringement if you do not have permission from the patent owner to do so.

Using, making or selling a patented invention without permission is called "direct infringement." You may be held liable for direct infringement even if you had no knowledge of the existence of the patent.

Since computer programs may also be protected by copyright, copying or distributing a computer program may infringe both a copyright and a patent.

INDUCEMENT TO INFRINGE

You may be liable for patent infringement even if you do not make, use or sell the program yourself, but you actively induce someone else to do so. Inducement liability may arise only if you knew a program was patented and you intended for a person to make an unauthorized use, manufacture or sale of it.

CONTRIBUTORY INFRINGEMENT

35 U.S.C. § 271(c) imposes liability for contributory patent infringement on anyone who sells "a component of a patented machine, manufacture, combination or composition, or a material or apparatus for use in practicing a patented process, constituting a material part of the invention, knowing the same to be especially made or especially adapted for use in an infringement of such patent, and not a staple article or commodity of commerce suitable for substantial non-infringing use...."

Selling access codes, keys, passwords or other things that allow unauthorized persons to use and/or copy patented software is an example of an activity that could result in contributory patent infringement.

TRADE SECRETS

While definitions vary from state to state, a trade secret is usually defined to include any compilation, method, process, device, program or formula:

1) that has economic value by virtue of not being generally known or readily ascertainable; and

2) as to which reasonable efforts have been made to maintain its secrecy.

The programming code of a computer program, therefore, may be a trade secret if it has economic value and reasonable efforts have been made to maintain its secrecy.

Measures that computer software creators and vendors sometimes employ to protect trade secrets include: confidentiality covenants in the licensing agreement; non-disclosure covenants with developers and testers; distribution only in executable form; and various kinds of security measures to prevent access to the source code.

Theft or disclosure of a trade secret with knowledge or intent that doing so will cause harm (including financial loss) to its owner, or will benefit a foreign government, is a federal crime. Misappropriation or disclosure of a trade secret may also expose you to civil liability under state law.

The First Amendment protects some disclosures, but use of a trade secret in violation of a confidentiality agreement or in breach of a fiduciary duty (such as the fiduciary duties owed by employees, officers and directors to the employers/entities they serve) is not protected by the First Amendment, and may expose you to liability for breach of contract or fiduciary duty in addition to liability for disclosure of the trade secret.

TRANSFERS

COMPUTER PROGRAM VS. TANGIBLE COPY

A purchase of digital media containing a copy of a software program does not transfer the copyright or patent in the computer program to the purchaser. Lawfully acquiring a copy of a program does not automatically give the buyer a right to make copies of it, or to distribute, lease, sell, or publish it. Most software vendors only sell licenses to use computer programs, not ownership of the programs themselves.

BREACH OF SOFTWARE LICENSE AGEEMENT

Violating the terms of a software license will expose you to liability for breach of contract. In addition, if the term you violate relates to one of the exclusive rights of copyright ownership, then you may also be liable for copyright infringement. For example, if a software license only permits you to make one copy of the software, and you proceed to make more than one copy, then you may be liable not only for breach of contract but also for infringement of the copyright in the computer program.

In some situations, violations of software licenses may also result in liability for patent infringement or trademark violations, or for unauthorized disclosure of a trade secret.

Software licenses are addressed in Chapter 21.

MALWARE AND SPYWARE

COMPUTER FRAUD AND ABUSE ACT

The Computer Fraud and Abuse Act, 18 U.S.C. § 1030 ("CFAA") makes it unlawful to knowingly cause the transmission of a program, code, information, or command, that intentionally causes damage to a computer without authorization. Both criminal and civil penalties may be imposed for a violation.

BUNDLING SPYWARE IN DOWNLOADABLE SOFTWARE

Some courts have applied the old common law cause of action for trespass to chattels to hold people accountable for bundling spyware in computer program files that they make available to users of their websites. "Trespass to chattels" basically refers to the act of making unwanted contact with another person's personal property, and requires a showing of some harm or injury to the property. A user's computer is "chattel." If including spyware in a program that is downloadable from your website causes some non-trivial kind of damage to a user's computer, then there may be liability for trespass to chattels. Courts have allowed recovery on the basis that taking up bandwidth on the user's Internet connection, or causing a user's computer to slow down, or taking up memory on a user's computer, or using screen space on a computer monitor, or reducing user productivity due to frustration, are substantial, not merely trivial, kinds of damage with respect to this kind of activity.

THE CONVENTION ON CYBERCRIME

The Convention on Cybercrime is a treaty to which the United States and several other counties are parties. Among other things, it requires member countries to criminalize the knowing and intentional creation or transmission of computer viruses or malware, as well as other things such as child pornography and computer-related fraud. It makes computer crimes extraditable offenses, and requires member countries to cooperate in investigations and prosecutions.

KEY POINTS:

❖ The literal elements of a computer program, such as source and object code, may be protected by copyright.

❖ Nonliteral elements of a computer program, such as the algorithm, are not protected by copyright.

❖ A computer program may be patented if it is novel.

❖ Data is not protected by copyright, but the selection and arrangement of them in a computerized database may be.

❖ Some unauthorized uses of a database may result in liability for misappropriation of information.

❖ Ownership of a disk is not ownership of the software on it.

❖ Potential sources of liability for violating a software license include patent, copyright and trademark infringement; misappropriation of a trade secret; and breach of contract.

❖ Do not transmit malware, spyware or other malicious code.

CHAPTER 7

Trademarks

Copying text or images from another website can raise trademark liability issues if what you are copying includes a brand name, logo, phrase, slogan, image, sound, or motion that is used in connection with the marketing of goods or services. Trademark issues can also arise if you use something confusingly similar to a brand identifier in material that is created for your website or blog (such as an advertisement, review, logo, html code, or domain name.) Not every mention of a brand name is a violation of trade-mark law, but it is important to know what kinds of things are trademarks, and what kinds of uses of them could put you at risk of liability.

A trademark can be nearly anything -- words, typographical character combinations, slogans, phrases, symbols, logos, drawings, photographs, packaging, sometimes even sounds, scents, motions, architecture, etc. If it is used to distinguish one person's or business's goods or services from the goods or services made or sold by others, it may be trademark.

A trademark for services is sometimes called a "service mark." A trademark indicating membership in an organization is called a "collective membership mark." A trademark indicating approval by an organization is called a "certification mark."

In some countries, trademark rights may arise by registration of the mark. In the United States, however, trademark rights arise through use, not registration. Registration can make it easier to enforce a trademark, but a valid trademark may exist, and be enforceable, even if it is unregistered.

INFRINGEMENT

You may be liable for trademark infringement if you use another person's trademark, or something similar to it, in a way that is likely to cause people to become confused about the origin, endorsement or sponsorship of goods or services. The classic example is marketing a product or service using a brand name that is identical or confusingly similar to one that someone else is already using.

DILUTION

You may be liable for trademark dilution if you use a famous mark in such a way as to cause it to lose its distinctiveness as a brand name ("dilution by blurring") or if you use it in such a way as to harm the reputation of the famous mark ("dilution by tarnishment.")

Liability for trademark dilution can arise even if consumers are not caused to become confused about origin, endorsement or sponsorship. Using a famous trademark to market another company's goods or services may be dilution by blurring even if the goods or services are so different that no reasonable person would be confused about whether they are made by the same company or not.

Liability for dilution by blurring arises when a famous and distinctive mark, or something that is so similar to the mark as to cause people to associate it with the famous mark, is used in commerce in a way that is likely to impair the distinctiveness of the famous mark. Liability for dilution by tarnishment arises when a famous and distinctive mark, or something that is so similar to the mark that people are likely to associate it with the famous mark, is used in commerce in a way that is likely to harm the reputation of the famous mark.

Using a famous trademark to sell lower-quality goods or services, and using the trademark in connection with a portrayal of a company or its products in an unwholesome or unsavory context, are examples of tarnishment. While the terms "unwholesome" and "unsavory" have not been defined with any great precision, it is clear that using a trademark, or a close variation of it, in sexual contexts, or in a way that implies sexual connotations, would qualify. Using a trademark or a close variation of it in a way that suggests an association with drugs or crime would probably qualify, too.

Noncommercial references to a brand name for the purpose of commentary or criticism should not result in liability for dilution by tarnishment. The Lanham Act exempts the following categories from dilution liability:

- nominative fair use;
- descriptive fair use;

- comparative advertising;
- news reporting and news commentary;
- parody, criticism or commentary;
- any non-commercial use of a mark.

A court may determine that a web site is commercial if it offers a product or service for sale or lease; displays links to commercial web sites; or if there is advertising on it (which can include a paid product review.) Nevertheless, even a commercial website is exempt from dilution liability when it uses a trademark solely for the purpose of criticism, commentary or parody, so long as the content is not false or misleading.

FALSE ADVERTISING AND UNFAIR COMPETITION

In addition to liability for infringement, you may also be liable for false advertising or unfair competition if you use another person's trademark in such a way as to create a false impression as to the origin, endorsement or sponsorship of particular goods or services.

Liability for false advertising is not limited to cases involving the creation of a false impression about the origin, endorsement or sponsorship of goods or services, though. Liability can arise under the provisions of the Lanham Act prohibiting false advertising whenever all of the following elements are present:

1) false or misleading statement or representation in an advertisement
2) having the capacity to deceive consumers
3) having a material effect on purchasing decision
4) having an effect on interstate commerce; and
5) likely damage as a result of the false advertising.

Use of another company's trademark in metatags to skew search engine results is one way to incur liability for false advertising under the Lanham Act.

CONTRIBUTORY LIABILITY

If you provide a venue (such as a web site) for someone else's infringing acts, then you may be held liable as a contributor to the infringement even though you did not personally do anything to cause confusion about the origin, endorsement or sponsorship of goods or services.

You may not be held liable for contributory infringement, however, if you neither knew nor should have known about the infringing activity. Also, you may not be held liable for contributory infringement unless you have direct control over the content appearing on a site.

If you do not actually know that infringing activity is taking place on your web site, but you have reason to believe that it might be occurring, and you deliberately fail to investigate, then a court may say that you "should have known" about it, and treat you the same as if you had actual knowledge of it. The law does not countenance willful blindness. On the other hand, if you had neither actual knowledge nor any reason to suspect that infringement might be occurring, then you should be safe from liability for contributory infringement.

"Direct control" means the ability and power to allow or remove content from a site. Website hosting services have been held to have direct control over the sites they host if they have the ability to disable individual IP addresses or prevent the transmission of trademark-infringing content in some other way.

Under the "should have known" prong of the contributory infringement standard, it may be said, as a general rule, that the more involved a web host is with an infringer's web site, the greater the risk he runs of being held liable as a contributory infringer, and the greater his duty to investigate becomes. While policing hosted sites for evidence of possible trademark infringement is not required, web hosts that are directly involved in the development of a site (e.g., by offering advice, or implementing search engine optimization for the site, etc.) should monitor these sites for any indication of possible trademark violations, and remove any hosted page or site that is infringing a trademark. And any web host, no matter how closely connected with a client's business he is, should remove allegedly infringing content immediately upon receiving a notice of infringement. Receiving a notice of infringement establishes actual knowledge of it.

A web host's contract with clients should require clients to obey all trademark laws. It would also be a good idea to include an indemnity clause, i.e., a provision requiring the client to pay any litigation costs and attorney fees incurred by the host in defending against a trademark infringement claim, including defending against contributory infringement claims. The contract should also set forth the client's representations and warranties that he either owns or has appropriate authority under a valid license for the trademarks that are used on the client's site, and that he has all necessary intellectual property rights for all content used on the site.

Of course, a contract between a web host and a webpage client will not immunize either of them from liability to a third party. Therefore, if the web host acquires any reason to believe a client may be engaging in trademark violations (such as registering and using a domain name that is another company's business name or brand name; or selling products or services using brand names, logos, slogans or product packaging that look or sound confusingly similar to those used by another company) he should immediately notify the client that the site will be taken down if the activity does not cease. If the client persists in the activity after receiving such a notice, then the web host should promptly take the site down.

The same kinds of considerations also apply to website owners and bloggers who accept user-provided content such as guest blogs, comments, etc. Although a website owner or blogger might not have a traditional formal contract with subscribers and users, a contract may be formed by requiring users to review and signify assent to Terms of Service by clicking on a "Yes" or "I Agree" button or box.

GOOD FAITH AND LACK OF KNOWLEDGE

Innocent infringement (using a mark in good faith and without knowledge of another person's exclusive right to use it) is not a defense to direct infringement. It is possible to succeed on an infringement claim without proving that the infringer knew he was using someone else's trademark; that he intended to deceive people; or that his use of the mark was in bad faith.

Although not a defense, an infringer's good faith can reduce the amount of damages that may be recovered. A trademark owner can require an infringer to turn over the profits he has made from his unauthorized use of the mark only if the infringement was in bad faith. Other damages – such as the trademark owner's own loss of earnings – may still be recoverable, however, regardless of whether the infringement was innocent or in bad faith.

Compensatory damages may be recovered against an innocent direct infringer, but not against an innocent contributory infringer.

Injunctive relief may be sought against publishers, printers and broadcasters of another person's infringing material on the basis of contributory infringement regardless of whether the infringement was innocent or not.

COMMERCIAL VS. NONCOMMERCIAL USE

Potential trademark infringement liability should only be a concern to you if you are using someone else's mark or something similar to it to sell, lease, offer or advertise goods or services. You do not have to worry about infringement liability for merely mentioning or referring to someone else's trademark if you are not using it for one of these purposes, so long as your statements in connection with it are not false or misleading.

The federal trademark statute, known as the Lanham Act, prohibits the unauthorized use "in commerce" of a trademark "in connection with the sale, offering for sale, distribution or advertising of goods and services." State laws vary, but all require a person claiming trademark infringement to prove that the use being made of a mark creates a likelihood of confusion with someone else's goods or services that are being marketed under the same or a similar trademark. For this reason, merely referring to someone else's trademark is not often very likely to result in liability for infringement.

The Lanham Act also excludes noncommercial uses of a trademark from the definition of dilution by tarnishment. Accordingly, you should not need to worry about potential dilution liability for things like an incidental display of trademarks in a photograph of a cityscape, or references to brand names in an unpaid product review.

USING TRADEMARKS IN METATAGS & DOMAIN NAMES

Metatags (or "meta elements") are elements that are used in html and xhtml documents to provide metadata about a web page. They are part of a web page's header section. Metatags can be used to specify a page's description, keywords, and any other words. They operate in the background; they normally are not seen by the web page reader. Web page developers sometimes insert keyword metatags in order to boost the likelihood that the page will turn up in search engine results, so that people with an interest in the topic related to the keyword will be more likely to visit the site.

Courts have held that using another company's trademark – or something confusingly similar to it -- in your domain name, or in metatags, as a means of increasing visitors to your website is a form of trademark infringement because it creates initial interest confusion among Internet users. If it is a famous trademark, you may also be liable for dilution.

Using another company's name in your domain name may also subject you to liability for cybersquatting, in some circumstances.

Using trademarks in metatags for the purpose of attracting people to a website does not come within any of the "fair use" defenses.

Several courts have held that using a competitor's trademark in a website's metatags is trademark infringement, dilution and/or false advertising. Certainly using a competitor's trademark as a metatag in a website advertising goods or services that directly compete with those of the mark's owner is more likely to result in liability than using a mark as a metatag for other purposes is. All things considered, though, it is probably never a good idea to use other people's trademarks in your metatags.

DEFENSES

Trademark law provides some exemptions and defenses to liability. Some of these derive from the underlying policy objectives served by trademark law; others are intended to promote First Amendment values of freedom of speech and press.

NOMINATIVE FAIR USE

Merely referring to a trademark, as distinguished from using it in a way that suggests something untrue about the origin, sponsorship or endorsement of a product or service, is not trademark infringement.

This kind of use is called *referential* or *nominative* use. It is also colloquially known as "trademark fair use."

To qualify for this defense, the referential use must be both truthful and not likely to confuse the public.

Merely mentioning a brand name or displaying a trademarked logo on your website should not, in itself, result in trademark liability, so long as the display is not likely to lead people to think the site is sponsored or endorsed by the trademark owner, and so long as you don't say anything false or misleading about the trademark owner or the product or service marketed under the trademark. Thus, "gripe sites," (web sites where people post their complaints about a particular product or service) may mention or display a company's mark or logo, so long as the "gripes" are not false or misleading.

Similarly, a repair service may refer to the brand names of products it repairs or services so long as it does not falsely state or imply that it is authorized by or affiliated with the owner of the trademark in some way. Likewise, a shop may sell brand-name replacement parts so long as it does not falsely hold itself out as an "authorized" seller or an "affiliate" of the trademark owner.

However it is denominated, what this doctrine essentially says is that you will not be held liable for trademark infringement or dilution just because you mention someone else's trademark in a statement, if the statement is truthful and not misleading; and so long as it does not confuse visitors to your site about the source, sponsorship or endorsement of particular goods or services.

This defense may be asserted only if three conditions exist:

1) the products or services to which you wish to refer are not readily identifiable without using the trademark;
2) only so much of the mark is used as is reasonably necessary to identify the product or service; and
3) the user does not state or imply sponsorship or endorsement by the trademark owner.

The defense is commonly associated with the right to use trademarks in news reporting, commentary, criticism, parody, and comparative advertising, but it can also apply in other contexts, too. An advertisement for an independent automotive repair shop stating that it specializes in fixing Volkswagens is an example. So long as the advertisement is clear that it is an independent shop and is not affiliated with or endorsed by the Volkswagen Company, this qualifies as nominative fair use of the Volkswagen trademark. If, on the other hand, the advertisement states or implies that the shop provides "authorized" or "approved" service, or is affiliated with, sponsored or endorsed by the Volkswagen company in some way, then nominative fair use cannot be raised as a defense to a trademark infringement claim.

DESCRIPTIVE FAIR USE

The descriptive fair use defense allows anyone to use ordinary words to describe their own goods or services even if those words happen to be part of someone else's trademark. For example, if the owner of the trademark, SWEETARTS, which is a telescoped composite of the words *sweet* and *tart*, were to sue you for infringement for advertising your product as "sweet and tart," you could assert the defense of descriptive fair use on the basis that you are merely using ordinary words that accurately describe your product or service.

The defense can also work for geographic descriptors. For example, a new car dealer who happens to have a sales location in Lincoln, Nebraska could advertise its "Lincoln store" even though someone else owns LINCOLN as a registered mark for sales of the Lincoln make of automobiles.

Using your own personal name in connection with your business is another example of descriptive fair use. If, for example, Samuel Adams decides to go into business using his own name as the name of his business, he could assert the Descriptive Fair Use defense if the beer maker were to sue him for infringement.

The defense is lost, however, if you start using the descriptive term as a trademark. A firm advertising "sweet and juicy oranges" could probably prevail using the Descriptive Fair Use defense if sued by the owner of the trademark SWEET 'N JUICY for infringement. If he were to start using "sweet and juicy" as a brand name for the oranges (in other words, as an identifier of the source of the oranges, such as by using that phrase on labels), then he will lose the protection of the Descriptive Fair Use defense.

The determinative test is whether a reasonable person would perceive the use of the word, symbol, etc. as an indicator of the origin of the goods. A prominent or differently stylized display of a descriptive word in an advertisement or a label is likely to create an inference that a descriptive term is being used as a trademark. Using the same descriptive word in a paragraph as an adjective to describe the goods is not likely to create an impression that the term is being used as a trademark.

The Descriptive Fair Use defense is available only if the descriptive use is truthful and done in good faith. "Bad faith," in this context, means using a mark with the intention of confusing consumers about the source of the goods or services, or with the intention of exploiting an existing trademark's reputation.

CRITICISM, COMMENTARY, AND PARODY

The fact that a person may be sued for trademark dilution by tarnishment might make you think that it is illegal to ever say anything bad about a particular product, service or company. Trademark law, however, attempts to respect First Amendment values of freedom of speech and press by shielding those who mention or display a trademark in the context of criticism, commentary, opinion, or parody from liability for trademark infringement or dilution. References to a trademark strictly for these purposes are normally fair use.

The Lanham Act, for instance, exempts the following from the definition of tarnishment:

a) nominative fair use;

b) descriptive fair use;

c) comparative advertising;

d) news reporting and news commentary;

e) parodying, criticizing, or commenting upon the famous mark owner or the goods or services of the famous mark owner; or

f) any non-commercial use of a mark.

A court may determine that a website is commercial if it offers products or services for sale or lease, or if there are links to commercial web sites, or if there is advertising, on it, which can include a paid product review. Nevertheless, even a commercial web site is exempt from dilution liability when it uses a trademark solely for the purpose of criticism, commentary or parody, so long as the content is not false or misleading.

As a general rule, it may be said that most expressive uses of a mark are probably fair use. In most cases, using a mark or logo in the course of communicating an idea about something other than the source, sponsorship or endorsement of particular goods or services is fair use. So long as nothing is sought to be suggested about those things, it may be said that expressive use of a trademark normally is permitted – provided, of course, it does not involve the communication of false or misleading information.

> *Example:* If I post the statement, "These Doritos brand chips are the best!" next to chips that I am selling online, and the chips I am selling look like but are not Doritos, then consumers are likely to mistakenly believe the chips I'm selling in these bags are Doritos brand chips, that is, the chips made by the company that owns the DORITOS trademark. This would be considered a non-expressive, commercial use; and I could be sued for infringement. If the chips are of lower quality than Doritos chips, I might also be sued for dilution by tarnishment. Publishing the same statement ("These Doritos brand chips are the best!") as part of a snack food review, on the other hand, should not cause any rational reader to become confused about the source of Doritos. A court would almost certainly rule the snack food review to be fair use, which I could assert as a defense if someone tried to sue me for infringement. Likewise, if I were to publish the statement, "Doritos are the worst chip I've ever tasted" in a snack food review, a court would almost certainly rule it is fair use (unless I fail to disclose an association with a competitor of Doritos), which I could assert as a defense if someone tried to sue me for dilution by tarnishment.

COMPARATIVE ADVERTISING

Companies may refer to a competitor's brand in their advertising. For example, the Toyota Company may advertise that its cars are better than Fords.

The right to engage in comparative advertising, however, does not include a right to make false or misleading statements. Suppose, for example, the

Toyota Company went further, and advertised that 90% of ASE-certified mechanics surveyed said they believe Toyota automobiles are better than Ford automobiles, when in fact no such survey exists. An argument might be made that this would be actionable as trademark dilution by tarnishment, although this argument would be extending the "tarnishment" doctrine beyond its original purpose of deterring the practice of portraying a company or its products in an unwholesome or unsavory way. In any event, there certainly could be liability for false advertising.

COLLATERAL USE

Referential use of a mark is also permitted if the trademarked product is a component part of another product or service, so long as the public would not be led to believe that the trademark owner is either the source or a sponsor or endorser of the other product or service. This is sometimes called "collateral use." An auto parts dealer selling "reconditioned Ford parts" would be an example. So long as he neither states nor implies that the parts are authorized or approved by Ford, the dealer should be safe from an infringement claim.

LOGOS

The nominative fair use defense may be invoked only if the products or services to which you wish to refer "are not readily identifiable without using the trademark." Since a brand may be identified by name, displaying the logo is not necessary to identify it. This raises the question: Is displaying a company's logo in the course of criticizing or commenting on the company or its products permissible?

An argument could be made that a company or its products are readily identifiable simply by using the company or product name, so nominative fair use could not be asserted as a defense when you display the company's logo (or any non-textual trademark) instead of simply referring to the company or its product by name. On the other hand, trademark law does not establish a hierarchy of trademark types. There is no reason to believe that word marks are superior to design logo marks for identification purposes, nor is there anything in the law that specifically requires the use of a word mark instead of a design logo mark for identification purposes whenever possible.

In any event, even if a court were to rule that nominative fair use does not apply to the use of logos, there can be no infringement liability unless the kind of use made of a trademark is likely to confuse consumers about the source, sponsorship or endorsement of a product or service. A display of a company's logo in the context of a critique of the company or its products and services, or a news report about them, is not very likely to confuse readers about the source, sponsorship or endorsement of the products or services being discussed. Of course, tarnishment liability may exist even if there is no likelihood of confusion, but the tarnishment statute specifically exempts commentary, criticism and news reporting. And the tarnishment exemptions are not subject to the requirement that the products and services not be readily identifiable without using the trademark.

Couldn't it be said that displaying the company's logo exceeds the scope of the exemption for criticism, commentary and news reporting? Again, trademark law does not set out a hierarchy pursuant to which word marks are preferable to other kinds of trademarks.

The owner of a trademarked logo may also have a copyright in the artwork embodied in the logo. There is a fair use defense for copyright violations, too, but it is governed by a separate set of standards and principles.

The law is still evolving in this area. If you want to be as safe as possible, use word marks instead of logos in your reporting, criticisms and commentaries about other companies and their products. If you do publish a company's logo as part of a criticism, commentary, or news report, though, be sure to do so in a way that is not likely to confuse anyone about the source, sponsorship or endorsement of the goods or services – or your website. Be sure to carefully evaluate the possible applicability or inapplicability of copyright fair use, as well.

DISCLAIMERS

While publishing a disclaimer on your web site will not necessarily insulate you from liability in every case, it can help you rebut a "likelihood of confusion" claim in an infringement suit. The disclaimer should be to the effect that the trademark(s) or logo(s) you reference on your web site is/are trademark(s) of XYZ Company. (But identify the actual company; don't just say, "XYZ Company.") If it is a registered trademark, then say so. Then expressly disclaim any affiliation with, or sponsorship or endorsement by, the trademark owner.

If you publish a fan site, then you should include a disclaimer on your web site to let visitors know that the site is not an "official" one, unless the trademark owner actually has authorized you to call yourself an "official" fan site. You should also provide a link to the trademark owner's site. This will not necessarily insulate you from liability in every case, but it can be helpful in terms of defending against a claim that your site misleads visitors into thinking that the site, the statements that you publish on it or the goods or services that you offer, are endorsed or sponsored by the trademark owner.

Disclaimers do not provide absolute protection from liability for trademark infringement, but they can go a long way toward building a defense against trademark infringement or dilution.

A disclaimer of affiliation, sponsorship or endorsement by the trademark owner will only help protect you from claims of trademark violations. It will not provide protection from a claim of copyright infringement, in those cases where a trademark is also protected by copyright. If you have reason to believe that a particular logo, motion, sound, etc. may be protected by copyright, and you are not sure that a copyright fair use doctrine clearly supports your display of it, then you should seek permission to display it on your site. If getting copyright permission is not feasible, but your reference to the trademark qualifies as trademark fair use, then you should refrain from displaying the artwork on your web site, and should refer to the brand by name instead.

MORE STRATEGIES TO REDUCE RISKS

First and foremost, avoid trying to capitalize on another company's trademark or goodwill. This is how most trademark violations, such as sound-alike brand names and similar-looking logos, begin.

Don't try to fool consumers into thinking your goods or services are those of another. And avoid misleading consumers to believe your goods or services are authorized, sponsored or endorsed by another person or company when they are not. If you want to say that you are an "authorized" dealer or repair service for X brand, for example, make sure you have something in writing that provides evidence that you really have been authorized by a person with appropriate authority to sell or repair X brand.

Refrain from publishing any false or misleading statements, especially if you run a "gripe" site.

Refraining from hosting advertisements or links to commercial websites is not necessarily required, and doing so will not necessarily insulate you from an infringement claim, but maintaining a noncommercial web site can be helpful in terms of building a defense against claims of trademark infringement or dilution. If that is not feasible, then you should at least try to refrain from hosting advertising for, or links to, the websites of companies that compete for business with the ones you criticize on your website.

GET A LICENSE OR PERMISSION

If there is any question about whether your intended use of a trademark is permissible, the best strategy is to get the trademark owner's permission in a written licensing agreement, and comply with it.

Sometimes a trademark, such as a drawing used as a logo, may also be protected by copyright. In these cases, you will need a license for both the copyright and the trademark.

KEY POINTS:

- ❖ Almost anything can be a trademark if it is used in connection with the marketing of goods or services.
- ❖ In the U.S., trademark rights arise from use, not registration.
- ❖ Choose a trademark that is different from others that are already being used to market products or services like yours.
- ❖ Avoid using a well-known trademark in a way that dilutes its distinctiveness, or damages its owner's reputation.
- ❖ Do not make false or misleading statements.
- ❖ Do not try to confuse consumers about the origin, sponsorship or endorsement of a product or service.
- ❖ Do not use a trade name or trademark in metatags.
- ❖ Do not use another's trademark or name in your domain name.
- ❖ Promptly remove any user-provided content that may infringe or dilute a trademark, or that is false or misleading.
- ❖ Trademark fair use includes:
  - Nominative fair use;
  - Descriptive fair use;
  - Comparative advertising;
  - News reporting;
  - Commentary;
  - Criticism;
  - Parody;
  - Non-commercial use.
- ❖ Publish disclaimers of affiliation, sponsorship or endorsement when you mention or display someone's trademark.
- ❖ The safest course is to ask for a license or permission.

CHAPTER 8

Information

At a time when it is possible to find information about almost anybody and anything by doing an online search, it is easy to get the impression that there are no limitations at all on the kinds of information that may be published to the Internet. In truth, however, the law imposes some very significant limitations. Some of these are designed to protect people's reputations and privacy. Others seek to prevent unfair competition and to ensure those who are invested in information a fair return on their investments. It is important for anybody who publishes or contributes to a website or blog to familiarize themselves with the various restrictions the law imposes on the disclosure of private or proprietary information.

PRIVACY RIGHTS

Numerous laws and regulations exist for the protection of an individual's personal privacy. The purpose of this body of law is to prevent and discourage the disclosure of personal or financial information as to which the subject of the information has a legitimate expectation of privacy. This could include such things as date of birth, address, driver license number, bank and credit card account numbers, criminal history, marital status, sexual orientation or activities, medical conditions, and other things.

Not all disclosures of personal or financial information about an individual are prohibited. In some circumstances the disclosure of even highly embarrassing information about a person is permitted. At the same time, some kinds of information may be disclosed only under court order.

The common law (judge-made law) protected privacy rights long before legislators and administrative agencies began enacting the detailed regulations that are in place now. A common law cause of action gives people the right to sue other people even if no statutes or regulations addressing the alleged wrong have been enacted. Laws and regulations enacted by legislators and administrative agencies generally do not supplant the common law; they supplement it. The logical starting point for an understanding of privacy rights, therefore, is the common law.

There are four basic kinds of common law invasion of privacy: publication of private facts, false light, intrusion, and misappropriation of personality.

PUBLICATION OF PRIVATE FACTS

Publishing facts about the private life of a person is an invasion of privacy if:

1) the facts are private, i.e., not generally known;
2) disclosure would be highly offensive to a reasonable person; and
3) the information is not newsworthy, i.e., not of legitimate concern to the public.

In order to prevail on this kind of claim, all three of these conditions must be satisfied. This means, for example, that even if a private fact about an individual is not generally known and is not newsworthy, publication of it is not actionable if disclosing it would not be offensive to a reasonable person. It also means that even if publication of a private fact would be highly offensive to a reasonable person, it may be permitted if it is newsworthy.

The facts do not necessarily need to be published in written form. Publishing a photograph of a person qualifies as a publication of "facts" about the person. It is not actionable as invasion of privacy, however, unless the facts disclosed in the photograph are private, their disclosure would be highly offensive to a reasonable person, and they are not a matter of legitimate concern to the public.

Information about a person's disabilities or medical conditions, or about the person's sexual orientation or activities, sexual organs or financial status are examples of private facts. Personally identifying information – such as Social Security number, driver's license number, and the like -- also come within the meaning of private facts.

Any fact that is already publicly available is not a private fact. For this reason, republishing something that someone else has already published to the Internet, or in a newspaper or magazine, is not actionable as a publication of a private fact. It might be actionable on some other basis, but not as an invasion of privacy of the "publication of private facts" variety. And unless the republisher was involved in some way with the original publication, the republisher would not be liable for publication of a private fact even if the original publication was itself an invasion of privacy.

A good example of this occurred when a former Congressional aide sued another former Congressional aide for writing about their private sexual relationship on her blog, and sued Anna Marie Cox of Wonkette for mentioning the blog piece on another web site. The court dismissed the "publication of private facts" claim against Cox because her comments were about something that had already been published online. The claim against the Congressional aide who originally published the facts may or may not have had merit, but there could be no liability for Cox because the original publication had caused the facts to cease being "private."

Even if it is clear that a private fact has been published, liability for publication of a private fact will not attach unless its disclosure would be highly offensive to a reasonable person. Descriptions of people's sexual organs and activities, sexually transmitted diseases or other medical conditions are examples of "private facts" the publication of which has been found to be highly offensive to a reasonable person. Publishing photographs of people engaged in sexual activity; or while they are nude or partially nude; or of a woman nursing a baby, or of a woman giving birth are also considered "publication of private facts."

This is not an exhaustive list.

Although a wedding may be private and not newsworthy, publishing photographs of it would not be considered highly offensive to a reasonable person. Accordingly, the publisher could not be sued for publication of private facts on this basis, in the United States.

Publishing photographs of military personnel engaged in prisoner abuse has been held to be inoffensive to a reasonable person, and therefore not actionable as a publication of private facts.

NO RIGHT OF PRIVACY IN PUBLIC PLACES

People generally do not have a legitimate expectation of privacy in the things they say or do in public. Put another way, the things people do in public places are public facts, not private facts. Therefore, liability for publication of private facts generally will not attach if you publish information about, or a photograph of, what someone did in public. For example, publishing a photograph of a couple engaged in amorous activity in their own bedroom would be a publication of a private fact, but a photograph of the same couple engaged in the same activity in a public place generally will not be actionable as a publication of a private fact.

On the other hand, there are some public places in which a person does have a reasonable expectation of privacy – public restrooms, for instance.

If the publication is for commercial or other advantage, then there may be liability for the appropriation of a person's name, voice or likeness regardless of whether any "private facts" are disclosed. For more information about publicity rights and misappropriation of personality, see Chapter 9.

NEWSWORTHINESS

Even if the facts published are private and their publication would be highly offensive to a reasonable person, there is no liability for publication of private facts if they are a matter of legitimate public interest. You cannot be held liable for publication of private facts if the private facts are newsworthy.

Courts have taken a fairly broad view of newsworthiness. The legitimacy of public interest in a particular matter has come to mean something like "genuineness." Thus, courts have held that there is a legitimate public interest in nearly every aspect of the private lives of politicians and public figures (e.g., celebrities, movie stars, professional athletes, people who commit crimes or engage in acts of heroism, etc. – basically anyone who has "injected himself into the public eye," whether voluntarily or involuntarily.) Courts have held that people have a legitimate public interest in nearly all events that do not take place exclusively within the confines of a place in which a person has a reasonable expectation of privacy.

Sometimes an event may be one of "legitimate" public interest regardless of where it occurs. Crimes, arrests, police raids, suicides, marriages, divorces, fires, accidents, natural disasters, drug overdoses, rare diseases, the discovery of a person long believed dead, police reports of an escaped animal, and many other things have been found to be matters of legitimate public interest irrespective of whether they happened in a private home.

Some courts have held that "information concerning interesting phases of human activity" and "all issues about which information is needed or appropriate so that individuals may cope with the exigencies of their period" are matters of legitimate public interest.[2] Under this standard, courts have found things like unusual love relationships, the location and living conditions of a former child prodigy, an Indian rope trick, and the personal characteristics of presidential campaign volunteers to be matters of legitimate public interest.

Courts tend to draw the line between newsworthiness and non-newsworthiness with reference to offensiveness. As one court put it: "The

---

[2] Campbell v. Seabury Press, 614 F. 2d 395, 397 (5th Cir. 1980.)

line is to be drawn when the publicity ... becomes a morbid and sensational prying into private lives for its own sake, with which a reasonable member of the public, with decent standards, would say that he had no concern."[3]

The media is allowed to communicate many kinds of facts about the private lives of newsworthy individuals, provided there is a logical connection between the facts and the matter of legitimate public interest. Thus, for example, a news story about a medical malpractice lawsuit may delve into the professional's marital life and mental health history. In one case, a court held that publication of a photograph of a patient inside a mental hospital is not actionable if the photograph was taken while the patient was walking next to a famous fellow patient, because the public has a legitimate interest in the mental and physical rehabilitation of public figures.

Unfortunately, court rulings in this area are not always consistent. For example, the sexual aspects of elected officials' lives typically are considered matters of legitimate public interest. In one case, however, the California Court of Appeals ruled that the fact that an elected student body president was a transsexual (born male and then underwent a sex-change operation) was not a matter of legitimate public interest – this, despite the fact that it was deemed newsworthy that she was the first "female" student body president who had ever been elected. The very next year, however, the same court held that the fact that a public figure (in this case, an otherwise private individual who engaged in a heroic act, namely, protecting President Ford from an assassination attempt) is homosexual is a matter of legitimate public interest. It is not really clear why the fact that a homosexual male is capable of performing a heroic act is considered newsworthy, but the fact that a transsexual female can be a capable elected official is not.

Newsworthiness can fade with the passage of time. And with the passage of time, it is also sometimes possible for a person who was once a public figure to become an "unknown," i.e., to become a private individual again. It doesn't happen very often, but it can.

You may publish facts that you find in public court records. There is an absolute First Amendment privilege to publish information obtained from such records. Some (but not all) states have extended the privilege to all public records. The privilege does not apply to sealed records.

INTRUSION

A common law cause of action for intrusion upon seclusion exists to compensate individuals for the anguish they suffer when their reasonable

[3] Virgil v. Time, Inc., 527 F.2d 1122, 1129 (9th Cir. 1975).

expectation of privacy in a place or thing (e.g., their homes, public restrooms, their phone conversations, or their mail) is disturbed. The classic examples are window-peeping, eavesdropping, and reading someone else's mail.

Hacking into someone's private email account is another example of intrusion upon seclusion. People generally have a reasonable expectation of privacy in their emails, unless they have done something to make them public.

Copying material from a person's public web site generally would not be an invasion of the website owner's privacy because it is not reasonable for an owner of a public website to expect what he publishes will remain private.

A cause of action for intrusion requires proof of four elements:

1) an unauthorized intrusion
2) that would be highly offensive to a reasonable person;
3) the place or matter intruded upon was private; and
4) the intrusion caused mental anguish or other damage.

The purpose of this cause of action is to redress the indignity of the intrusion itself. Neither publication nor publicity need be proven.

"Intrusion," in this context, means interrupting a person's solitude or seclusion, either as to his person or as to his private affairs, in a way that would be highly offensive to a reasonable person. Surreptitiously taking a picture of another person might be actionable if the manner of taking the picture would be highly offensive to a reasonable person.

The intrusion must occur at a place or with respect to a matter about which the complainant has a reasonable expectation of privacy. People have a reasonable expectation of privacy with respect to the contents of their mail, for example, and they also have a reasonable expectation of privacy in their dwellings and certain other places, such as restrooms.

FALSE LIGHT

"False light" refers to the portrayal of a person in a false or misleading way. The elements of the legal cause of action are:

1) publication
2) of a false or misleading statement or depiction of a person
3) that would be highly offensive to a reasonable person.

Although commentators have pointed out that doing so tends to blur the distinction between this cause of action and defamation, some courts hold that the statement need not be about something that is personal, private or secret in order to be actionable as "false light" invasion of privacy. To these courts, it is the portrayal of a person in such a way as to falsely attribute some action, inaction or characteristic to him that is the gravamen of this tort.

Altering information or a photograph of or about a person in order to cause visitors to your site to have a misimpression about the person would be an example of "false light" invasion of privacy, if the effect is to cause reasonable people to believe something highly offensive about the person.

Liability for "false light" invasion of privacy may exist even if no factually false information has been communicated. Liability may be predicated on a misleading depiction of a person's character, history, activities or beliefs.

Of course, publishing factual text or an unaltered photograph is not as likely to result in "false light" liability as publishing altered text or "photoshopped" pictures is. On the other hand, it is possible for even an unaltered photograph or news story to portray a person in a false light. This can happen if information conveyed is presented out of context, or if your presentation of the material on your web page creates a false impression about the person.

Suppose, for example, that the text appearing on another web site truthfully reports that Bob McKinsey attended a family picnic at which he was seen engaging in "social intercourse with numerous people." If you were to publish the statement that Bob McKinsey attended a family picnic at which he was seen engaging in "intercourse with numerous people," your statement, technically, would not be false. Nevertheless, you would be exposed to potential liability for "false light" invasion of privacy because a reasonable person probably would understand the word "intercourse," standing alone, to refer to sexual intercourse. Disclosure of the fact that a person engaged in sexual activity with different people while attending a family picnic most likely would be highly offensive to a reasonable person.

The same kind of thing can happen with unaltered photographs. Suppose that Bob McKinsey is seen reaching for a hamburger bun at the picnic. A photographer snaps a picture at such an angle that the hamburger buns are not visible, but somebody's derriere is. Publishing such a photograph might be actionable as "false light" invasion of privacy if a reasonable person would interpret the photograph as communicating that Bob McKinsey was reaching out to grab someone's bottom. Whether a reasonable person would draw that inference depends on a lot of different factors. Liability would almost certainly attach, though, if accompanying text suggests, encourages or buttresses a particular interpretation. For example, if the photograph was captioned, "Bob McKinsey certainly likes 'buns'!" then liability for "false light" invasion of privacy would be somewhat less uncertain.

The bottom line is this: Just as you should not knowingly publish false information about a person, so you should not publish statements or photographs of or about a person which, although literally true, are likely to create a false impression about that person. Don't try to misrepresent facts through the manipulative or clever use of language or photography.

Note that unless they can prove actual malice (knowing falsity or reckless disregard for the truth), public officials cannot sue for false light invasion of privacy with respect to their official acts or duties.

MISAPPROPRIATION OF NAME, VOICE OR LIKENESS

Appropriating another person's personality (name, voice or likeness) is a form of invasion of privacy, and it may also be a form of unfair competition or false advertising. Because its primary focus is to redress misappropriations of publicity rights, it is addressed in Chapter 9.

FINANCIAL AND PERSONALLY IDENTIFYING INFORMATION

A number of statutes and regulations have been enacted to protect the privacy of certain kinds of information and data collected from customers and website users. These typically include personally identifying information (social security numbers, for example) and financial information (bank and credit card account numbers, for instance.)

In addition to refraining from publishing anyone's social security number, bank account or credit card account numbers, you are also required to implement adequate measures to protect the security of such information.

You must disable access to personal identifying and financial information (social security numbers, account numbers, etc.) immediately upon learning that it has been published to your website or blog, or that security has been breached. In addition, you must notify users of the breach. If that means taking down your site completely, then that is what you must do.

REQUESTS FOR REMOVAL

Many (but not all) people who sue for invasion of privacy would not have done so if the site owner had simply removed the offending material when asked. One of the best ways to improve your chances of being sued for a large amount of money is to refuse to remove material that wrongfully invades someone's privacy.

EUROPE

European countries tend to be more protective of privacy rights than the United States is. For example, a European court has allowed a celebrity to sue a photographer for taking pictures of the celebrity's private wedding. American courts, by contrast, generally limit recovery to situations in which the private matter would be offensive to a reasonable person.

Several countries have laws protecting the privacy of correspondence.

The U.K. and British Commonwealth countries prohibit the disclosure of "confidential information." The scope of this protection is fairly broad. Basically, the test is whether the nature of the information and the circumstances surrounding the communication of the information support a conclusion that it was intended to be held in confidence. There is no liability for information that is easily obtainable through other means, though. It is a defense that disclosure was necessary to further some important public interest (e.g., protection of public health or safety) or to disclose iniquity on the part of a public official.

PRIVACY POLICY

If you plan to share a user's name, contact or other information with others, you need to include a notice to users, in your privacy policy, that you may do that. (Example: "We reserve the right to share your information with our partners so that they may provide services to you.") In addition, you need to let users know that they can opt out of having their information shared, and let them know how to do that.

PROPRIETARY INFORMATION

Personal privacy laws serve the purpose of protecting individuals from emotional, reputational or financial harm. There is another branch of privacy law that serves a different purpose, namely, protecting the interests of information gatherers, developers and owners in receiving a fair return on their investments of time and money to obtain information.

MISAPPROPRIATION OF INFORMATION

Misappropriation is a broad term referring to any use of the property of another without permission. The property may be tangible or intangible.

Copyright, trademark and patent infringement are examples. Copyright and trademark law, however, do not protect information. Meanwhile, patent law only protects certain kinds of inventions. In some circumstances, the common law gives certain people the right to prevent or recover damages for the disclosure of information even if it is not protected by copyright, trademark or patent law. Even if repeating facts and information found on other web sites does not infringe a copyright, trademark or patent, it could give rise to liability for misappropriation of information in some cases.

The cause of action for misappropriation of information derives from state unfair competition law. It was first expounded in *International News Service v. Associated Press*, 248 U.S. 215 (1918). In that case, one news service was "scooping" the other by accessing and publishing the news stories gathered by the other news service before the other service had a chance to publish them. The Court held that the news service that had expended effort gathering the information could sue the other news service for appropriating the information to its own use in a way that prevented the first news service from exploiting it commercially.

Although courts in some states have refused to do so, courts in several jurisdictions recognize a cause of action for misappropriation of information.

Whether a particular state has adopted the doctrine or not, it is clear that it cannot be expanded to include rights protected by copyright or patent law. Federal copyright and patent laws preempt state law to the extent a state law conflicts with, or regulates the same things as, either of these sets of federal laws do. For this reason, states can establish a cause of action for misappropriation of the information, but not for misappropriation of the manner of expressing it. Copyright law only protects expression, not information. Similarly, there can be no state law cause of action for copying an invention, since that involves rights protected by federal patent law.

There is no copyright protection for expression when it is the only way of conveying the underlying idea or information. In that situation, the idea is said to have merged with the expression. Contest rules are an example. The statement, "The temperature in New York City today is 46°F" is another example. Nothing more is expressed in this sentence than the information that the temperature in New York City today is 46°F. The more "bare bones" an expression of a fact is, the more likely it is that it will be deemed to be a merger of an idea and its expression. When that happens, copyright protection vanishes; federal preemption should no long apply; and liability for a state law misappropriation claim may be possible – provided all the necessary elements of such a claim are established.

The line of demarcation between expression and information is not always clear. In *Barclay's Capital Inc. v. Theflyonthewall.com, Inc.*, 650 F. 3d 876 (2nd Cir.

2011), a federal court held that a stock advisor's stock recommendations are expressive, not informational. Therefore, publishing them without permission could be a violation of copyright law, but could not be the basis for a state law misappropriation claim because preempted by federal copyright law.

Within those limitations, states that have recognized this tort have adopted differing requirements for recovery. Some only require a showing that the plaintiff expended time and/or other value acquiring information; that a competitor used it to his own advantage without compensating the one who acquired it; and that the plaintiff suffered damage as a result. Others impose stricter requirements, such as that the information was gathered at a cost; that it is time-sensitive; that the defendant is in direct competition with a product or service offered by the plaintiff; and that allowing others to "free-ride" on the efforts of the information-gatherer would threaten the existence or quality of the goods or services the plaintiff offers.

REDUCING THE RISK OF MISAPPROPRIATION LIABILITY

Because of the above-described dynamic between copyright law and state misappropriation law, it might begin to seem as if no reporting of information obtained from other websites is permitted: If what you are copying is expressive, then you risk liability for copyright infringement; but if it's not, then you risk liability for misappropriation of information. This can be a real problem for web sites that aggregate news stories. It can also be a problem for anyone who likes to report on his own website the interesting pieces of information he discovers on other websites.

Unfortunately, there is no way to insulate yourself completely from being sued for either copyright infringement or misappropriation when you repeat information gathered from other websites on your own website. There are some things you can do to reduce your exposure to liability, though.

First, to reduce the risk of copyright infringement, avoid copying news and informational items verbatim. Use your own words.

Another strategy is to copy only a small quantity of material. The fair use doctrine (which is addressed in Chapter 14) sometimes permits copying of small amounts of content from a copyrighted work. It is very risky to rely on that defense, though, because there is no quantitative definition of what a small amount is. Contrary to popular belief, copying only a small amount of copyrighted material does not guarantee that you will be protected by the fair use defense, particularly if the seemingly small amount you copy is the heart of the work. The best way to avoid copyright infringement liability when repeating information acquired from another website is to refrain from copying at all. Instead, use your own words to convey the information.

Next, to reduce the risk of misappropriation liability, refrain from publishing information that still has commercial value for the original gatherer of the information. As a rule of thumb, the newer the information is, the greater the risk of liability for misappropriation. Therefore, think twice before re-publishing information you have obtained that is time-sensitive (such as stock tips; inside information about businesses that could affect investment decisions; the play-by-play or scores of sporting events as they are occurring, etc.)

You are at greater risk of liability for misappropriation if your provision of such information is in direct competition with the person or business that gathered the information and your publication of it impairs the ability of the original information-gatherer to commercially exploit it

Your risk of liability is also greater if the information-gatherer has taken measures to protect the commercial value of the information, such as by requiring payment to access the information. Conversely, if the information-gatherer has already published the information on a public web page (i.e., one that is freely accessible, without payment, to anyone with an Internet connection), and the information is not exclusive to that website (i.e., if the same information already appears on other sites), then your risk of liability for misappropriation is very low.

Your risk of liability for either copyright infringement or misappropriation of information is at its lowest if you use your own words to convey the information (don't just copy and paste text from another site); the information you report is not "hot news" (i.e., it is already widely available from numerous sources available to the public); and making it available for free on your site would not diminish the information-gatherer's ability to exploit it commercially (such as where she has already published it online for any member of the public to view, free of charge.)

Of course, your risk of liability will decrease considerably if you get written permission from the information source to republish it.

TRADE SECRETS

Most states have laws in place that are designed to protect a business's trade secrets. Many are based on the Uniform Trade Secret Act (UTSA.) Publishing a business's trade secret may subject you to liability for damages.

A trade secret can be any kind of information – a formula, recipe, plan, design, pattern, customer list, supplier list, financial data, personnel information, physical device, method, process, computer software, or "know-how" related to a business.

More specifically, a trade secret is any information that:

1) is secret;
2) gives a business a competitive advantage; and
3) a business has made reasonable efforts to keep secret.

You may be liable for misappropriation of a trade secret if you:

a) obtain it by improper means (e.g., theft, bribery, or breach of confidentiality agreement); or
b) publish or use it, knowing or having reason to know that someone else acquired it improperly.

Reverse engineering normally is not considered an improper means of obtaining information, unless doing so violates a term of a contract (such as a provision in an end user license agreement.)

To qualify as "secret," the information must not be generally known to or readily ascertainable by competitors. For this reason, information that has already been published on another public website generally is no longer considered secret. If, however, the information has only been published on an obscure site, or it is quickly taken down after being published, it may continue to be treated in the law as a secret, at least if you know or have reason to know that it was obtained by improper means.

Remedies may include damages and injunctive relief. Damages may be in an amount that will compensate the business for its loss as a result of the misappropriation, or a royalty on any profits made by using the trade secret. Punitive damages and attorney fees may be awarded if the disclosure or use was willful or malicious. Attorney fees may be awarded to the defendant if the court determines the misappropriation claim was filed in bad faith.

The First Amendment may be asserted as a defense if the trade secret involves a matter of public concern. For example, disclosure that there are toxic chemicals in a food vendor's "secret sauce" probably would be constitutionally protected. On the other hand, use of trade secrets in violation of a confidentiality agreement or in breach of a fiduciary duty (such as the fiduciary duties owed by employees, officers and directors to the employers or organizations they serve) is not protected by the First Amendment.

FEDERAL CRIMES

Theft or disclosure of a trade secret with knowledge or intent that doing so will cause harm (including financial loss) to its owner is a federal crime. 18

U.S.C. § 1832. A violation is punishable by a fine of up to $5 million and up to 10 years imprisonment.

Appropriating or disclosing a trade secret without authorization is an even more serious crime if it is done with intent to benefit, or knowledge that it will benefit, a foreign government. 18 U.S.C. § 1831. A violation of this provision is punishable by a fine of up to $10 million and up to 15 years imprisonment.

These provisions are part of the Economic Espionage Act, 18 U.S.C. §§ 1831-39. Under the Act, appropriating or disclosing a trade secret means copying, duplicating, sketching, drawing, photographing, downloading, uploading, altering, destroying, replicating, transmitting, photocopying, delivering, sending, mailing, communicating, or conveying it without authorization.

Children's Online Privacy Protection Act

The Children's Online Privacy Protection Act imposes restrictions on the collection of information from children under 13. The Act applies to commercial websites.

KEY POINTS:

- ❖ Avoid publishing:
  - personal or financial information collected from site visitors
  - information about a person that is not generally known if disclosure of it would be offensive to the average person
  - information obtained from another website unless it is already freely available on more than one website
  - trade secrets.
- ❖ Implement security measures to prevent access to financial and personally identifying information.
- ❖ If there is a security breach, disable access and notify users immediately.
- ❖ Establish a privacy policy and adhere to it.
- ❖ Respect people's privacy when gathering information for your website or blog.
- ❖ Use your own words when publishing information obtained from other websites.

CHAPTER 9

Personality
(name, voice, likeness)

PUBLICITY RIGHTS

Everybody has an exclusive right to his or her own identity. Other people cannot exploit that right without permission. If they do, they may be sued for misappropriation of name, voice or likeness (or as it is sometimes called, "misappropriation of personality.")

In many states, appropriating another person's personality is also considered a form of invasion of privacy.

The elements of a cause of action for misappropriation of name, voice or likeness are:

4) unauthorized use
5) of another person's name, voice, likeness, or other identifying characteristics
6) for commercial gain or other advantage.

The gravamen of this cause of action is the commercial use of another person's personality without permission. Thus, liability may arise not only from the unauthorized use of a person's name or of a photograph of the person, but also from the unauthorized use of the person's voice or a recognizable drawing of the person.

Any publication of a person's name or voice, or a photograph or drawing of a person, raises potential misappropriation of personality issues. The most common way to incur liability is by publishing a person's name or image in an advertisement for a product or service without the person's permission, or in a way that suggests the person's endorsement of a particular product or service. But liability can arise in other ways, too.

COMMERCIAL OR OTHER ADVANTAGE

Not every display of a person's name, voice or likeness gives rise to misappropriation liability. Liability for misappropriation arises only if the person's name, voice or likeness is used for commercial or other advantage. Displaying a person's name, voice or likeness on a purely noncommercial website, for reasons other than to bring some advantage to the user, is not misappropriation. In some cases, it might be wrongful for another reason such as invasion of privacy (see Chapter 9), but it would not be actionable as misappropriation.

Liability for misappropriation of personality for commercial advantage may arise even if the person's name, voice or likeness is not used to state or imply an endorsement or other connection to a particular product or service. If you have advertising on your site and advertising revenue is tied to the number of hits your site receives, then including a person's name, voice or likeness on your website as a means of attracting visitors to your site could be considered a use for commercial advantage.

Unless a particular state statute provides otherwise, the gain or advantage need not be a commercial or pecuniary one. A few states have enacted statutes limiting liability to commercial uses, but others, such as California, have not. Political popularity is an example of a noncommercial advantage. Using a person's name, voice or likeness to state or imply the person's endorsement of a candidate would be an example of misappropriation for noncommercial advantage.

At least one court has held that using another person's name as a keyword in competitive advertising does not violate the person's exclusive publicity rights.[4] If the name is also a trademark, however, then it might be a violation of trademark law.

PHOTOGRAPHS

Misappropriation of name or likeness, and invasion of privacy, are the causes of action that should be of particular concern to you if you are publishing or copying photographs of people on your website. The most

---

[4] Habush v. Cannon, 346 Wis. 2d 709 (Wis. App. Ct. 2013).

common way to incur liability is by publishing a person's image in an advertisement for a product or service without the person's permission. It may arise in other ways, too, though. If revenue from your website is linked to the number of clicks on it, then publishing a person's photograph to get more clicks would be a use of the person's likeness for commercial advantage. And using a person's photograph to state or imply that person's endorsement or sponsorship of a product, service, business or political candidate could be considered a use of the person's likeness for commercial or other advantage.

NEWSWORTHINESS

The use of a person's name or likeness in connection with reporting on a newsworthy incident is permitted. For example, a website may publish a photograph of people attending a political rally without violating the privacy or publicity rights of the individual participants depicted in the photograph. A political rally is newsworthy.

UNFAIR COMPETITION AND FALSE ADVERTISING

The statutory or common law of about half the states recognize a person's exclusive right to use his name or personality for commercial or other advantage. Even in states that do not recognize such a cause of action, however, the right of publicity may be protected under the law of unfair competition. Misappropriation of a person's name, likeness or voice for the purpose of misrepresenting or "passing off" a product or service as being made, sponsored or endorsed by that person is a form of unfair competition.

The federal Lanham Act authorizes a person to sue for false advertising. Using a person's name, voice or likeness in a way that falsely suggests the person's manufacture, sponsorship or endorsement of a product or service may be actionable as false advertising under the Lanham Act.

LICENSES AND PERMISSIONS (AKA "RELEASES")

The best way to reduce the risk of liability for misappropriation of personality is to refrain from using other people's names, voices or likenesses to your advantage.

If you do choose to make such a use, however, then you should obtain written permission (sometimes called a release) from the person in question.

This certainly should be done if you intend to use the person's name, likeness or voice for a commercial purpose such as a product or service endorsement. Consent is a defense to misappropriation.

Because some states allow a cause of action for misappropriation for non-pecuniary advantage, you should also secure such a release when you intend a use for noncommercial advantage. For example, if you are running for office, you should get a person's written permission before identifying the person to the public as someone who supports your candidacy.

It is also not a bad idea to obtain permission when you intend to use a person's name, voice or likeness in a way that might otherwise expose you to liability for invasion of privacy. See Chapter 9

Children are deemed incapable of giving a valid consent. A parent or legal guardian must give consent on their behalf. Depending on state law, an incompetent, coerced, defrauded or traumatized person also may be incapable of giving consent on her own behalf.

When copying a photograph taken by somebody other than yourself, or a drawing made by someone else, you may need to obtain permission from both the photographer/artist and the subject of the photograph/drawing. This is true whether you are using it for commercial purposes or not. Liability for copyright infringement can attach irrespective of motive.

Get permissions in writing, and signed. That will make it easier to prove that consent was given.

An example of a model release is provided in Appendix V. A general purpose request for permission to use copyrighted material, which may be adapted to use as a request for permission to use a photograph, appears in Appendix IX.

KEY POINTS:

❖ **Get permission before using a person's name, voice or likeness for commercial or other advantage.**

❖ **If website revenue is tied to the number of visitors (or "clicks") the site gets, publishing a well-known or controversial person's photograph to it might be considered a commercial use.**

❖ **Newsworthiness may be a defense to misappropriation of personality in some cases.**

CHAPTER 10

Defamation

Publishing a statement about a person, group, business or organization may subject you to liability for defamation (libel) if it is false or misleading. Damage awards in defamation cases can be astronomical, sometimes in the millions of dollars. Litigation costs and attorney fees can be expensive, as well. Therefore, it is important for every website owner and blogger to exercise caution when publishing a statement about a person, group, business or organization.

The elements of a cause of action for defamation are:

1) publication of a statement to a person other than the plaintiff
2) that is false;
3) that is understood to be about the plaintiff
4) that tends to damage the plaintiff's reputation
5) with either negligence or intent.

In cases involving public officials, public figures, or matters of public concern, actual malice may also need to be proven in order to establish a right to recovery for defamation. (See below.)

Written defamation is sometimes called *libel*. Oral defamation is sometimes called *slander*.

The copyright definition of publication does not apply to defamation law. Communication of a statement to a third party is all that is needed to establish "publication" for purposes of defamation law. Displaying, broadcasting, downloading, or making something available for download on an Internet web site, or transmitting a statement via email, are all forms of "publication" for purposes of defamation law.

There is no requirement that a person must actually be named. Providing enough information so that a reader can figure out who it is will suffice.

Knowledge of the falsity of the information will almost certainly result in liability, but it is also possible to be held liable for defamation even if you are not aware that the information is untrue. A defamation claim may be predicated on either negligence or intent. Publishing something without having a reason to believe it is true could be considered negligence.

On the other hand, if the false statement relates to a public official, public figure, or a matter of public concern, then mere negligence is not enough. Instead, it would need to be shown that you published the information with actual malice. "Actual malice" exists when a person either publishes something knowing that it is false, or publishes something with a reckless disregard for its truth or falsity.

A person who republishes someone else's defamatory statement as if it were fact may be just as liable for defamation as the person who published the original statement. Accordingly, checking the reliability of sources is important.

The elements of a cause of action for defamation are different in other countries. In British Commonwealth countries, for example, truth must be asserted, if at all, as a defense. In the United States, the plaintiff has the burden of proving falsity. Also, unlike the U.S., British Commonwealth countries do not require public officials and figures to prove actual malice.

GROUP LIBEL

Group libel means a publication of a false statement that damages the reputation of a group of persons. The general rule in this area is that there is no defamation liability if the group is large, but there may be liability to each member if the group is small.

The rule is subject to some qualifications. Defamation of a large group may result in liability if an individual member can demonstrate special application of the defamatory matter to him. And defamation of a small group results in liability to an individual member only if the defamatory matter applies to every member of the group and not just to the group collectively, or if the group is so small that the statement necessarily applies to every member.

Correspondence schools, wineries, trading-stamp concerns, and antique dealers are examples of groups that courts have held to be too large to provide a basis for a claim of defamation by an individual member even if something provably false about the group is published.

Examples of groups as to which courts have permitted an individual member to sue for defamation even though not specifically named include:

"the Fenstermaker family;" the staff of doctors at a particular hospital; the occupants of a particular house; the jury in a particular case; a specified county commission; a specified board of town trustees; a specified election board; the administrative board of a particular university; a group of coroner's physicians.

Not all courts are in agreement. For example, some courts have held that a false statement that a particular apartment building is a house of ill-repute defames every tenant in the building. Other courts have held that it does not.

When a basis for group libel exists, the fact that the publisher did not intend his statement to include every member of the group is irrelevant. For example, if a writer publishes the false statement, "Some of the teachers employed by Flyover School District No. 16 are adulterers," the fact that the writer had Alice Jones and Bob Cricket in mind when he wrote it is not a defense to a defamation action brought by Flyover teacher Fred Mertz.

DAMAGE TO REPUTATION

For defamation liability to attach, it is not enough to show that a statement is false. It must also be shown that it damages a person's reputation, in the sense that it subjects a person to hatred, contempt, or ridicule; decreases good will; or causes others to shun, avoid, or lose confidence in the person. Falsely reporting that a person performed a heroic act, for example, normally will not result in defamation liability because this kind of statement, even if false, normally does not damage a person's reputation. For the same reason, inaccuracies in details that do not have any impact on reputation will not result in liability for defamation.

DEFAMATION PER SE ("LIBEL PER SE")

Certain kinds of statements are presumed to cause damage to reputation, and in some states, may also be presumed to be false and malicious. These kinds of statements constitute defamation per se, effectively shifting the burden of proof to the defendant to show that the statements are truthful, that he did not act with malice, and that the plaintiff did not suffer any damage.

Examples of statements that are defamatory per se:

- that a person has a sexually transmitted disease;
- that an unmarried person is unchaste;

- that a person has committed a crime of moral turpitude;
- disparaging a person's professional character or standing.

In some states, a statement that a married person committed adultery is also considered defamatory per se.

Other kinds of statements may be defamatory, as well. For statements that are not defamatory per se, though, proof of a harmful effect on the person's reputation will be required.

PRE-EXISTING BAD REPUTATION

A person's pre-existing bad reputation may be asserted as a defense to defamation. Since damage to reputation must be proven in order to establish a right to recovery for defamation, there can be no recovery if the plaintiff has nothing to damage. Thus, for example, if you falsely accuse a known, convicted thief of stealing something, he may have difficulty proving that your statement harmed his reputation.

On the other hand, if you publish a statement that causes a person's reputation to go from bad to worse, then you may be held liable for the incremental damage to reputation that you caused.

In practice, a court is more likely to award reduced, or even nominal, damages in cases such as these than to dismiss the lawsuit altogether on the basis of a pre-existing bad reputation. Accordingly, making up bad things to "pile on" someone who already has a poor reputation is not a smart thing to do.

TRUTH AS A DEFENSE

Since the making of a false statement is part of the definition of defamation, the truthfulness of a statement is a defense.

To improve your chances of being able to assert this defense, rely on primary source materials (e.g., public records), not secondary ones (e.g., a New York Times report of something it says is in a public record.)

Many people think they cannot be held liable for defamation if they quote another person's statement, so long as they correctly attribute the statement to that person. Admittedly, there is some logic in this notion. If A's statement is only that B made a particular statement, and if it is, in fact, true that B made that statement, then it would seem that A's statement is true and that A therefore is not guilty of making a false statement regardless of whether B's statement is true or not. Unfortunately, that is not the law. Accurately publishing a quotation of someone else's statement may result in liability for defamation if that person's statement is false. Courts treat a republisher of a false statement the same as the original publisher of the statement.

> *Example:* You publish on your blog the statement, "As John Smith has recently reported on his blog, 'Clyde Jones is a convicted murderer.'" If it turns out Clyde isn't really a convicted murderer, then both you and John Smith may be sued for defamation. The fact that John Smith really did publish the quoted statement on his blog is not a defense.

Of course, if you republish a false statement and add a statement of your own to the effect that the statement is not true, then you are not likely to be held liable for defamation. In that situation, a court is not likely to hold that you are republishing a false statement in a way that harms a person's reputation.

> *Example:* You publish on your blog the statement, "According to John Smith's blog, 'Clyde Jones is a convicted murderer,' but this is not true. Clyde Jones is not a convicted murderer." In this situation, only John Smith could be sued for defamation. No reasonable person would construe a statement that a particular individual is not a murderer as a reason to think less of him.

INNUENDO

Truth is not a defense when a technically truthful statement is presented in such a way that a reasonable reader would construe it as implying something false and defamatory.

> *Example:* John and Bernard participate in a civil rights march. Hillary does not. Bernard issues a statement that he participated in the march. John meets Hillary in a setting completely unrelated to civil rights marches. He then declares that he never met Bernard during those marches but that he "did meet" Hillary. Technically, John's statement is true. A reasonable reader, however, would construe his statement as implying that Hillary took part in the march and that Bernard is a liar. If Bernard is a private figure, John could be at risk of liability for defamation even though his statements are technically true.

Sometimes the positioning of materials on a web page can suggest something false and defamatory. For example, displaying a photograph of an identifiable person directly adjacent to an article about the rise in sexually-transmitted diseases might cause a reader to infer that the pictured individual is a person with a sexually-transmitted disease. Whether that inference is reasonable or not would depend on all the facts and circumstances in a particular case. The important point is that you, as a website owner or blogger, need to be thinking not only about how to say what you want to say, but also about how to avoid implying what you do not intend to say.

To prevail on a truth defense, both the statement and the innuendo (if any) must be true.

HYPERBOLE, SARCASM, RHETORIC

If you publish a blog or operate a website, you need to be aware that liability for defamation is based on a reader's reasonable interpretation of a statement, not the author's intended meaning. You may be held liable for defamation on the basis of a hyperbolic, sarcastic or rhetorical statement even if you did not intend people to take the statement literally. If a reasonable reader could mistake your statement for a statement of fact, then you may incur defamation liability regardless of what your intended meaning was.

> *Example*: To drive home the point that she is angry about XYZ Corporation's role in increasing women's cervical cancer rates, Joan publishes a blog post declaring, "XYZ Corporation is raping women!" Since corporations are not humans, no reasonable reader would interpret this statement literally. On the other hand, if Joan were to publish the statement, "The CEO of XYZ Corporation is raping women!" to make the same point, then she may be liable for defamation. Although she may only have intended to use the word 'rape' as a hyperbolic metaphor, a reasonable reader could interpret her statement as meaning that the CEO is sexually assaulting women.

If no reasonable reader would interpret a statement as a factual one, then there is no liability for defamation. For example, if a user posts the comment, "Oh yeah, like I'm so sure the XYZ Corporation is increasing cancer rates in women. Come on!" a reasonable reader would interpret this as sarcasm, not as an allegation that XYZ Corporation actually is increasing cancer rates in women. Accordingly, XYZ Corporation would probably lose if it attempted to sue the user for defamation.

OPINIONS

Only false statements of fact can qualify as defamation. Opinions cannot.

It is important to understand, however, that a statement of opinion about a fact is still a fact statement. Prefacing your factual statements with "I think" or "In my opinion" will not insulate you from defamation liability. The determinative question is neither what your subjective intention is nor what form of words you use. Rather, it is whether a reasonable person would interpret your statement as an allegation of fact.

Juries are instructed to consider all the circumstances surrounding the statement, including the precision with which your statement was made, the likelihood of your familiarity with the facts, your reason for making the statement, and the like. If the fact-finder concludes that you were really making an allegation of fact while purporting to only express an opinion, then you may be held liable for defamation.

Statements reflecting a necessarily subjective judgment about the quality of a thing are more likely to be considered opinions than statements about objectively verifiable facts are. The statement, "Ed Jones is the best candidate for president" is more likely to be deemed an opinion than "In my opinion, Ed Jones accepted campaign contributions from a foreign government."

Reporting of your own emotional response to a person, even if expressed with hyperbole, generally will not expose you to defamation liability. For example, the statement, "I get a huge uneasy feeling when I see John Doe hugging young girls" probably will not expose you to defamation liability.

In some places, this defense may be called the right of fair comment.

CONSENT

Consent can be a defense, at least in theory. It is difficult to imagine a situation in which a person would give his consent to the publication of a false and defamatory statement of fact about himself, but if that could be proven to have occurred in a particular case, then it may be asserted as a defense.

PUBLIC OFFICIALS AND PUBLIC FIGURES

The U.S. Supreme Court has construed the First Amendment freedom of the press as imposing some limitations on the law of defamation with respect to public officials and public figures. Specifically, the Court has declared that public officials and public figures cannot recover punitive damages in defamation cases. Moreover, to recover anything at all, they must prove actual malice. This means either knowledge of the falsity of the statement or reckless disregard for whether it is true or not. Consequently, a news media outlet cannot be sued for defamation for publishing a false statement about a public figure if it did not know the statement was false, and its lack of knowledge was due to mere negligence rather than a reckless disregard for the truth.

Although "reckless disregard" means something more than mere negligence, a person may be found to be acting with reckless disregard for the truth for failing to investigate an allegation before publishing it. For example, if the truth of a matter could easily have been found by conducting an Internet search, but the reporter published a false statement without conducting such a search, then the reporter may be said to have been acting with reckless disregard for the truth.

A person becomes a public official by seeking or holding political office.

A person may become a public figure by voluntarily injecting himself into a public issue, such as by being a vocal advocate with respect to a matter of public concern. Sometimes a person can involuntarily become a public figure, too. A person who is accused of a serious crime, for example, may not have done anything to draw attention to himself. Nevertheless, he may be deemed a public figure.

Sometimes a person is considered a public figure only with respect to the activity giving rise to her status as a public figure. A woman who publicly advocates for abortion rights, for example, does not become a public figure with respect to her personal shopping habits. In these cases, the person is said to be a limited purpose public figure.

When it is not clear whether a person is a public or private figure with respect to a particular activity or aspect of the person's life, courts tend to prefer characterizing the person as a private person with respect to that activity or aspect.

In the United States, public figures cannot sue for defamation unless they can prove actual malice. This is true even with respect to matters of private concern. Thus, gossip about a celebrity's personal and romantic relationships is fair game, so long as it is done without actual malice. This is not always true in other countries, however. Some countries require proof of malice only if the matter is one of public concern. In those countries, a celebrity or other public figure might be able to sue for the publication of a false statement about a matter of private concern, such as her personal relationships, without having to prove that the publisher was actuated by malice.

LACK OF KNOWLEDGE

A public official or public figure, including a person who is the subject of a matter of public concern, cannot recover damages for defamation unless the false and defamatory statement was published with either actual malice or a reckless disregard for the truth or falsity of the statement. Therefore, lack of knowledge is a defense to a defamation claim brought by a public official or public figure, or someone who is the subject of a matter of public concern, unless the information was published with reckless disregard for the truth.

MATTERS OF PUBLIC CONCERN

A showing of actual malice is required in cases where a private person sues for defamation for a website owner's or blogger's false statement in connection with a matter of public concern. Unlike public officials and public figures, a private person may recover punitive damages.

A thing is not a matter of public concern merely because the public finds it interesting. Gossip about a person's relationship(s), for example, may be interesting to a large segment of the public, but for legal purposes it is not considered a "matter of public concern."

PRIVATE PERSONS AND PRIVATE MATTERS

A private person may sue for defamation on the basis of the publication of a false statement about a matter of private concern without having to prove actual malice.

RETRACTIONS

Many states have enacted statutes limiting the amount of damages that may be recovered for defamation if the plaintiff timely demands a retraction and the defendant promptly publishes a retraction in the manner, and within the time frame, specified in the statute. The retraction statutes of some states only apply to newspapers, television and radio broadcasters, however.

In some states, failure to demand a retraction may prevent the recovery of certain kinds of damages, such as punitive damages.

Failure to publish a retraction after receiving a demand that is accompanied by facts rebutting the false statement is evidence of actual malice. Accordingly, if you receive a demand for retraction, even if it is from a public official or public figure, and it is accompanied by facts rebutting your false statement, then you should promptly publish a retraction.

In some countries, such as the U.K. and Australia, an early offer of an apology and settlement is a defense if the court determines the settlement offer was reasonable. There are conditions on this rule, however. You should consult with an attorney if you are considering pursuing this route.

PRIVILEGES

Privilege may also be a defense in some cases. There are two kinds of privilege relevant to defamation: absolute and qualified.

An absolute privilege exists to make false and defamatory statements:

- in judicial proceedings;
- by legislators during legislative debates;
- during political speeches and broadcasts;
- by top government officials;
- to one's spouse.

Even though false statements made in these contexts may not always be actionable as defamation, there may be other legal penalties for this kind of conduct. A person who makes a false statement under oath in court, for example, may be charged with the crime of perjury.

The privilege in the above-described situations is absolute, meaning the person making the statement cannot be sued for defamation even if the statement is outrageous and even if the person knows it is false.

A qualified privilege exists to make certain kinds of false statements so long as you are not acting intentionally, recklessly, or with malice, hatred, spite, or ill will. Different states recognize different kinds of qualified privilege, and define differently the level of negligence or intent that must exist in order to qualify for the privilege.

Some examples of contexts in which a qualified privilege may exist (depending on state law) include:

- statements appearing in governmental reports of official proceedings;
- statements made by lower-level government officials;
- testimony given during legislative proceedings (e.g., during a legislative hearing to which the public is invited to give testimony or make statements);

- statements made in self defense;
- warnings to others about a danger or harm;
- statements about an employee communicated by a former employer to a potential new employer;
- statements made in a published book or film review.

Republishing another person's false and defamatory statement should not result in liability for defamation if the original statement was absolutely privileged. Republishing another person's false and defamatory statement may result in liability, however, if either the original falsehood or the republication of it was intentional, reckless, or made with malice, hatred, spite, or ill will.

A republisher's immunity from liability exists only if he republishes the original statement fairly and accurately. Taking a snippet of a speech, conversation or testimony, and republishing it out of context in such a way as to create a defamatory misimpression of what the original speaker intended to say is not "fair and accurate" reporting. A republisher who does this loses the protection of the privilege.

Example: During a legislative session, Rep. Hauser declares, "A yes vote on this bill would send a message that this legislature is a bunch of homicidal maniacs." Bob then posts, "According to Rep. Hauser, 'this legislature is a bunch of homicidal maniacs.'" This is not a fair report of what Rep. Hauser said, so Bob's privilege is lost.

CRIMINAL LIBEL

Some states and countries have made libel (the written forms of defamation) a crime.

Prosecutions for criminal libel are rarer in the United States than in other countries. Increasing sensitivity to real or perceived discrimination, however, may change that. Laws in a number of states now call for stronger penalties for crimes when they are motivated by bias or prejudice ("hate crimes.") On the other hand, the First Amendment protects even racist and insulting speech so long as it is not directed to inciting or producing imminent lawless action, and is not made with the intention to threaten or intimidate. Statements about public figures that are made without actual malice are protected by the First Amendment.

Of course, since the First Amendment only applies in the United States, it would not be a defense to the criminal libel statutes of other countries.

TRADE LIBEL

Publication of a false and defamatory statement that damages the reputation or goodwill of a business is trade libel (or "disparagement.") Damages, however, are recoverable only for pecuniary loss, such as loss of business income or customers.

KEY POINTS:

❖ Opinions, hyperbole, parody and satire can, but do not usually, result in liability for defamation.

❖ You may make a false statement about a public official or figure, or a matter of public concern, unless you act with actual malice, knowledge of falsity, or reckless disregard for the truth.

❖ To reduce the risk of liability for defamation:

- don't publish false or misleading statements;
- don't try to portray someone in a false light;
- write about things of which you have personal knowledge;
- rely on primary sources, not secondary sources;
- don't rely on anonymous sources;
- investigate and verify before publishing;
- Focus on public officials and figures, not private individuals;
- Write about matters of public concern, not private matters;
- Don't characterize an allegation as fact;
- Attribute information to its source;
- Consider how readers might misinterpret what you say;
- Promptly publish a retraction when you are wrong.

CHAPTER 11

Pornography, hate speech & other restrictions

Despite the popular view of the Internet as the last frontier of free expression, it is actually subject to a large and growing amount of regulation, both in the United States and abroad. In some cases, the penalties can be quite severe.

OBSCENITY

Obscenity is not protected by the First Amendment. Both federal and state statutes provide for the imposition of severe penalties for possessing, distributing or displaying it.

Various kinds of activities in connection with obscenity are also prohibited, including using an interactive computer service to send or receive it.

Aiding and abetting another person's violation of obscenity laws is also a federal offense. The penalty for the federal crime of selling, distributing, or receiving obscene material using the Internet, or aiding and abetting such activity, may consist of a fine and up to 5 years in prison. In addition, a person convicted of a violation of federal obscenity laws must register as a sex offender.

In 1973 the U.S. Supreme Court, in *Miller v. California*, 413 U.S. 15, 24 (1973), delegated the role of defining obscenity to the States, declaring that it is whatever "the average person, applying contemporary community standards," says it is. The "community" to which the Court referred was the particular city, town or state whose obscenity law or ordinance a person stood accused of violating – in other words, the community in which the material is found. Thus, material transmitted from a liberal community that does not consider it obscene, to a conservative community that does regard it as obscene can result in an obscenity conviction against the person who transmitted it into the conservative community.

Because the Internet is accessible in virtually every community, and there is no effective way to restrict content to specific geographic areas, the almost certainly unforeseen consequence of the Court's 1973 ruling is to give the least tolerant community the power to be the ultimate arbiter of moral standards for the entire country.

The federal circuit courts of appeals are split as to whether local community standards should be applied to determine whether an Internet communication is obscene or not. According to the 9th Circuit, a national standard must be applied instead.[5] The 11th Circuit disagrees, maintaining that individual members of a local community are the ones who should get to decide what is obscene in that community.[6]

Despite this uncertainty, the U.S. Supreme Court has made it clear that obscenity must not only be of a sexual nature, but it must also be "patently offensive." The Court seems to have intended that stereotypically male-oriented ("hardcore") pornography may come within a government's definition of obscenity, but stereotypically female-oriented ("soft-core") pornography may not. In any event, a legislature must define in its laws which specific kinds of portrayals of sexual activity are "patently offensive."

To meet constitutional requirements, no communication may be considered obscene unless the average person in the community finds that, taken as a whole, it:

1) appeals to prurient interests (i.e., an erotic, lascivious, abnormal, degrading, shameful, or morbid interest in nudity, sex, or excretion);
2) describes or depicts sexual activity in a patently offensive way (i.e., sexual intercourse or other sex acts, whether actual or simulated; masturbation; excretory functions; lewd exhibition of genitals or sadomasochism); and
3) lacks serious literary, artistic, political, or scientific value.

Since beauty and artistic merit are matters of subjective opinion, the third factor seems to condition freedom of expression on the positive reception of a creative expression by a handful of armchair art critics. It may be questioned whether this approach is consistent with the values sought to be protected in the First Amendment. Nevertheless, this is the standard that the Supreme

---

[5] United States v. Kilbride, 584 F.3d 1240 (9th Cir. 2009)
[6] United States v. Little, 365 Fed. Appx. 159, 2010 WL 357933 (11th Cir. Feb. 8, 2010).

Court has announced, so it is the framework within which you will need to operate if you do not wish to run afoul of obscenity laws.

It is important to note that all three of the elements described above must be proven before a communication may be deemed obscene. Therefore, it may be inferred that most depictions or descriptions of nudity are not obscene (unless the pose or context makes it "lewd.") It can also be inferred that a depiction of sexual activity is not, in itself, obscene, unless it is also "patently offensive." And even a patently offensive depiction of sexual activity cannot be deemed obscene unless, in addition, it lacks any serious value, artistic or otherwise.

OBSCENITY INVOLVING A MINOR

Material involving a minor may be deemed to be obscene even though it does not meet the three-prong Miller test if it:

1) depicts an image that is, or appears to be, a minor engaged in graphic bestiality, sadistic or masochistic abuse, or sexual intercourse; and
2) lacks serious literary, artistic, political, or scientific value.

CHILD PORNOGRAPHY

Obscenity involving a minor may be prosecuted under general obscenity laws or separate laws, such as 18 U.S.C. § 1466A. Section 1466A makes it a crime to knowingly produce, distribute, receive, or possess with intent to transfer or distribute visual representations, such as drawings, cartoons, or paintings that appear to depict minors engaged in sexually explicit conduct and are deemed obscene. The penalty for a violation of this statute consists of a fine and a minimum of 5 years in prison. Registration as a sex offender is required. The penalty for a second or subsequent offense, or for a violation that involves a depiction of a child engaged in sadomasochistic activity, or for a violation involving sexual abuse of an actual child, can be life imprisonment.

Federal laws impose criminal penalties for child pornography whether the material qualifies as "obscene" or not. The Prosecutorial Remedies and Other Tools to end the Exploitation of Children Today Act ("PROTECT Act") specifically prohibits advertising, promotion, distribution, presentation, and solicitation of child pornography.

18 U.S.C. § 2252 prohibits the sale, possession with intent to sell, Internet transmission, or receipt, or knowing reproduction, of a visual depiction of a minor engaging in sexually explicit conduct. Knowing possession,

reproduction, or access with intent to view such material is also illegal, whether or not there is also intent to sell or further distribute the material.

In addition to fines, the statute provides mandatory minimum prison sentences upon conviction of a violation of this statute.

THE DEFINITION OF CHILD PORNOGRAPHY

Any material that meets the definition of obscenity will also meet the definition of child pornography if any of the participants in the depicted sexual activity is a minor (i.e., under the age of 18.) However, material does not have to be obscene in order to be child pornography.

Unlike obscenity, a depiction of nudity alone may be a violation of child pornography laws. A picture of a naked child violates child pornography laws if it is sexually suggestive, even if no actual sexual activity is depicted.

Pornographic images that are created or modified to look like they depict a minor qualify as child pornography even if no photograph of a child's nude body has ever been taken. For example, using photo-editing software to superimpose the face of a child onto a photograph of a nude adult striking a sexually suggestive pose could qualify as child pornography.

18 U.S.C. § 2256 limits the definition of child pornography to visual depictions (photographs, videos, digitally-generated images, and created images.) It does not matter whether a depiction has been "activated" for viewing or not. Electronically stored data are considered child pornography if they will yield depictions of child pornography when read by a computer.

It is a defense to a charge of possession or access without intent to sell or distribute, that the defendant possessed no more than two items containing such a depiction, did not show it to anyone other than the police, and promptly took steps to either destroy it or report it to the police.

Under 18 U.S.C. § 2252A (a) (3) (B), speech accompanying or seeking the transfer of child pornography is also punishable criminally. In addition, sending material in a way that "reflects the belief, or is intended to cause another to believe" that it contains child pornography is illegal. Offers to provide or obtain child pornography are not protected by the First Amendment even if the materials in question do not actually contain any child pornography.

TRANSMITTING OBSCENE OR HARMFUL MATERIAL TO A CHILD

Under 18 U.S.C. § 1470, it is a federal crime to knowingly transfer or attempt to transfer obscene matter using the U.S. mail or any facility of interstate commerce (such as the Internet) to a minor who is under 16 years of age. Penalties for violation of this law include fines and up to 10 years imprisonment.

47 U.S.C. § 231 also makes it illegal to knowingly make a commercial communication via the Internet that includes obscenity and is available to any minor who is less than 17 years of age.

Under 47 U.S.C. § 223 it is a crime to use the Internet to knowingly make or solicit, and transmit child pornography, or an obscene image, comment, request, suggestion, proposal or communication:

a) with the intent to harass, abuse or threaten someone;

b) to a person who is under 18 years old; or

c) using an interactive computer service in a way that makes it available for display to a person who is under 18 years old.

It is also a federal crime to knowingly allow a telecommunications facility to be used for these kinds of activities.

An employer or principal may be held vicariously liable for an employee's or agent's violation of this law only if the employee or agent was acting within the scope of his employment or agency, and the employer either knowingly authorized or ratified the conduct or recklessly disregarded it.

Laws prohibiting the display of obscenity or child pornography to a minor also exist at the state and local levels.

Both civil and criminal penalties may be imposed for violation of these laws.

Implementing measures to restrict access to minors is a defense to the crime of sending or making obscenity or child pornography available to minors, provided the measures are taken in good faith, are reasonable, and are appropriate under the circumstances. Requiring use of a verified credit card, debit account, adult access code, or adult personal identification number, may also provide a defense to these kinds of charges.

MAKING HARMFUL MATERIAL ACCESSIBLE BY CHILDREN

The Child Online Protection Act ("COPA"), codified at 47 U.S.C. § 231, makes it a crime to knowingly make any communication for commercial purposes using the World Wide Web, if it is:

1) harmful to minors; and

2) available to a person who is under 17 years of age.

Material is deemed harmful to minors if it is a communication, picture, image, graphic image file, article, recording, writing, or anything else that is either:

a)   obscene; or

b)   a depiction, description or representation of an actual or simulated sex act or sexual contact, an actual or simulated normal or perverted sexual act, or a lewd exhibition of genitals or a post-pubescent female breast, in a way that:

   1)   is patently offensive with respect to minors under 17;

   2)   the average person, applying contemporary community standards, would find, taking the material as a whole and with respect to minors under 17 years of age, is designed to appeal to, or is designed to pander to, the prurient interest; and

   3)   taken as a whole, lacks serious literary, artistic, political, or scientific value for minors under 17 years of age.

In addition to imprisonment, a fine of $50,000 per day may be imposed for each day that this law is intentionally and knowingly violated. In addition, a civil penalty of $50,000 per day may be imposed.

This statute does not apply to:

a)   telecommunications carriers providing a telecommunications service;

b)   business providing Internet access service;

c)   business providing an Internet search tool; or

d)   person engaged in the transmission, storage, retrieval, hosting, formatting, or translation (or any combination thereof) of a communication made by another person, without selection or alteration of the content of the communication.

Deleting material in the belief that it is offensive is permitted, and does not constitute "selection or alteration" of material for purposes of subparagraph (d).

Restricting access by minors to material that is harmful to minors is a defense, if access by minors is restricted in one of the following ways:

a)   by requiring use of a credit card, debit account, adult access code, or adult personal identification number;

b)   by accepting a digital certificate that verifies age; or

c)   by any other reasonable, technologically feasible measures.

Information gathered in any of these processes must be protected from disclosure to anyone other than the individual providing it, if over 16 years of age, or the individual's parent or legal guardian, if the individual is less than 17 years of age.

COPA is of questionable constitutionality. At least one court has held that it violates the First and Fifth Amendments because it is unconstitutionally vague and overbroad. The U.S. Supreme Court has declined a request to quash an injunction against its enforcement. (See below.) You will need to make your own assessment, though, which should be made in consultation with an attorney.

DECEIVING A MINOR INTO VIEWING HARMFUL MATERIAL

18 U.S.C. §§ 2252B and 2252C prohibit the use of misleading domain names, words, or digital images on the Internet with the intent to deceive a minor into viewing harmful or obscene material.

The definition of "harmful," for purposes of this law, is broader than the definition of obscenity. A communication may be deemed harmful to a minor if it:

1) depicts nudity, sexual activity, or excretion;
2) appeals to the prurient interest of minors,
3) is patently offensive to prevailing standards in the adult community with respect to what is suitable material for minors; and
4) lacks serious literary, artistic, political, or scientific value for minors.

PORNOGRAPHY IN LIBRARIES

Website owners are not required to ensure that pornographic images on their sites are not viewed in libraries. As a condition of receiving federal funds, however, the Children's Internet Protection Act ("CIPA") requires all public libraries to install software that blocks obscene or pornographic images from being viewed on their computers.

CONSTITUTIONALITY

The U.S. Supreme Court has declared that obscenity and child pornography are kinds of speech that are not protected by the First Amendment. For this reason, the First Amendment is not available as a defense to an obscenity or child pornography charge.

Although obscenity and child pornography are not constitutionally protected, the First Amendment does impose limitations on how a government may define these terms. Accordingly, the First Amendment may still be invoked to challenge an obscenity or pornography law, or laws prohibiting "harmful" or "offensive" material, on the grounds that it is either:

a)   overbroad, i.e., burdens both protected and unprotected speech; or

b)   so vague that it has a chilling effect on protected speech.

A law is overbroad, in the First Amendment sense, if it is so worded that it proscribes both protected and unprotected speech.

The prohibition against vague criminal laws is also an aspect of Due Process under the 5th and 14th Amendments. It would be fundamentally unfair to punish a person for a crime without first giving him adequate notice of the particular conduct that is proscribed.

Thus, in *Reno v. ACLU*, 521 U.S. 844 (1997), the Supreme Court struck down a provision of the Communications Decency Act that prohibited the display of a patently offensive comment, image or other communication in a way that it could be seen by a minor. The Court held that the undefined phrase, "patently offensive" was unconstitutionally vague and overbroad.

Congress responded by enacting the Child Online Protection Act ("COPA.") In *Ashcroft v. ACLU*, 535 U.S. 564 (2002), the U.S. Supreme Court held that "contemporary community standards" is not so overbroad or vague as to violate the constitution.

The Court did not decide whether other provisions of COPA were constitutional. In 1999, a federal district court granted the American Civil Liberties Union's request for an injunction against enforcement of COPA on the basis that its other provisions were likely to be unconstitutionally vague and overbroad. In 2004, the U.S. Supreme Court issued a decision allowing the injunction against enforcement to stand. Then in 2008, the Third Circuit Court of Appeals, in *ACLU v. Mukasey*, 534 F.3d 181 (3d Cir. 2008), ruled that COPA is unconstitutionally vague and overbroad. The U.S. Supreme Court has denied review of that decision. As it stands now, therefore, COPA is a law that is of uncertain constitutional validity, but it remains on the books until somebody pursues a successful First Amendment challenge to it.

STATE SECRETS

Some information gathered or maintained by a government is intended to be kept secret. Troop movements, ongoing criminal investigations, anti-terror operations, surveillance and intelligence-gathering activities are some examples. The penalties for unauthorized disclosure can be severe. A website owner or blogger who works with a government source to obtain and publish confidential government information may be charged as a co-conspirator.

In some cases, a whistleblower statute may permit disclosure of such information if disclosure is for the purpose of revealing official misconduct. Whistleblower statutes, however, do not authorize immediate disclosure of such information. Instead, the person seeking to reveal the protected information must go through the government channels that have been established for the handling of such situations.

If you find yourself in a situation where a government insider has or plans to divulge information about government operations to you for purposes of publication, you should retain an attorney.

TERRORISM AND INSURRECTION

The USA PATRIOT Act was enacted almost immediately after the September 11, 2001 terrorist attacks on the World Trade Center. It gave the U.S. government sweeping powers to investigate suspected terrorists, members of terrorist organizations, and those who aid or support them. Although it expired in 2015, Congress renewed its major provisions that year, in the USA Freedom Act. Many other countries have enacted similar laws. In some cases, merely associating with, or expressing support or agreement with a suspected terrorist organization is a crime. In some countries, a false report of a terrorist attack is also a crime.

Governments do not have a sense of humor when it comes to terrorism. In one case, for example, a British airline passenger expressed his upset over a flight delay by jokingly tweeting that the airline had a week to get its act together or he was "blowing the airport sky high!" He was investigated under the U.K. version of the USA PATRIOT Act, and ultimately convicted on a nuisance charge.

Moral: Don't even joke about terrorism.

FRAUD

Publishing false or misleading statements can subject you to liability for fraud.

Fraud is both a civil and a criminal wrong, with slightly different elements and standards of proof applying in each realm.

Fraud is actionable both at common law and pursuant to various state and federal statutory enactments. Definitions vary from jurisdiction to jurisdiction. The required elements also vary depending on whether the claim is based on statutory or common law. The essence of all fraud, though, is the intentional misrepresentation or concealment of a material fact(s) on which a person relies to his or her detriment.

To prove a claim of common law (not statutory) fraud, it is necessary to establish each of the following elements:

1) intentional representation of a material fact
2) that is false or misleading
3) with the intent to induce
4) and that actually does induce
5) reasonable reliance
6) causing
7) economic loss to another.

Basically, common law fraud involves intentionally deceiving another to induce him to alter his position to his detriment.

An "intentional misrepresentation of a material fact" is a broad enough concept to include a deliberate omission of a known fact, if nondisclosure is likely to mislead a person.

Remedies for fraud range from compensatory and punitive damages, to equitable remedies like injunctions and rescission ("undoing" a deal procured by fraud.) Fraud may also be raised as a defense to the enforcement of a contract.

There are numerous kinds of fraud, both at common law and by virtue of statutory enactments. The basic take-away from all of them is that you should never try to induce people to take an action, or to refrain from taking an action, by providing them with false or misleading information, or by failing to provide them with information that would be likely to influence their decisions if they knew about it.

"PHISHING"

"Phishing" refers to the practice of posing as someone else for the purpose of deceiving people into sending financial or personal information to you. It is most commonly done by sending an email message directing the recipient to follow a link or visit a named website to provide information falsely claimed to be necessary to "maintain" or "update" an account or record.

Setting up a website, or a page or link on a website, for the same purpose would also be a form of "phishing."

If someone takes the bait and sends financial, personal or private information in response to these kinds of phony solicitations or notices, she may sue the "phisher" for fraud.

"SPAM"

"Spamming," i.e., sending people unwanted email messages, is not inherently fraudulent. Certain kinds of spam may be fraudulent, though. For example, sending email messages that display a falsified return email address could be actionable as fraud. The economic loss in this situation need not be extensive. For example, it may simply consist in the spammer's use of storage space on the email service provider's computer system.

USING BOTS TO CLICK ON "PAY-PER-CLICK" ADVERTISEMENTS

An advertiser commits fraud if it uses bots to click on its advertisement in order to boost revenues under a pay-per-click arrangement.

MISREPRESENTATION

A blogger or website owner may be liable for intentional misrepresentation. The cause of action is very similar to fraud.

Several states also allow recovery for negligent misrepresentation. In these states, damages may be recoverable against a website owner or blogger for publishing false or misleading information even though there is no evidence of any actual intention to deceive anybody.

The elements of a cause of action for negligent misrepresentation are:

1) failure to exercise reasonable care in obtaining or communicating information;
2) causation;
3) pecuniary loss; and
4) justifiable reliance.

The owner of a commercial website that offers third parties a place to sell their property normally is not under any duty to protect buyers from unscrupulous third-party sellers. But if the website owner makes a statement to the effect that "all sales are safe" or some other assurance to similar effect, then liability for negligent misrepresentation may arise if the owner fails to check out the sellers to ensure that they are, in fact, trustworthy, etc. In some circumstances, a representation such as this could also be construed as a warranty, giving users an additional cause of action against the site owner for breach of warranty (contract.) Accordingly, it is not a good idea to include representations like this on your website unless you are prepared to take full financial responsibility for any sales that go wrong.

NEGLIGENCE

Liability can arise not only from intentional wrongdoing, but also from careless acts or omissions, i.e., negligence.

Negligence is a broadly defined term encompassing any failure to exercise the care that a reasonably prudent person would exercise in similar circumstances.

The four basic elements of any negligence claim are:

1) Duty to exercise the requisite standard of care;
2) Breach of the duty;
3) Causation (causal link between breach and damage); and
4) Damage.

The first element, of course, is pivotal, yet it is difficult to define with precision. It really requires two kinds of determinations: (1) whether a particular person owes a duty to someone; and (2) what the applicable standard of care is. In making these determinations, courts primarily consider the extent to which harm is reasonably foreseeable from a particular kind of act or omission; the nature of the connection or relationship between the person harmed and the person sought to be held liable; and whether it is fair and reasonable to impose liability.

A website owner who collects identifying information and/or financial information about users may have duties to utilize reasonable security measures to prevent access to the information, and to notify users if security is breached. Failure to do so may expose the website owner to liability to its users for negligence.

Statutes often impose and define obligations. When they do, the statute itself, being the source of the duty, may provide guidance about the applicable standard of care. Conduct or inaction that breaches an obligation imposed by a statute is called negligence per se.

If you hold yourself out as a professional, or if you are one, dispensing advice via the Internet exposes you to a risk of liability for professional negligence (also called "malpractice.") Doctors, lawyers, and certain other professionals are held to a higher standard of care than the one that applies to a "reasonably prudent person." The question in these cases is not what a reasonably prudent person would have done under the circumstances, but what a reasonably prudent doctor (or lawyer, etc.) would have done under the circumstances. In most situations, a reasonably prudent doctor most likely would examine a patient and consider a number of possible diagnoses before dispensing medical advice specific to an individual's particular symptoms and health history. If the advice given turns out to be incorrect and it causes injury to the reader, the doctor could be sued for professional negligence (also known as malpractice.)

Two kinds of causation must be proven in any negligence case: actual and proximate. Actual causation requires proof that the complained-of injury or damage would not have happened but for the defendant's breach of duty; or proof that the defendant's act or omission materially increased the risk of the complained-of injury occurring. Proximate cause (sometimes called "legal cause") is really only a limitation on liability for actual causation. Basically, it means that a person will not be held liable for harm that is not reasonably foreseeable to result from the act or omission in question.

Historically, it has been necessary to prove that some sort of physical and/or economic injury pecuniary loss resulted from the negligent act or omission. Damages to compensate for non-pecuniary injury, such as pain and suffering, mental anguish, and emotional distress could also be awarded, but only if some sort of pecuniary loss was first established (medical or psychotherapeutic bills, property repair or replacement costs, loss of income, or the like.) This is still the rule in many jurisdictions, but some states now permit recovery without proof of pecuniary loss.

INFLICTION OF EMOTIONAL DISTRESS

A growing number of states recognize a cause of action for intentional infliction of emotional distress. Four elements must be proven:

1) extreme and outrageous conduct;
2) intent to cause, or reckless disregard of likelihood of causing, emotional distress;
3) causation (actual and proximate); and
4) emotional distress.

Not every insult or annoyance is actionable. Mere rudeness is not enough. Instead, the conduct must be so extreme as to "exceed all bounds of that usually tolerated in a civilized community."[7]

Some states also allow recovery for negligently inflicted emotional distress.

The First Amendment may provide a defense if the speech concerns a public official or a public figure. There is some authority that a public official or public figure may not sue for infliction of emotional distress unless she proves actual malice.

THREATS

18 U.S.C. § 875 makes it a federal crime to transmit a communication containing:

a) a demand for a ransom or reward for the release of a kidnapped person;

b) a threat to kidnap a person;

c) a threat to injure a person (i.e., inflict bodily injury); or

d) a threat, for purposes of extortion, to injure property or reputation or to accuse someone of a crime.

State laws also make the communication of a threat a crime. Definitions vary from state to state, but in general the crime of making a threat means intentionally communicating a serious (not joking) expression of intention to commit an illegal act of violence against a particular person or group of persons.

In some circumstances, such as where it causes the recipient to suffer emotional distress, a threat may also result in civil liability.

A true threat of bodily harm generally receives no First Amendment protection. But a threat transmitted via the Internet may be protected by the First Amendment if the speaker did not act with either the intent to actually carry it out or knowledge that the words used would cause the person at whom it is directed to fear actual harm. The fact that some person subjectively felt threatened, or that a reasonable person would have felt threatened, is not enough, if the speaker did not have actual intent to do harm, and was merely negligent in the phrasing of a communication.

It is not clear whether speech that is transmitted with reckless disregard for whether it might cause someone to feel threatened, but without either

---

[7] RESTATEMENT (2d) TORTs, Section 46.

intent or actual knowledge that it would, is protected by the First Amendment.

HARASSMENT AND STALKING

Most states make it unlawful to stalk or harass another person. Some make it a crime; some make it actionable as a civil wrong; and some provide both criminal and civil remedies.

These laws are usually worded broadly enough that they would apply to the use of an Internet website or blog to stalk or harass someone.

Definitions vary from state to state. Typically, they require proof of some unwanted or offensive conduct or contact that is intended to and/or does cause fear or annoyance to a particular person.

The quickest way to run afoul of online harassment laws is to create a web page for the purpose of being mean to a private individual. Repeatedly sending emails or posting mean and/or embarrassing content about a person is another way. These are just examples. They are not the only possibilities.

Interstate stalking is a federal offense. 18 U.S.C. § 2261A(2) makes it a crime to use an interactive computer service or an electronic communication service or system (e.g., a website, blog, or email service) to harass, injure, kill, intimidate, or place another person under surveillance with the intent to do so, if it causes such person to be placed in reasonable fear of death or seriously bodily injury to himself, an immediate family member, or a spouse or intimate partner of that person; or could reasonably be expected to cause substantial emotional distress to any such people.

Courts have held that a student's online activities can provide a basis for disciplinary action against the student up to and including expulsion. This does not violate the First Amendment rights of students even if the online activity occurs off school grounds and on the student's own time.

If you don't like someone, or if you are angry at someone, resist the temptation to use the Internet to try to annoy, embarrass, scare, or make them feel bad.

HATE SPEECH

Article 20 of the International Covenant on Civil and Political Rights (ICCPR) prohibits "advocacy of national, racial or religious hatred that constitutes incitement to discrimination, hostility or violence." It has been adopted by many countries. The U.S. has become a party to it, as well, but subject to reservations and declarations, including that it is not self-executing. That means it does not have legal force and effect in individual cases in the U.S. unless and until implementing legislation is enacted.

Although crimes motivated by bias or prejudice may be punished more severely than other kinds of crimes, the First Amendment imposes limitations on the regulation of speech itself.

The First Amendment protects even racist, sexist and other forms of "hate speech" so long as it does not contain fighting words, a threat of imminent harm, or solicitation to commit a crime, and so long as it does not come within the definition of harassment.

> *Example:* Donald hates black people, so he establishes a website called IHateBlacks.com, at which he lists all kinds of negative stereotypes about black people, and states that he sees nothing wrong with burning crosses. So far, his speech is protected by the First Amendment. Even if he invites readers to a cross-burning event he is planning, his speech is still protected. If he goes further, announcing specific plans to burn a cross for the purpose of intimidating a particular individual, then his speech is not protected by the First Amendment.

Most countries have more restrictive hate speech laws. For example, some European countries prohibit the distribution or display of Nazi symbols, anti-Semitism, and/or expressions of denial about the Holocaust. Several Middle Eastern countries prohibit blasphemy, which under Sharia law means expressions of disrespect for the Islamic religion or Mohammad. Penalties can be severe, up to and including death.

DISCRIMINATION

Laws, regulations and ordinances prohibiting various kinds of discrimination exist at all levels of government – federal, state, and local. Website owners and bloggers are not exempt from these. For example, if a law, regulation or ordinance prohibits race, sex, religious, and/or disability discrimination in employment, housing or public accommodations, then website owners and bloggers are under the same obligation to abide by those laws as everyone else is. This may include an obligation to refrain from publishing or displaying discriminatory employment or housing advertisements on your website, for example.

A "place of public accommodation" means a hotel, restaurant, theater or the like, that is generally open to the public. To qualify for protection from discrimination under the federal Civil Rights Act, a place of public accommodation must be a physical structure. A website, blog or Internet chat room is not a place of public accommodation. They are the legal equivalent of private clubs. Therefore, restrictions against discrimination in granting access to a public accommodation do not apply. On the other hand, restrictions against advertising or promotion of discrimination in employment, housing or a public accommodation, do apply to online advertisements and promotions.

There is some case law suggesting that an Internet-based service is a place of public accommodation for purposes of the Americans with Disabilities Act.[8] An online video subscription service may be required to accommodate deaf persons by providing a closed-captioning feature.

DISCLOSING IDENTITY OF SEXUAL ASSAULT VICTIM

Several states have enacted laws making it a crime to publish the name of an alleged sexual assault victim.

Penalizing the publication of information, or allowing a rape victim to sue for damages on the basis of such publication, violates the First Amendment if the information is acquired from a lawfully obtained public record. An unredacted police report that is released to the media or the public is a lawfully obtained public record.

The First Amendment may not protect a publisher who obtains information by unlawful means.

DESCRIBING AN ABORTION PROVIDER AS A PERSON WHO HAS COMMITTED CRIMES AGAINST HUMANITY, IN A MOCK-UP OF AN OLD WEST "WANTED" POSTER

The Freedom of Access to Clinic Entrances Act subjects a person to both criminal penalties and civil liability if the person intimidates or interferes with another person's attempt to obtain or provide reproductive health services. In *Planned Parenthood v. American Coalition of Life Activists*, 90 F.3d 1058 (9th Cir. 2002), the 9th Circuit Court of Appeals ruled that posting Old West style "Wanted" posters identifying specific doctors known to perform abortions violates this provision of the law. The Court reasoned that threats are not

---

[8] National Association of the Deaf v. Netflix, Inc., 869 F. Supp. 2d 196 (D. Mass. 2012).

constitutionally protected, and interpreted the "Wanted" poster, in conjunction with the accusation of "crimes against humanity," as an implied threat to doctors who perform abortions.

INTERFERENCE WITH CONTRACT OR BUSINESS ADVANTAGE

Inducing a person to breach a contract with a third party may subject you to liability for interference with contract. The elements that must be proven to establish a right to recovery for interference with contract are:

1) Existence of a contract;
2) Knowledge of the contract;
3) Intentional procurement of the contract's breach;
4) Lack of justification;
5) Causation of injury (which may be economic); and
6) Damage.

Interference with someone else's prospective business advantage can also subject you to liability for damages. Unlike interference with contract, this kind of claim requires no proof of any actual contract. Instead, a right of recovery exists upon proof of all of the following elements:

1) intentional interference with an existing or potential business or economic relationship;
2) for an improper purpose or means (e.g., to drum up business for yourself);
3) causation; and
4) injury.

BREACH OF CONTRACT

A blogger or website owner is not immune from common law liability for failing to perform an obligation required of him under a contract.

Contracts may be oral, written, or implied by conduct.

To be enforceable, a contract must be supported by consideration. A promise to do something, or to give something, while getting absolutely nothing in return is not enforceable as a contract. On the other hand, if a promise has the effect of inducing a person to do or refrain from doing something, to his detriment, a court may hold the promisor to his promise despite the lack of consideration, under the equitable doctrine of promissory estoppel.

Breaching a contract (such as a non-compete agreement) in order to get customers who might otherwise have gone to the other party to the contract puts you at risk of liability for both breach of contract and interference with prospective business advantage.

EMPLOYMENT CONTRACTS

It is not unusual for employment contracts to provide that an employee may be terminated or disciplined for doing or saying certain things, or for disclosing certain kinds of information. A website or blogger is not exempt from such provisions.

A website or blogger who is employed should carefully review the employment contract and employee handbook, if any.

Unless a contract provides otherwise, an employer may fire an employee for any reason or for no reason at all. This means that an employer may fire an at-will employee simply because he doesn't like the employee's blog, or disagrees with a post to it.

Under the National Labor Relations Act (NLRA), an employer is prohibited from restricting an employee's right to talk about wages or working conditions with other employees, and cannot prohibit an employee from telling other people who his employer is. Thus, an employer cannot restrict an employee's right to post comments about wages and working conditions to social media or his blog.

The NLRA does not protect an employee from being terminated or disciplined for merely griping about the employer, the company, or the job, if the complaint is not about wages or working conditions.

The NLRA only provides protection for "concerted activity" by multiple employees. Posting to a website or blog to which no coworkers are connected does not qualify for NLRA protection. An employer may discipline or fire an employee for complaining on her own behalf without any "intended or actual group action to improve working conditions."

The NLRA also does not protect employees from being fired or disciplined for making threats of physical violence.

And the NLRA does not protect an employee from being fired or disciplined for making a statement that constitutes a violation of the employment agreement. For example, if an employment contract prohibits an employee from disclosing trade secrets, then the NLRA does not prohibit the employer from firing or disciplining the employee for doing so.

CONFIDENTIALITY AGREEMENTS

Confidentiality agreements are commonly made in a number of different situations. An attorney may have a confidentiality agreement with a client; an employer may have one with its employees; a merchant may have one with a credit card processing service; a journalist may have one with his sources of information; and so on.

Like any other contract, disclosing information in violation of a confidentiality agreement may result in liability for damages for breach of contract. Depending on the circumstances, disclosure of confidential information may violate other laws, too, such as laws prohibiting attorneys from disclosing client confidences.

Many states have enacted shield laws that protect journalists from having to disclose the identities of anonymous sources. In these states, a court may require a journalist to disclose the identity of a source only if the information is highly relevant and necessary to a claim, and cannot be obtained from other available sources. Shield laws vary from state to state, and courts in different states are not in agreement on the question whether bloggers are "journalists" for purposes of shield laws. Accordingly, if you are a blogger working with an anonymous source, it would be a good idea to include in your contract an agreement that you may disclose the source's identity if a court orders you to do so. It would also be a good idea to familiarize yourself with any applicable shield laws.

Many non-U.S. countries have no shield laws. It is not uncommon for American journalists to be arrested and jailed for contempt in foreign countries for disobeying a court order to reveal their sources.

Moreover, in many of the U.S. states that have shield laws, regular publication is required. And in some states protection only extends to newspaper, television and radio reporters, not to website owners and bloggers.

UNFAIR COMPETITION

Unfair competition is a broadly defined source of common law liability for any kind of dishonest or unethical activity that is engaged in for the purpose of either harming a competitor's business or unfairly trading on a competitor's good reputation. Many of the specific kinds of torts described elsewhere in this book – such as counterfeiting or "passing off" goods using a competitor's trademark; communicating false and disparaging information about a competitor or a competitor's goods or services; or fraudulent or misleading advertising – are also forms of unfair competition.

SOLICITATION AND INCITEMENT

Solicitation of crime means requesting, commanding or encouraging someone to commit a crime. It is a crime even if it doesn't succeed.

Advocacy of crime in the abstract, on the other hand, is not solicitation. Musing that "What we need in this country is a violent revolution" is very unlikely to provide sufficient grounds for a solicitation charge. To support a solicitation charge, the advocacy must be for the commission of a specific crime. "I urge you to burn down a mosque right now!" might support a solicitation charge.

Incitement of crime refers to speech that is intended to and likely to produce imminent crime. It, too, is a crime.

TRESPASS TO CHATTELS

Historically developed as a way to make people pay for the loss of value of an animal or other personal property they have injured or damaged, the common law cause of action known as "trespass to chattels" is now being applied to impose liability for various kinds of unwanted Internet activity.

The elements of a cause of action for trespass to chattel are:

1) intent to interfere with another person's rights in personal property;
2) physical interference with possessory rights (which may include rights of use and enjoyment of the property);
3) in personal property;
4) causation; and
5) injury to the property (which may include diminution in usefulness or value.)

Basically, trespass to chattels means damaging another person's personal property, or decreasing its value.

The measure of damages for a trespass to chattels claim is the diminution in value of the property attributable to the trespass.

SPAM

An email system is the personal property of an Internet Service Provider (ISP). An ISP may have a cause of action for trespass to chattels if a hacker uses the system to send emails without the ISP's permission, or if a person uses the service in a manner that is not authorized by the terms of service. Thus, if the terms of service prohibit the sending of "spam" emails, then using the service to send such emails would expose the user to liability not only for breach of contract, but also for trespass to chattels.

Spammers who "spoof" the origin of the email messages they send may also be liable for trespass to chattels.

Because injury to property is required, small amounts of spamming that do not make an appreciable impact on a server's operations or disk storage space might not result in common law liability for trespass to chattel. There may be statutory liability, however, under the Computer Fraud and Abuse Act (CFAA) and the Controlling the Assault of Non-Solicited Pornography And Marketing Act of 2003 (CAN-SPAM).

"SCRAPING"

Using spiders and robots to gather ("scrape") information from other websites may be a form of trespass to chattel. Some courts have treated websites and servers as "chattel" (a legal term for an item of personal property that somebody owns.)

At common law, damage or injury to another person's chattel is a wrongful act for which a person may be sued. Computer hardware is certainly personal property. Sending electrons to make contact with it will suffice as "physical" contact with the property. Increased use of disk space and processing time may suffice as an "injury" to the property, since those things decrease the value of the property to users. If the electrons interfere with another person's use or enjoyment of his computer, hard drive, processor, or server, then liability for trespass to chattels should actually be fairly clear. This may happen when access to the server significantly reduces its available memory and processing power.

Robotically and repeatedly performing search functions on a website/server for information/data can be a trespass to chattel if it has the effect of significantly reducing available memory or processing power. It may also be a trespass to chattels if others could make the same use, and the combined use could have such an impact.

INCLUDING SPYWARE IN DOWNLOADS

Including spyware in a program that is downloadable from your website may make you liable for trespass to chattels, if the spyware causes some non-trivial kind of damage. Taking up bandwidth on the user's Internet connection, or causing a user's computer to slow down, or taking up memory on a user's computer, or using screen space on a computer monitor, or reduced user productivity due to frustration, are all deemed to be substantial, not merely trivial, kinds of damage with respect to this kind of activity.

CONVERSION

Conversion is a common law cause of action that is intended to compensate a personal property owner for another person's unlawful exercise of dominion and control over the property. This can include wrongfully withholding possession, or wrongfully withholding the means of obtaining possession, of another person's property. Theft is the classic example of withholding possession. Wrongfully refusing to relinquish possession of a key to a car is an example of conversion of a car by withholding the means of obtaining possession of it.

The elements of a conversion claim are:

1) exercise of dominion or control over personal property;
2) another person's right to immediate possession of it;
3) demand for possession;
4) failure to return the property after demand is made;
5) duty to return the property (i.e., it is being withheld wrongfully); and
6) the property is specifically identifiable.

The remedy for conversion is a "forced sale" of the property at its full value. This means that the person who is guilty of conversion keeps the property but will be ordered to pay the rightful owner its full value.

Early common law held that conversion only applied to tangible personal property, not to intangibles like intellectual property. This is still the case for copyrights and patents. Because federal law preempts these fields, courts have not extended the common law conversion doctrine to apply to misappropriation of copyrights and patents.

A few states continue to apply the rule to all other forms of intellectual property, as well. The modern trend, however, is to extend the cause of action to apply to any forms of intellectual property that are not preempted by federal law.

CONVERSION OF A DOMAIN NAME

Some states, including California, authorize a cause of action for conversion of a domain name. Thus, if a person wrongfully persuades a domain name registrar to transfer someone else's domain name to him, and then refuses to transfer it to the rightful owner after demand is made, then he may be liable for conversion of the domain name.

UNAUTHORIZED USE OF TRADE SECRETS AND INTANGIBLES

Courts in a growing number of states are extending the cause of action for conversion to apply to more kinds of intellectual property besides copyrights and patents. For example, in several states courts have extended it to apply to trade secrets, and also to electronic records, such as customer lists. In some situations, an activity may be actionable on a theory of conversion as well as on a theory of misappropriation of information, giving the aggrieved party a choice of remedies.

Of course, there can be no recovery for conversion of any kind of personal property unless each of the elements of a cause of action for conversion is proven.

HACKING

The Computer Fraud and Abuse Act ("CFAA") is a federal law making it a crime to access a protected computer and get information from it without authorized access, or in a way that exceeds the authority granted. Gaining access to a password-protected website without permission would be an example.

The CFAA also makes it unlawful to traffic in passwords or other identifiers to help others gain unauthorized access to a protected computer.

A protected computer is one that is:

a)   used exclusively by a financial institution;
b)   used exclusively by the U.S. government;
c)   used by or for a financial institution or the U.S. government; or
d)   used in interstate or foreign commerce or communication.

A civil action may be brought under the CFAA if the unauthorized access was gained knowingly and with intent to defraud, something of value was obtained as a result, and the defendant's conduct caused at least $5,000 damage to the plaintiff over a one-year period. The damage can include the cost of returning the computer to its previous condition; lost revenue; or other consequential damages incurred due to the interruption of service.

Spamming, in the sense of harvesting email addresses and transmitting them through an email server or service can be a violation of the CFAA. Using a software program to "scrape" data from another website, in excess of the authority granted in the terms of service, can also be a violation of the CFAA.

VIRUSES, WORMS, AND OTHER MALICIOUS CODE

The CFAA also makes it unlawful to knowingly cause the transmission of a program, code, information, or command, that intentionally causes damage to a protected computer, without authorization. Both criminal and civil penalties may be imposed for a violation.

A civil action may be brought under the CFAA only if the defendant's conduct caused at least $5,000 damage over a one-year period. The damage can include the cost of returning the computer to its previous condition; lost revenue; or other consequential damages incurred due to the interruption of service.

A protected computer is one that is used:

a)   exclusively by a financial institution;
b)   exclusively by the U.S. government;
c)   by or for a financial institution or the U.S. government; or
d)   in interstate or foreign commerce or communication.

THE CONVENTION ON CYBERCRIME

The Convention on Cybercrime is a treaty to which the United States and a number of other counties are parties. Among other things, it criminalizes the knowing and intentional creation or transmission of computer viruses or malware, as well as computer-related fraud. Signatories to the Convention agree that computer crimes are extraditable offenses, and the Convention calls for cooperation among member countries in the investigation and prosecution of computer crimes.

UNAUTHORIZED ACCESS FOR UNLAWFUL PURPOSE

The CFAA also penalizes any conduct that is committed "in furtherance of any criminal or tortious act" in violation of federal or state law.[9] Accordingly, gaining unauthorized access to another person's computer in order to commit a crime or civil wrong against that person would be a violation of the CFAA.

Providing false information (such as a fake profile on a MySpace account) for the purpose of harassing or inflicting emotional distress on another computer user would be an example.

PRODUCT LIABILITY

A manufacturer or seller of a product may be liable to a consumer if the consumer suffers harm as a result of a defect in the product.

In *James v. Meow Media, Inc.*, 300 F.3d 683, 688 (6th Cir. 2002), the 6th Circuit Court of Appeals rejected an attempt to hold the creator of Internet content liable for injury allegedly caused by viewing the content. In that case, the plaintiff sued the makers of videogames, movies, and Internet content, claiming these products desensitized viewers to violence, and impelled a viewer to shoot classmates. The court differentiated between a container of content (such as a disk or digital file), which may be a product, and the communicative expression contained within it, which is not.

Product liability is more likely to be a concern for commercial website owners than for owners of noncommercial websites and blogs. A website owner might be liable for defective products he offers for sale on his website, but a court is not likely to treat the content of the website itself, or the expressive content of digital media offered or sold via a website, as a "product" for purposes of product liability law.

CONSUMER PROTECTION

People and businesses that use websites to make sales, or to advertise goods or services, must comply with a panoply of regulations at various levels of government – local, state, federal, and sometimes international.

---

[9] 18 U.S.C. § 1030(c)(2)(B)(ii).

WEBSITES AND BLOGS WITH ADVERTISING

It is not necessary to sell or offer to sell a product or service on your website or blog in order to be subject to certain consumer protection regulations that are applicable to commercial websites. Even if you set up a website or blog for a noncommercial purpose (such as commenting on current events; reviewing books, products or movies, etc.), it still may be necessary to comply with federal and state consumer protection and commercial regulations if you display other people's advertisements on your site.

PRODUCT REVIEWS

You also may need to comply with consumer protection and commercial regulations if you receive money for a product or service review that you publish on your site. A paid review is essentially an advertisement, so you will need to comply with all laws related to advertising.

Being given free product in the hope that you may write a review of it is the legal equivalent of receiving payment for the review. The ensuing review is considered an advertisement, so you will need to comply with all laws related to advertising.

Federal Trade Commission (FTC) rules require you to publish a disclosure of your relationship with a company that pays for a review, or provides free product in the hope that you will provide a review, and you must indicate that payment has been received for the review or endorsement. Your opinion must also be truthful, which means that you cannot endorse or write a review of a product unless you have actually used it. And you must give your honest opinion of it. These rules and requirements also apply to product reviews or endorsements set out in user comments on other people's websites or blogs.

The disclosure must be conspicuous but it need not be elaborate. It may be something as simple as, "ABC Company sent me ABC brand product to try, and here is my opinion about it...."

LINKING

Although legal issues around hypertext linking to other websites most often are raised in the copyright and trademark context, providing a link to a website or blog that contains unlawful or actionable material may expose you to criminal or civil liability in other situations, too. Providing a link to a website might be considered a form of aiding, facilitating or encouraging the display or distribution of materials at the site. This can be a dangerous risk to take in cases where the linked-to site may be engaged in distributing illegal content such as obscenity, child pornography, material that is harmful to minors, illegal narcotics, copyright circumvention tools, etc.

Linking to a site normally will not result in liability unless you knew or should have known the site contained unlawful content.

CONTEMPT OF COURT

Judges are becoming increasingly involved in attempting to regulate the content of websites and blogs, especially in family court and juvenile proceedings. It is not uncommon for a judge to issue an order directing a website owner or blogger to refrain from posting specified kinds of content and/or to remove specified content. Violation of such an order is contempt of court, and is punishable by confinement to jail and possibly a fine.

Publishing false and defamatory information about a judge, or suggesting that a judge is biased or guilty of some other violation of judicial ethics, or insulting a judge or court in some other way, is also contempt of court, and may result in the issuance of an injunction and possibly jail time.

In some cases, a First Amendment defense may be available.

WEBSITE CONTENT AS EVIDENCE

That old Miranda suggestion that "Everything you say may be used against you in a court of law" sounds like a cliché, but it is true. In fact, it applies with at least as much force to website owners and bloggers as it does to those who are the subject of a custodial interrogation. Nearly everything a person posts online becomes accessible to the public, and remains accessible to many people even after the person thinks she has deleted it.

Although the rules of evidence prohibit hearsay evidence (unsworn, out-of-court statements) there are many exceptions to that rule. Moreover, the hearsay rule only prohibits the use of an out-of-court statement to prove the truth of the matter asserted. It does not prohibit the use of out-of-court statements as evidence of state of mind, such as motive, intent, ill will, etc. As a website owner or blogger, you need to be aware that website content and blog posts are increasingly being used as evidence against people in court. A blog post threatening or revealing animosity toward a particular person, for example, might be used as evidence of ill will or motive or intent to harm the person.

Deleting material from a computer or server does not usually remove all records of it.

Also be aware that posting material anonymously will not necessarily protect your identity from being discovered. Even if you create an anonymous or pseudonymous user name, law enforcement is generally capable of tracing email messages and Internet postings to the IP addresses from which they were sent.

Finally, be aware that courts tend to be inclined to issue subpoenas to obtain access to computers that may provide evidence of the author or publisher of a website or blog post. First Amendment arguments have not met with a great deal of success in this area.

LAWS OF OTHER COUNTRIES

The liabilities, defenses and immunities discussed in this book relate primarily to U.S. law. The laws of other countries are different. Unlike the United States, for instance, many countries allow public figures to sue publishers without having to prove actual malice.

A number of countries impose much stricter limitations on Internet transmissions than the Unites States does. Here are some examples:

- Afghanistan: apostasy; atheism (death penalty)
- Belarus: defamation of a head of state
- Brunei: insulting royalty
- Denmark: insulting royalty
- Egypt: defamation of a head of state
- Ethiopia: "outrages against the constitution" (death penalty)
- France: strict regulations re: wine and liquor advertisements
- Germany: Holocaust denial; defamation of a head of state
- Greece: defamation of a head of state
- Iran: apostasy; atheism; homosexuality (death penalty)
- Kazakhstan: defamation of a head of state
- Kuwait: insulting royalty
- Malaysia: apostasy; atheism (death penalty)
- Maldives: apostasy; atheism; defamation of a head of state
- Mauritania: apostasy; atheism; homosexuality (death penalty)
- Morocco: insulting royalty
- Netherlands: insulting royalty

- Nigeria: apostasy; atheism; homosexuality (death penalty)
- North Korea: attempting to leave the country
- Pakistan: atheism; blasphemy (death penalty)
- Poland: defamation of a head of state
- Qatar: apostasy; atheism (death penalty)
- Saudi Arabia: apostasy; atheism; homosexuality; witchcraft (death penalty)
- Singapore: insulting a public servant
- Somalia: apostasy; atheism (death penalty)
- Spain: insulting royalty
- Sudan: apostasy; atheism; homosexuality (death penalty)
- Switzerland: defamation of a head of state
- Syria: expression of opposition to the government; membership in the Muslim Brotherhood (death penalty)
- Thailand: insulting royalty
- United Arab Emirates: apostasy; atheism (death penalty)
- Yemen: apostasy; adultery; homosexuality (death penalty)
- Zimbabwe: defamation of a head of state

This is not an exhaustive list. Many additional content-specific regulations exist in many countries.

Website owners, operators and bloggers should be careful about traveling to other countries. Before entering a country, they should review the laws of that country to ensure they have not been guilty of transmitting prohibited content into the country via their website or blog.

ANONYMOUS AND PSEUDONYMOUS PUBLISHING

You might think that publishing anonymously or using a pseudonym will protect you from lawsuits. It will not. The state or a person who believes he has a legal claim against you may initiate a court proceeding against "John Doe" and then ask the court to issue a subpoena to your web hosting service requiring it to reveal your identity. The First Amendment protects the right to anonymous expression, but the rights it protects are not absolute. In deciding whether to issue a subpoena to require disclosure of an anonymous website owner's or blogger's identity, a court will weigh the First Amendment interest against the state's interest in disclosure and a party's need for the information in order to redress claimed injury.

There may be legal steps you can take to fight a subpoena, or to protect your anonymity (e.g., a motion to seal the record, and/or to make an appearance in the proceeding without revealing your identity), but ultimately if a court is persuaded that at least a prima facie case exists, it will probably issue the subpoena.

Of course, courts in other countries may issue orders requiring the disclosure of a website owner's or blogger's identity without regard to First Amendment concerns.

KEY POINTS:

- ❖ Avoid publishing:
  - Obscenity;
  - Child pornography;
  - State secrets;
  - Advocacy, aid or support of terrorism;
  - Discriminatory advertising;
  - Fraudulent statements or misrepresentations;
  - Solicitation or incitement of crime;
  - Threats;
  - Harassment;
  - Material likely to cause extreme emotional distress;
  - Material the publication of which breaches a contract;
  - Material intended or likely to induce a breach of contract;
  - Material intended to interfere with a business, or to unfairly discourage potential customers from doing business with a company;
  - Offer to help gain unauthorized access to a computer or web page;
  - Description of abortion providers as being guilty of crimes against humanity;
  - The name of an alleged sexual assault victim, unless it is in a public record;
  - Information a court order prohibits you from disclosing;
  - Links to sites containing unlawful content.

- ❖ Stalking people online is illegal.
- ❖ Avoid using software that robotically searches other websites.
- ❖ Avoid transmitting viruses, worms or other harmful code.
- ❖ Websites with sexual content must prevent access to minors.
- ❖ Hacking is illegal, as is helping or offering to help others do it.
- ❖ Exercise reasonable care in the operation of your website.
- ❖ Posting anonymously or pseudonymously will not protect you from liability.
- ❖ Content protected in one country may be prohibited in another.

CHAPTER 12

User-provided content

There are a variety of circumstances in which the law may hold a person responsible for someone else's actions. When people get together to plan a crime, each person who participated in the conspiracy will be held responsible for the acts of the individual who is actually sent out to carry out the crime. An employer will be held vicariously liable for the actions of its employees if they are within the course and scope of employment. Principals are liable for the actions of their agents. Parents are sometimes held responsible for their children's misdeeds. And a person who facilitates another person's wrongful act, such as by providing a forum for it, may share responsibility for it. When a person aids, facilitates or provides a means for another person to commit a wrongful act, he is said to incur *contributory liability* for the act.

This should be of concern to you if you operate an interactive Internet service, a web hosting service, a website or blog to which others (such as guest bloggers) contribute content, or a website or blog to which users may post comments or contribute other kinds of content. What is your liability if someone uses your website or other Internet service to make false and defamatory statements about another person, or posts private information or an unauthorized photograph of another person, or posts false or misleading information that results in injury to people who rely on it?

PUBLISHERS, DISTRIBUTORS AND CONDUITS

At common law, the legal standard for contributory liability varies depending on whether the person sought to be held liable is considered a publisher, a distributor, or merely a communication conduit.

A conduit is a service that facilitates communications between other parties but has no legal power to screen or control the content of the communications it processes. Telephone companies and the post office are examples. Conduits are not subject to contributory liability for communications transmitted by others using their services. Bloggers, website owners and web hosts generally do not come within the definition of a conduit, however, because they usually have the power to monitor and control the content of communications on the sites they own or manage.

A distributor is a person who distributes copies of another person's statement. Unlike a mere conduit, a distributor has both the opportunity and the legal ability to review the content of the publications it distributes. The classic examples are newsstands, libraries, and bookstores. To avoid imposing an onerous censorship obligation on distributors, the policy of the law is to exempt distributors from contributory liability unless a particular distributor actually knows that the copies being distributed contain defamatory material (or material that is actionable on some other basis, such as invasion of privacy, fraud, etc.), or is aware of circumstances that would make it reasonable to conclude that he should have known that they did.

A publisher is someone who actually has some editorial control over the content of a publication. The classic example is a book or magazine publishing company. A publisher has the legal ability to prevent defamatory or other tortious content from appearing in the publications it produces. Because it has this power, a publisher may be held liable for contributory defamation to the same extent as the author of the statement is liable for defamation. The same is true with respect to material that is tortious for some other reason, such as that it invades somebody's privacy. A publisher of another person's statement generally bears the same legal responsibility for it as if she had been the one who originally made the statement.

At common law, the fact that a website owner screened user-provided content for objectionable material caused her to be classified as a publisher of user-provided content. As a result, a person using parental controls to filter website content theoretically could incur "publisher" liability for all website content contributed by users. A major purpose of the Communications Decency Act is to immunize people from any liability that might arise as a result of taking steps to screen or filter user-provided content.

COMMUNICATIONS DECENCY ACT

Before the enactment of the Communications Decency Act (CDA), courts classified web services as either distributors or publishers on the basis of how much editorial control they exercised over user-provided content. In *Cubby v. CompuServe, Inc.* 776 F. Supp. 135 (S.D.N.Y. 1991), a court ruled that

CompuServe was merely a distributor, not a publisher, when it provided subscribers with access to a variety of different forums run by third parties, because it did not review the content of posts to the forums before they appeared on the site. By contrast, in *Stratton Oakmont v. Prodigy*, 23 Media L. Rep. 1794 (N.Y. Sup. Ct. 1995), Prodigy was determined to be a publisher, not merely a distributor, because it had implemented editorial control measures for the purpose of ensuring it would be a "family friendly" service. Specifically, it had adopted content guidelines and used a software program to screen submissions. Because of this, Prodigy was held liable for defamatory user-provided content.

This result did not sit well with "family values" legislators who wanted to encourage web service providers to freely censor user content. Therefore, when Congress enacted the Communications Decency Act in 1996, it included a provision titled "Protection for Good Samaritan blocking and screening of offensive material." This provision expressly prohibits any provider or user of interactive computer services from being treated as a publisher of information provided by another person. Codified at 47 U.S.C. § 230, it further provides that "[n]o cause of action may be brought and no liability may be imposed under any State or local law that is inconsistent with this section."

Section 230 has been construed as giving distributors immunity, too.[10]

What this means is that generally a web hosting service, website owner, or blogger that allows third parties to post content to a site cannot be sued on the basis of user-provided content. The statute basically makes the question of the level of editorial control over user-provided content irrelevant. And it means that immunity may continue to exist even if the service provider (website owner, etc.) has knowledge or reason to know of objectionable content.

The Communications Decency Act differs in this respect from the Digital Millennium Copyright Act (DMCA.) Under the DMCA, a website owner or web-based service provider is subject to liability if he fails to follow the procedures relating to the removal of content upon receiving notice of claimed copyright infringement. Because the CDA does not apply to copyright claims, it has no affect on the DMCA's notice-and-takedown provisions. A website owner or service provider might incur no liability for defamation as a result of failing to remove user-provided content after receiving notice that it is defamatory, but she could incur liability for copyright infringement if she fails to remove user-provided content after receiving notice that it infringes a copyright.

---

[10] Barrett v. Rosenthal, 40 Cal. 4th 33 (2006)

Section 230 distinguishes between an interactive computer service and an information content provider. Information content providers are responsible for the content they provide. An interactive computer service is not responsible for content provided by an information content provider.

An interactive computer service is any information service, system or access software provider that provides or enables computer access by multiple users to a server. This language is broad enough to cover most blogs, forums, listservs, website hosting services, and interactive websites. An information content provider is "any person or entity that is responsible, in whole or in part, for the creation or development of information provided through the Internet or any other interactive computer service."

Generally, an interactive computer service provider is immune from liability for removing, failing to remove, or editing user provided content. The immunity generally exists even if the provider knows or has notice of the objectionable nature of the content.[11]

Although Section 230 immunizes a web service provider from liability for failing to remove content after receiving notice of its objectionable nature, a website owner may incur liability if he makes a promise to somebody to remove something, and then fails to do so. (See discussion of "promissory estoppel," below.)

An interactive service provider may also lose its immunity by so editing user-provided content as to become an information content provider. Specifically, if a service provider's edits have the effect of transforming non-tortious content into tortious content, then the service provider may be held liable for the tortious content it provides. For example, if a website owner changes a user's statement from "Bob McKinsey is not a burglar" to "Bob McKinsey is a burglar," then the website owner may be liable for defamation if Bob McKinsey is not, in fact, a burglar. In this situation, the information that McKinsey is a burglar was not provided by a user; it was created by the website owner.

Although Section 230 shields bloggers and website owners from liability for content created by third parties, it does not shield bloggers and website owners from liability for their own statements. This means that bloggers and website owners may become information content providers, thereby losing Section 230 immunity, if they do things that go beyond merely hosting an interactive website or allowing users to post content, that make them even partially responsible for the creation or development of user content.

The mere act of reviewing and republishing user-provided content normally is not construed as assuming even partial responsibility for the

---

[11] Zeran v. America Online, 129 F.3d 327 (4th Cir. 1997)

creation or development of the content. A website owner's invitation or encouragement to users to submit a specific kind of objectionable material could be construed as assuming partial responsibility for the creation or development of the objectionable content, though. For example, although a website owner generally is immune from liability for publishing a nude photograph of a person that a user took without the subject's permission, he might incur liability if he specifically invites users to submit nude photographs of people that were taken without their permission.

Contracting for, and/or acquiring ownership of or publication rights in, user-provided content does not result in loss of Section 230 immunity unless the contract specifically seeks or encourages objectionable content. Contractual provisions in a website's terms of service to the effect that the website owner has the right to remove or edit user-provided content, or that all user-provided content becomes the property of the website owner do not have the effect of making the website owner an "information provider" with respect to such user-provided content. Section 230 immunity remains. On the other hand, if a website owner knows that users are obtaining information through illegal means, and continues to pay them for it anyway, then the website owner may be deemed to be partly responsible for developing the information, thereby losing Section 230 immunity. Also, at least one court has held that soliciting objectionable content or soliciting the gathering of information by illegal means, or making an advance offer to pay for such material, results in a website owner's loss of Section 230 immunity.

Section 230 immunity also may not exist if the user who provides the content also happens to be the blogger's or website owner's employee or agent. An employer or principal is vicariously responsible for the actions of his employees and agents. An employment or agency relationship may exist where a website or blog owner hires or commissions someone to create content for the site. In these situations, actions of the employee or agent are treated as if they were the actions of the employer, provided the actions were taken during the course and within the scope of the employment or agency. In other words, notwithstanding Section 230, a website or blog owner may be liable for the content her employee or agent produces for her.

Section 230 immunity also is lost when a person conspires with the information content provider to publish the objectionable material. Co-conspirators are liable for each other's actions to the extent they are taken in furtherance of the conspiracy.

To sum up, a blogger or website owner generally is immune from most kinds of tort liability for hosting, reviewing, editing, or soliciting user content, so long as she does not solicit, create or work with another person to create the offensive portion of it. Immunity from liability may be lost if:

a) the user who posts the content is an employee or agent of the website owner and the posting of the content is during the course and within the scope of the employment or agency;

b) the website owner promises to remove the offensive content and then fails to do so;

c) the website owner engages in conduct that is unlawful in itself, independent of the publication of the content – such as falsely warranting the reliability or safety of user-provided content;

d) the website owner edits the post in a way that creates offensive content;

e) the website owner actively encourages or solicits the offensive portion of the user-provided content; or

f) the website owner is involved in a conspiracy with the information content provider to create or disseminate the objectionable material.

IMMUNITY FOR REPUBLISHING CONTENT OBTAINED ONLINE

The Communications Decency Act provides immunity from liability not only for interactive computer service providers but also for users of interactive computer services. This has been construed to mean that a user of an interactive web service is immune from liability for republishing content obtained through the Internet. Therefore, if a person obtains defamatory information from Website X and posts it to Website Y, then both the owner of Website Y and the user who posted the content on Website Y are immune from liability for defamation. Only the original creator of the content on Website X would be liable for it. Interactive website owners and bloggers are classified as both users and interactive computer service providers.

This immunity does not apply to infringements of intellectual property rights.

IMMUNITY FROM CONTRIBUTORY LIABILITY FOR DEFAMATION

Section 230 generally provides protection from contributory liability for defamatory content submitted by a user. Contributory liability for defamation may arise, however, if you publish or republish content knowing it is false and defamatory, or if you so alter the meaning of user-provided content as to transform it from an unobjectionable statement to a statement that is false and defamatory.

Inviting users to submit false information about a person might also subject you to liability for contributory defamation. In that situation, a good argument may be made that your act of extending such an invitation to users makes you partially responsible for the creation or development of the information.

Section 230 is not the only defense to a defamation claim. There are several other kinds of defenses, including certain privileges that may be asserted in some circumstances. See Chapter 10.

The CDA is a U.S. law. Section 230 immunity from contributory liability may protect a web host, website owner or blogger from a judgment issued in an American court, but it does not necessarily provide protection from the entry of judgments in foreign countries. Fortunately, Congress has acted to protect American web hosts, website owners and bloggers from foreign judgments imposing contributory liability for defamation. The SPEECH Act says a foreign court judgment for defamation cannot be enforced in the United States if the result would have violated Section 230 had it been litigated in a U.S. court.

IMMUNITY FROM CONTRIBUTORY LIABILITY FOR INVASION OF PRIVACY

A person may be liable for another person's invasion of some else's privacy if he contributes to it some way. Contributory liability for invasion of privacy may arise by facilitating another person's publication of private facts, or facilitating another person's portrayal of a third party in a false light, or facilitating another person's intrusion upon a third party's seclusion. This could happen, for example, where a user posts material that violates another person's privacy rights to a website's discussion forum or as a comment to a blog.

Since an information content provider is defined as any person who is even partially responsible for the creation or development of information, it is not likely that Section 230 would immunize a web service provider from liability for inviting users to submit objectionable content. For example, a website that expressly invites users to post unauthorized photographs or private facts about people almost certainly would incur contributory liability for invasion of privacy.

An internet service provider also may become an information content provider, and thereby lose its immunity from liability, if its edits of user-provided content substantially alter the meaning of the user-provided content. Specifically, if a service provider's edits have the effect of transforming unobjectionable user content into content that invades someone's privacy, then the service provider may be held liable for the invasion of privacy. For example, if you change a user's statement from "Bob McKinsey enjoys attending family picnics" to "Bob McKinsey, who is an alcoholic, enjoys attending family picnics," then you may be liable for "false light" invasion of privacy if Bob McKinsey is not an alcoholic, or you may be liable for publication of private facts if he is. Likewise, if a user submits a photograph of Bob McKinsey reaching for a hamburger bun at a picnic, and you photoshop it to substitute an image of somebody's bottom in place of the hamburger buns, then you may be liable for "false light" invasion of privacy. In these situations, it is clearly the editor, not the user, who is creating the content that violates Bob McKinsey's privacy rights.

Although Section 230 shields bloggers and website owners from liability for invasions of privacy by third parties, it does not shield bloggers and website owners from liability for their own invasions of other people's privacy.

IMMUNITY FROM CONTRIBUTORY LIABILITY FOR DISCRIMINATION

What liability might you incur if a user posts a discriminatory message to your website, such as a message that he is seeking a roommate but prefers to have a straight white male roommate?

Section 230 prohibits courts from treating any provider of an interactive computer service (such as bulletin boards and websites and blogs to which users may post content) as a publisher of information provided by another person. Further, "[n]o cause of action may be brought and no liability may be imposed under any State or local law that is inconsistent with this section." This means that you should not have to worry about liability for other people's discriminatory posts to your website.

An interactive computer service loses its immunity to the extent it becomes an "information content provider," though. Since an information content provider is defined as any person who is even partially responsible for the creation or development of information, Section 230 would not immunize a web service provider from liability for encouraging the service to be used by others to practice discrimination. Thus, it has been held that a website service that enables people to locate roommates is contributorily liable for housing discrimination if it instructs users to complete a form that asks them to state their preferences with respect to the sex or sexual orientation of the roommate they are seeking.

Although Section 230 shields bloggers and website owners from liability for the statements and acts of third parties, it does not shield bloggers and website owners from liability for their own statements and acts.

IMMUNITY FROM CONTRIBUTORY LIABILITY FOR EMOTIONAL DISTRESS

Section 230 may be asserted as a defense to a claim of intentional or negligent infliction of emotional distress. It may also be asserted as a defense against an employer's liability for an employee's use of an employer-provided Internet service (or access to Internet service) to inflict emotional distress on others, if the employer has no knowledge and does not authorize or ratify the conduct.

IMMUNITY FROM CONTRIBUTORY LIABILITY FOR NEGLIGENCE

Section 230 immunity applies to negligence claims. A blogger or website owner cannot be held liable for publishing, republishing, or failing to screen, review, or censor user-provided content.

IMMUNITY FROM CONTRIBUTORY LIABILITY FOR UNFAIR COMPETITION

Courts have held that Section 230 immunity applies to state law claims of unfair competition.[12]

IMMUNITY FROM CONTRIBUTORY LIABILITY FOR FRAUD

Section 230 immunity applies to claims for fraud and misrepresentation. On the other hand, intellectual property claims are excluded from Section 230. Accordingly, it would seem that Section 230 immunity does not apply to trademark claims that are based on the use of a trademark as a false designation of origin, endorsement or sponsorship.

It is not clear whether trade secrets are intellectual property or not. If they are, then Section 230 will not immunize you from liability for trade secrets that a user wrongfully posts to your website or blog.

IMMUNITY FROM THIRD-PARTY BENEFICIARY LIABILITY

The law sometimes permits a person to enforce the terms of a contract to which he is not a party. This may occur if the contract, or one or more of its terms, is intended for his benefit. When a user agrees to a website's terms of service in connection with posting content to the site, the user is entering into

[12] Perfect 10, Inc. v. CCBill, LLC,340 F. Supp. 2d 1077 (C.D. Cal. 2004)

a contract with the website owner. If the terms of service prohibit the posting of content that violates a third party's rights, then the contract may be said to be for the third party's benefit, and therefore enforceable against the website owner by the third-party beneficiary.

Section 230 immunizes a website owner from liability to the third-party beneficiary under such circumstances.

IMMUNITY FROM LIABILITY FOR BREACH OF CONTRACT

Section 230 prohibits an interactive website owner (or other web service provider) from being held liable for restricting access to obscene, lewd, lascivious, filthy, violent, harassing or other material she considers objectionable. If a website owner does restrict access to such content, she cannot be held liable for breaching an agreement to provide users with a forum for unrestricted, robust speech.

IMMUNITY FROM LIABILITY FOR OTHER KINDS OF CAUSES OF ACTION

Section 230 provides immunity from liability for a lot of different kinds of things outside the area of intellectual property, including nuisance, cyberstalking, interference with business advantage, violations of securities regulations, and others.

APPLICABILITY TO PROMISSORY ESTOPPEL

"Promissory estoppel" is an equitable doctrine (judge-made legal principle) that prevents a defendant from objecting to the enforcement of a promise she has made if the promisee relied on the promise to his detriment. Craigslist, for example, was held liable for user-provided content notwithstanding Section 230 because it had promised a customer who had requested the removal of objectionable content that the company would "take care of it," but it never did, and the customer relied on the promise to her detriment.

Other courts, however, have come to the opposite conclusion, holding that Section 230 does immunize web service providers from liability for promissory estoppel with respect to the removal of user-provided content.

The safest course for a website owner or blogger to take is to refrain from making promises to remove content that someone finds objectionable. And if you do decide to make such a promise in a particular case, be certain that you can deliver on your promise very promptly.

NOT APPLICABLE TO TRADEMARK AND COPYRIGHT CLAIMS

Section 230 of the Communications Decency Act expressly provides that it is not a defense to a trademark or copyright claim.

Courts are split on the question whether the exception for intellectual property claims applies to both state and federal law claims. Some say it does; others say it applies only to federal law claims.

The Digital Millennium Copyright Act provides qualified immunity from copyright infringement liability for user-provided content. To qualify, however, it is necessary to comply with the conditions and requirements set out in that law. These are described in Chapter 15.

APPLICABILITY TO PUBLICITY RIGHTS CLAIMS

Section 230 expressly exempts intellectual property claims from its coverage. It says, "Nothing in this section shall be construed to limit or expand any law pertaining to intellectual property." Courts are not in agreement as to whether this means that state law claims relating to the right of publicity, such as the unauthorized use of a person's name or likeness, come within the purview of this exclusion or not.

APPLICABILITY TO TRADE SECRET CLAIMS

It is not clear whether state law claims of misappropriation of trade secrets come within the exclusion for intellectual property claims or not.

SECTION 230 AS A DEFENSE TO CRIMES

Section 230 is not a defense to any federal crime, but it may be a defense to state criminal charges against a web service provider that are predicated on the publication of user-provided content.

Although Section 230 may not be asserted as a defense to a federal crime, it may be asserted as a defense to a civil lawsuit for damages that is predicated on a website owner's commission of a federal crime.

INTERNATIONAL LAW

The Communications Decency Act is a U.S. law. While some other countries have laws that provide similar protections and immunities, most do not. In those countries that have not enacted such a law, a website owner or blogger may have contributory liability for user-contributed content. Courts in other countries can, and have, issued judgments against U.S. companies and individuals for user-contributed actionable content to a public Internet website that is accessed by citizens of that country. A website owner or blogger should be wary about throwing caution to the wind on the basis of an assumption that the CDA will protect him.

INDEMNIFICATION

Although Section 230 insulates a website owner or blogger from many kinds of liability, it is still not a bad idea to include an indemnification clause in your terms of service and in your contracts with guest bloggers and other contributors of content to your website or blog. An indemnification clause requires a person to pay your damages, attorney fees and costs in the event you are sued for contributory liability on the basis of the person's contribution to your website or blog.

KEY POINTS:

- ❖ **Who may be held liable for other people's conduct:**
  - • **Co-conspirators**
  - • **Employer (for actions of employee)**
  - • **Principal (for actions of agent)**
  - • **Parents (for actions of child)**
  - • **Facilitators of another's act ("contributory liability.")**
- ❖ **The Communications Decency Act is good news for web hosting services and website operators because it usually immunizes them from liability for user-provided content.**
- ❖ **The CDA only protects interactive service providers, not information providers.**
- ❖ **Substantial edits to user-provided content puts you at risk of being treated as an information provider.**
- ❖ **You may not get CDA immunity if you specifically solicit unlawful or actionable content for your website.**
- ❖ **The CDA is not a defense to intellectual property claims.**

PART TWO

Copyright Defenses

CHAPTER 13

The public domain

The public domain is simply the universe of works which, for whatever reason, are not protected by copyright law. When none of the exclusive rights of the kind that copyright law protects exist, a work is said to be in the public domain.

Anyone may freely use material that is in the public domain without risking liability for copyright infringement. The fact that something is in the public domain, however, does not mean that using it is free of risk. Publication of material that is in the public domain may still be a violation of other law, such as trademark, misappropriation, unfair competition, defamation, privacy, or other laws.

There are several reasons a work may be in the public domain. A copyright owner may voluntarily dedicate the work to the public domain. Alternatively, it may be a kind of subject matter that does not receive copyright protection, such as the title of a book, or a short phrase or slogan. At one time, it was not uncommon for a copyright to be lost through abandonment or lapse, such as where a copyright owner failed to file a timely renewal, or published a work without a copyright notice on it. Due to changes in the law, that is not likely to happen anymore.

Today, most copyrighted works that enter the public domain do so as a consequence of the passage of the applicable period of time specified in the federal Copyright Act.

Determining whether an older work is in the public domain is not always easy. The validity and duration of a copyright in an earlier work must be determined with reference to the law that was in effect at time, not current law. Copyright law has undergone numerous changes over the past fifty years, and they have not been uniform throughout the world. As a result, it is necessary to know if, when and in which country a work was first registered or published, and to familiarize yourself with both former and current law.

DEDICATION TO THE PUBLIC DOMAIN

The owner of the copyright in a work may voluntarily dedicate it to the public domain. That is to say, she may release all rights in the work to the public. This is done by including a statement that the work is in the public domain (or "is dedicated to the public domain.")

The decision to release a work into the public domain is irrevocable.

It is important to distinguish between works that an author releases into the public domain from works that an author makes available to the public free of charge. Unless a free work is expressly dedicated to the public domain, it remains protected by copyright. Most freeware and shareware, for example, has not been released into the public domain. They may be used without the payment of a fee, but unless they are expressly dedicated to the public domain, any reproduction or further distribution of them would violate copyright law, as would the making of derivative works from them.

Only the copyright owner has the power to dedicate a work to the public domain. Accordingly, a person relies on a "dedication to the public domain" statement on a website at his own risk.

Creative Commons offers a way for copyright owners to arrange to have their works enter the public domain sooner than they normally would. It does this by allowing copyright owners to either dedicate their works to the public domain immediately or, in the alternative, enter into a "Founders' Copyright" agreement with Creative Commons. This agreement consists of the sale of the copyright to Creative Commons for a nominal sum, with an exclusive license back from Creative Commons for 14 or 28 years. As part of the agreement, a copyright owner may choose to require that users of the dedicated work attribute it to the author.

WORKS PUBLISHED BEFORE JANUARY 1, 1978

Today, copyright is exclusively a matter of federal law. Prior to 1978, however, federal copyright protection only arose upon publication. Until a work was published, an author had only common law copyright rights under state law.

For works first published before January 1, 1978, federal copyright protection existed only upon publication, not upon creation of the work.

The 1976 Copyright Act, which became effective January 1, 1978, preempted the field of copyright by extending federal copyright protection to authors before publication, as well as after.

"Publication," in this context, means distribution of copies to the public, or offering to do so. It does not include performance; display (such as a public display of a painting in a museum); or showing a work to a limited number of people for a limited purpose. Circulating a research paper among one's peers, for example, would not qualify as "publication" of the paper.

WORKS IN SOUND RECORDINGS PUBLISHED BEFORE 1978

Before January 1, 1978, publishing a sound recording of a musical or literary work only had the effect of publishing the sound recording; it did not have the effect of publishing the musical composition or literary work. Thus, unless published in some other way, such as sheet music, a song and its lyrics, if any, remained "unpublished" for copyright purposes despite the release of multiple copies of recordings of performances of the song. For this reason, it was a common practice for publishers and record companies to register musical compositions as unpublished works in order to secure the benefits of federal registration. Beginning with musical works first published after 1977, distributing copies of a sound recording of a performance of a musical composition is publication of both the sound recording and the musical and/or literary work embodied in it.

SOUND RECORDINGS MADE BEFORE FEBRUARY 15, 1972

Copyright protection for sound recordings did not begin in the United States until February 15, 1972. As a result, sound recordings made in the U.S. before February 15, 1972 are not protected by federal copyright law. They may be protected by state law, though. A California statute, for example, protects intellectual property rights in pre-1972 sound recordings.

Although U.S.-made pre-1972 sound recordings are not protected by federal copyright law, the musical or literary works performed on them may be. And some pre-1972 sound recordings are protected by foreign copyright.

DURATION OF COPYRIGHT

The general rule is that copyright protection lasts for the life of the author plus 70 years. For co-authored joint works, it lasts for the life of the last surviving author plus 70 years.

These rules are subject to three important exceptions: works made for hire; anonymous or pseudonymous works; and works published before 1978.

WORKS MADE FOR HIRE

The term of a work made for hire is the earlier of:

a) 95 years after publication; or
b) 120 years after the work was first fixed in a tangible medium.

ANONYMOUS AND PSEUDONYMOUS WORKS

The duration of a copyright in a work by an anonymous or pseudonymous author is the same as that for work made for hire, if the author is never identified. If, within this period, an interested person identifies the author of an anonymous or pseudonymous work to the Copyright Office, then the duration is the life of the identified author plus 70 years.

WORKS FIRST PUBLISHED BEFORE 1978

The life+70 rule was established by the Copyright Act of 1976, effective January 1, 1978. Before then, a system of renewable copyright terms keyed to the date of publication or registration, not to the author's life, was in place. For this reason, the "life of the author plus 70 years" rule cannot be used to calculate the duration of a copyright in a work that was published or registered before January 1, 1978.

The original rule, as set out in the Copyright Act of 1909, was that the term of the copyright was 28 years from the date of first publication or registration, whichever occurred earlier. It was renewable for a second 28-year term, for a total of 56 years. The total duration of a copyright, therefore, was 56 years from the earlier of the date of publication or the date of registration, provided the copyright was renewed in a timely manner.

For works first published before January 1, 1978, a copyright had to be renewed during the last year of the original term. If it wasn't, then the copyright lapsed and the work entered the public domain.

In order to file a renewal registration, an original registration has to be filed, too, if that hasn't already been done.

RENEWAL TERM EXTENSIONS

A series of Congressional enactments beginning in 1962 and continuing into the 1970's extended the lengths of renewal terms of copyrights that were in their renewal terms at the time of the enactment. These enactments affected copyrights that had been secured (registered or first published) between September 19, 1906 and December 31, 1918, to the extent they had been timely and properly renewed prior to the enactment in question. The intent was to prevent copyrights from expiring before a new copyright law (the Copyright Act of 1976) could be enacted. The effect of these enactments may be summarized as follows:

For copyrights subsisting in their renewal terms on...	the renewal term was extended to...
September 19, 1962	December 31, 1965
August 28, 1965	December 31, 1967
November 16, 1967	December 31, 1968
July 23, 1968	December 31, 1969
December 16, 1969	December 31, 1970
December 17, 1970	December 31, 1971
November 24, 1971	December 31, 1972
October 25, 1972	December 31, 1974
December 31, 1974	December 31, 1976
December 31, 1976 to December 31, 19777	a duration of 47 years

These extensions only applied to copyrights that still existed on the date of the enactment in question – i.e., copyrights that had not been allowed to expire as a result of failing to timely renew them. They did not extend the duration of the original term, nor did they eliminate the requirement of renewing a copyright within the last year of the original term. If a timely renewal had been filed, then these enactments extended the duration of the renewal term in the manner indicated above. If a copyright had been permitted to expire due to failure to timely renew it during the last year of the original term, it was lost. These enactments did not revive any expired copyrights.

The Copyright Act of 1976 extended the renewal term to 47 years (i.e., an additional 19 years), for those works that were still in existence on January 1, 1978. This meant that the total possible duration of copyright (original + renewal terms) was set at 75 years for any renewable-term copyright that was in existence on January 1, 1978.

The extension applied to any copyrights that were in their original term on January 1, 1978, and to any copyrights that were in their renewal term at any time between December 31, 1976 and December 31, 1977, inclusive; and to copyrights that were in the last year of their original term during that time period and for which a timely renewal application had been filed.

The Sonny Bono Copyright Term Extension Act of 1998 added twenty more years to the renewal term, thereby extending the renewal period from 47 to 67 years, bringing the total copyright term (original + renewal) to 95 years. The extension applies to all renewable-term copyrights that were still in existence as of the effective date of the Act, which was October 27, 1998.

The Act also provides that the term runs through the end of the calendar year in which the copyright would otherwise expire.

1978 CHANGES TO THE BEGINNING AND END DATES OF RENEWAL TERMS

Prior to January 1, 1978, the renewal copyright term began the day after 28 years after the date of first publication or registration. The terms of all copyrights that were in existence on January 1, 1998 were extended to run through the end of the calendar year in which they would otherwise expire. This meant that if a copyright was in its original term on January 1, 1998, then the renewal term would begin on January 1st of the 29th year following the date the copyright was originally secured (usually, the date of first publication.) If a copyright was in its renewal term on January 1, 1978, then the renewal term will expire on December 31st of the year in which the renewal term is set to expire.

An exception to this rule exists for works that were first published before March 1, 1989, with a year date in the copyright notice that was earlier than the actual date of publication. In those cases, the renewal term is tied to the year date set out in the copyright notice, not the actual date of publication.

AUTOMATIC RENEWAL OF CERTAIN PRE-1978 WORKS

Amendments to the Copyright Act that were enacted in 1992 made renewal automatic for works that were still in their original term as of the effective date of the Act, which was June 26, 1992. This meant that for works registered or first published between January 1, 1964, and December 31, 1977, inclusive, it was no longer necessary to apply for renewal; it happened automatically.

The Copyright Act of 1976 established a single-term system for copyrights, and linked the duration of most copyrights to the life of the author rather than the date of publication. Specifically, it set the term of most copyrights at the life of the author plus 70 years. (Works for hire, and anonymous and pseudonymous works, are subject to a different rule.) This new system went into effect on January 1, 1978. The renewable-term system was retained for works that were registered or first published before January 1, 1978.

The elimination of the renewal requirement did not apply retroactively, however. The Act only eliminated the renewal registration requirement for works that were still in their original term on June 26, 1992. It did not restore copyright in works that had already entered the public domain due to failure to renew the copyright before the expiration of the original term.

Although renewal registration was no longer required beginning June 26, 1992, it continued to be permitted. The Act permitted any renewable copyright that was still in its original term as of June 26, 1992 to be registered anytime during the renewal period. The requirement of renewing during the last year of the original term was eliminated for this category of works, though. For works that were in their original term on June 26, 1992, failure to file a renewal registration prior to the expiration of the original term would no longer result in forfeiture of copyright protection.

Under the 1992 Act, the copyright in a work that had been published or registered before January 1, 1978 and was still in its original term on June 26, 1992 was renewed automatically, and renewal registration was entirely optional. This meant that copyrights in works first published or registered between January 1, 1964 and December 31, 1977, inclusive, were automatically renewed. Although it was not required, a renewal registration could be filed either during the last year of the original term, or anytime during the renewal term. In either case, a renewal registration could not occur unless there was an original registration. If an original registration had not been filed, then both the original and the renewal copyright could be registered together, and this could be done during the last year of the original term or at any time during the renewal term.

Although renewal of copyrights in works first published between 1964 and 1977, inclusive, became automatic by virtue of Congressional enactments, renewal registration of such works is still permitted. There are some benefits to doing so. One of the most important of these is that a renewal registration filed during the last year of the original term gives rise to a presumption of validity of the copyright and of the facts set forth in the registration (authorship, ownership, etc.) A renewal registration that is filed during the renewal term does not.

The various renewal provisions and extensions described above only apply to works for which copyright had been secured prior to January 1, 1978, i.e., works that had been registered or first published before then. They do not apply to works created on or after January 1, 1978. They also do not apply to works that were created before January 1, 1978 but were neither published nor registered until after December 31, 1977.

Of course, a work may enter the public domain sooner than the scheduled time if it is dedicated to the public domain, or if a necessary renewal is not timely and properly filed, or if a notice or other formal requirement is not satisfied.

OWNERSHIP OF THE RENEWAL RIGHT

The author generally owns the renewal right. If the author is not living, then the renewal right belongs to:

- The widow, widower, or children of the author;
- If no widow, widower or children, then the author's executor;
- If no will, widow, widower or children, then the author's next of kin.

Exceptions and qualifications are described below.

POSTHUMOUS WORKS

The person who secured the copyright in a posthumous work owns the right to renew it.

For renewal registration purposes, a work is posthumous if it was unpublished when the author died and the author had not assigned the copyright or exploited any rights in the work during his lifetime. An author's heirs or estate do not have a renewal right in a posthumous work.

COMPILATIONS

The renewal right in a compilation belongs to the owner of the copyright in the compilation. The author of a contribution to a compilation retains the renewal right for his individual contribution, though.

WORKS FOR HIRE

The employer (or person who commissioned the work for hire) owns the right to renew it. The actual author of the work has no renewal rights.

WORKS CREATED AND COPYRIGHTED BY CORPORATIONS

A corporation owns the renewal right in works originally registered in the corporation's name, even if the work is not a work made for hire. For example, a work created by non-employee stockholders or directors of the corporation is not a work for hire, but if the corporation registers a copyright in the work, then the corporation owns the right to renew it.

This rule does not apply to situations in which an individual author has assigned or licensed a copyright in a work to the corporation.

PRE-1978 WORKS PUBLISHED WITHOUT COPYRIGHT NOTICE

A work published on a visually perceptible copy of it without a copyright notice, or with a notice that was not in proper form, entered the public domain on the first date of such publication.

As of December 31, 1977, a copyright notice was not considered sufficient if it had any of the following defects:

- failure to include at least one copyright indicator, which could be the word "Copyright," the abbreviation "Copr." or the symbol © -- or, for sound recordings, the symbol ℗
- name of the copyright proprietor (or, for sound recordings, a recognizable abbreviation or a generally known alternative designation of the copyright owner) omitted;
- year of publication omitted;
- notice is in a foreign language;
- notice is not located in a place/position authorized by regulations;
- elements of notice (date, year, and a copyright word or symbol) are so dispersed that they are not all identified as part of the copyright notice (but a producer's name appearing anywhere on the label or container of a sound recording is deemed to be "identified" with the notice if no other name appears in conjunction with the notice);
- notice is not visible without tearing the copy apart;
- notice is illegible;
- notice is so small that a magnifying glass is needed to read it (unless ordinary use of the copy requires magnification, such as microfilm or a motion picture);
- notice is on a detachable tag;
- notice is on a wrapper or container that is normally removed and discarded when the copy is put to use (but the notice may be placed on a container that is designed and expected to remain with the copy, such as an album cover or CD case);
- notice is restricted or limited exclusively to a non-copyrightable

element, either by virtue of its position on the work, by the use of asterisks, or by other means;

- name is of someone who had no authority to secure copyright in his name;
- year stated in the notice is more than one year after the actual publication date;
- year is more than one year after the date of copyright registration, in cases where the copyright was secured by registration of an unpublished work rather than by publication; year is more than one year after the first foreign publication date, in cases where the work was first published in a foreign country.

ADDITIONAL REQUIREMENTS FOR SOUND RECORDINGS

1) ℗ symbol, the word "Copyright," or the abbreviation, "Copr."
2) year of first publication; and
3) name (or a recognizable abbreviation or a generally known alternative designation of the copyright owner.)

There are some exceptions to these requirements, particularly for works published between January 1, 1978 and March 1, 1989, as to which a 5-year curative period was allowed.

Since a phonorecord is not a visually perceptible copy of a musical, dramatic or literary work, the publication of a literary, musical or dramatic work on a phonorecord without the copyright notice, although possibly causing loss of copyright protection in the sound recording, did not result in loss of copyright in the literary, musical or dramatic work embodied in it.

ADDITIONAL REQUIREMENTS FOR AUDIOVISUAL WORKS

For audiovisual works, the notice could be displayed when the work was performed (such as a notice that is displayed on the screen when a motion picture is played), provided it was displayed near the title, with cast, credits, and similar information, at or near the beginning or end of the work. For works lasting no more than one minute, the notice could also be located on the leader of the film or tape immediately preceding the work. In the case of a copy that was distributed to the public for private use, it was also acceptable for the notice to appear on the container for the copy of the work.

Federal regulations should be consulted for more detailed information about copyright notice requirements that were in force on particular dates.

WORKS PUBLISHED BEFORE MARCH 1, 1989 WITHOUT COPYRIGHT NOTICE

FIVE-YEAR CURATIVE PERIOD

The Copyright Act retained many of the formal notice requirements that existed for works first published before January 1, 1978, but sought to ameliorate the harsh consequences of an omission or error by giving the copyright owner a five-year period to correct the problem before the work would finally enter the public domain.

NOTICE REQUIREMENTS

A copyright notice was required on all works first published after 1977 and before March 1, 1989. Different notice requirements applied to different kinds of works and embodiments of them. Requirements common to all copyright notices were:

1) legible;
2) not concealed;
3) placed in a position required or allowed by regulations, and in all cases must be so located as to give reasonable notice of the claim of copyright;
4) includes a name; includes a date that is not more than one year after the first publication date;
5) if consisting primarily of U.S. government material, it must include the additional statement required by federal regulations.

ADDITIONAL REQUIREMENTS FOR VISUALLY PERCEPTIBLE COPIES OF A WORK

Although publication was not required in order for a work created during this period to be protected by copyright, copyright protection could be lost if the work was published without a proper copyright notice affixed to it.

All visually perceptible copies of a work had to contain all three of the following elements:

1) © symbol, the word "Copyright," or the abbreviation, "Copr."
2) year of first publication; and
3) name, or an abbreviation or generally known alternative designation.

The year of publication was not required to be placed on greeting cards, postcards, stationery, jewelry, dolls, toys, or any useful article, to protect the copyright in a pictorial, graphic, or sculptural work that was reproduced on such item.

Placement on a dust jacket was not adequate to protect the copyright in the book, and placement in a book was not adequate to protect the copyright in dust jacket content, because a dust jacket is removable from the book.

For compilations and derivative works, the date of publication of the compilation or derivative work suffices. A single copyright notice applicable to a collective work as a whole is acceptable to indicate copyright protection for all the contributions in the collective work, except for advertisements, regardless of who owns copyright in the individual contributions or whether they were published previously. A separate contribution to a collective work may have its own notice of copyright, though, without affecting the adequacy of the copyright notice for the collective work.

On the other hand, if the owner of the copyright in the collective work is not the same as the owner of the copyright in an individual contribution, and that individual contribution does not have its own notice, then the contribution itself (not the collective work as a whole) may be deemed to have been published with an erroneous notice.

A notice for the collective work does not serve as notice for any advertisements inserted on behalf of persons other than the copyright owner of the collective work. Such advertisements should each have a separate notice in the name of the copyright owner of the advertisement.

Federal regulations govern the required location and position of the notice. For books and periodicals, the title page, the page immediately following the title page, either side of the front or the back cover, or the first or the last page of the body of the work are acceptable. For periodicals, additional possibilities include the page containing the masthead; or adjacent to a prominent heading, at or near the front of the issue, containing the title of the periodical and any combination of the volume and issue number and the date of the issue.

For a separate contribution to a collective work, acceptable positions include: under a title appearing at or near the beginning of the contribution; on the first page of the main body of the contribution; immediately following the end of the contribution; or on any of the pages where the contribution appears if the contribution consists of no more than 20 pages, the notice is reproduced prominently, and the application of the notice to the particular contribution is clear.

For works published in machine-readable copies, acceptable positions include: near the title or at the end of the work, on visually perceptible printouts; at the user's terminal upon sign-on; continuous display on the terminal during use; or on a label that is securely affixed to the copies or to a container used as a permanent holder for the copies.

For audiovisual works, the notice is acceptable if it is displayed when the work is performed (e.g., a notice that is displayed on the screen when a motion picture is played), provided the notice is displayed near the title, with cast, credits, and similar information, at or near the beginning or end of the work. For works lasting no more than one minute, the notice may also be located on the leader of the film or tape immediately preceding the work. In the case of a copy that is distributed to the public for private use, it is also acceptable if the notice is on the container for the copy of the work (e.g., DVD case.)

For pictorial, graphic or sculptural works that are reproduced in two-dimensional copies, the copyright notice must be affixed permanently to the copy. It may be placed on the front or back; or on any backing, mounting, framing, or other material to which copies are durably attached. For works reproduced in three-dimensional copies, the notice must be affixed permanently to the copy, and it may be placed on any visible portion of the work; or on any base, mounting, or framing or other material on which the copies are durably attached. If it is impractical to affix a notice to the copies directly or by means of a durable label, a notice is acceptable if it appears on a tag or durable label attached to the copy so that it will remain with it as it passes through commerce. For works reproduced in copies consisting of sheet-like or strip material bearing multiple or continuous reproductions of the work, such as fabrics or wallpaper, the notice may be applied to the reproduction itself; to the margin, selvage, or reverse side of the material at frequent and regular intervals; or, if the material contains neither a selvage nor a reverse side, to tags or labels attached to the copies and to any spools, reels, or containers housing them in such a way that the notice is visible in commerce.

For sound recordings, the necessary elements of the copyright notice were:

1) ℗ symbol, the word "Copyright," or the abbreviation, "Copr."
2) year of first publication; and
3) name (or a recognizable abbreviation or a generally known alternative designation) of the copyright owner.

Since a phonorecord is not a visually perceptible copy, the publication of a literary, musical or dramatic work on a phonorecord without the copyright notice, although possibly causing loss of copyright protection in the sound recording, would not result in loss of copyright in the literary, musical or dramatic work embodied in it.

The requirements described here are not necessarily exclusive or exhaustive. Consult the federal regulations for more detailed information about the requirements that were in force on the date relevant to your query.

EXCEPTIONS TO THE COPYRIGHT NOTICE REQUIREMENT

Omission of a proper copyright notice does not cause a work published during this period to enter the public domain if:

a) it was omitted from only a small number of copies;
b) the notice was removed without the copyright owner's authorization;
c) the publisher had breached an express written agreement to place the notice on copies of the publication; or
d) the work was registered either before a copy with the omitted notice was published, or within five years after such publication; and an effort was made to add the notice to all copies after the omission was discovered.

If none of the first three exceptions apply, then a work published without a proper copyright notice entered the public domain 5 years after the publication without the requisite notice affixed, unless the work was registered either before or within 5 years after the publication of the first copy with the omitted notice and an effort was made to add the notice to all copies after the omission was discovered.

Some kinds of errors did not cause a work to enter the public domain, but could have other adverse consequences. Publication of a copyright notice erroneously naming the wrong person as the copyright owner could be corrected by registering the work in the name of the actual owner, or recording a document executed by the person named in the notice that shows the correct ownership. If this was not done, then an innocent infringer who was misled by the notice and obtained an assignment or license from the person named in the notice would have a complete defense against a claim of infringement.

COPYRIGHT NOTICE DATE EARLIER THAN PUBLICATION DATE IN WORKS PUBLISHED BEFORE MARCH 1, 1989

Usually, and subject to the exceptions noted above, failure to comply with requirements for the placement of a copyright notice on published copies would cause the work to enter the public domain. If the only error is that the date indicated in a copyright notice that has been placed on a published work is earlier than the actual date of publication, then the work does not enter the public domain as a result of the error. Instead, the term of copyright is deemed to begin in the copyright year indicated in the notice, not the year of actual publication.

A copyright notice that indicates a year later than the actual date of publication does not have this effect. In this situation, the actual year of publication marks the beginning of the copyright term.

A copyright notice containing a date that is more than a year after the actual date of publication is treated as a complete omission of a copyright notice. Subject to the exceptions noted above, such an omission would cause the work to enter the public domain.

ELIMINATION OF THE NOTICE REQUIREMENT

For works first published on or after March 1, 1989, the copyright notice is optional. Publication without the copyright notice does not cause loss of copyright protection for any work first published on or after March 1, 1989.

Elimination of the notice requirement is not retroactive. With the exception of certain foreign works that may be restored from the public domain (See below), entry into the public domain is irrevocable.

MANUFACTURING REQUIREMENT

Books, periodicals, lithographs and photoengravings published before July 1, 1986 were required to be manufactured in the United States in order to receive federal copyright protection. This requirement also applied to any illustrations contained in a book or periodical to which the requirement applied, to the extent the illustrations were produced by a photoengraving or lithographic process.

The manufacturing requirement did not apply to:

- dramatic works;
- lectures, sermons, addresses;
- musical compositions;
- maps;
- any work not manufactured by typesetting, lithographic or photo-engraving process;

- pictorial illustrations representing subjects that were located in a foreign country and that illustrate a scientific work or reproduce a work of art;
- Braille books or periodicals;
- foreign language book by a foreign author first published in a foreign country;
- English language work published in a foreign country that qualifies for ad interim protection;
- unpublished works.

To register a work, it was necessary to sign a sworn affidavit of compliance with the manufacturing requirement. Knowingly filing a false affidavit resulted in forfeiture of the copyright.

Though English language works generally were subject to the manufacturing requirement, foreign language books generally were subject to the manufacturing clause only if first published in the United States. If the author was a U.S. national or domiciliary when a foreign language book was first published, however, then the book had to be manufactured in the United States. If the book was manufactured abroad, copyright in the United States was lost upon publication; ad interim copyright could not be secured; and renewal registration would not be possible.

The manufacturing requirement expired on July 1, 1986.

AD INTERIM REGISTRATION

Registration of an English-language book that was manufactured in a foreign country was permitted if, within 30 days after publication in a foreign country, the author or owner made a request to reserve the copyright, deposited a copy, and filed a statement of the name and nationality of the author and copyright proprietor and date of publication with the U.S. Copyright Office. Doing this gave the applicant ad interim copyright protection which lasted until 30 days after the deposit of the copy with the U.S. Copyright Office.

If the applicant published a U.S. edition in compliance with the manufacturing requirement within the 30 day period, and applied for interim registration within the 30-day period, then the work would receive a full 28-year term of copyright.

For works first published abroad after March 2, 1921, the 30-day period was later extended to 60 days, and the time frame for publishing an edition in compliance with manufacturing requirements was lengthened to 4 months. In

1949, the ad interim registration period was extended to 6 months, and the time frame for publishing an edition in compliance with manufacturing requirements was lengthened to 5 years. As with the 30-day, 60-day, and 4-month periods that had been provided for in the earlier versions of the ad interim law, publication of a U.S. edition in compliance with the manufacturing requirement during the relevant period qualified the work for registration for a renewable 28-year term, provided publication and registration occurred during that period. If either compliance with the manufacturing requirement or full registration did not occur within that period, then the work received no federal copyright protection.

Effective September 16, 1955, and pursuant to the Universal Copyright Convention ("U.C.C."), works of foreign origin were exempted from the manufacturing requirement if they originated in a country that was a signatory to the U.C.C. and a "UCC notice" consisting of the © symbol accompanied by the name of the copyright proprietor and the year of first publication was properly affixed to published copies of the work. Further, any ad interim protection that had been secured for a work originating in a U.C.C. country was automatically extended to the full term. These provisions did not apply to works of American citizens and domiciliaries that were published abroad or to works that were first published in the United States.

In its final form before it expired, the Act permitted manufacture in either the United States or Canada. Subject to certain limitations such as an exception for books for government, educational, religious or scholarly use, it expressly prohibited importation of certain kinds of foreign-made books and periodicals. At the same time, though, it specified that while a violation of the prohibition against importation (as distinguished from the filing of a false affidavit) could be raised as a complete defense to a claim of infringement, the violation did not affect the validity of the copyright itself.

Transitional provisions in the Copyright Act extended the term of ad interim copyrights subsisting or capable of being secured on December 31, 1977 to the same term as ordinary copyrights that existed on that date. If a work was first published on or after July 1, 1977, and was otherwise eligible for ad interim copyright protection, then registration could be made at any time during the six-month period beginning July 1, 1977, i.e., until December 31, 1977. In other words, the terms of any ad interim copyrights that existed on December 31, 1977, and of any copyrights in works that were first published outside the United States between July 1, 1977 and December 31, 1977, inclusive, that were otherwise eligible for ad interim registration, were made subject to the same rules as to duration as any other copyright that existed on December 31, 1977.

The manufacturing requirement expired on July 1, 1986.

RESTORATION OF COPYRIGHTS IN FOREIGN WORKS

To comply with international treaties, Congress has provided for the restoration of copyrights in certain foreign works.

To be eligible for restoration, each of the following conditions must exist:

1) at least one author was a citizen or domiciliary of a foreign country that is a signatory to the World Trade Organization Agreement on Trade-Related Aspects of Intellectual Property Rights (TRIPS) or Berne Convention, or an adherent to the World Intellectual Property Organization (WIPO) Copyright Treaty or the WIPO Performances and Phonograms Treaty, or the subject of a proclamation under 17 U.S.C. § 104A, subsection (g); or the work must have been first published in such a country and not published in the United States within 30 days after such first publication;

2) the work is still protected by copyright in its nation of origin;

3) it is in the public domain in the U.S. only because of one the following:

   a) failure to satisfy a formality (such as registration, renewal, copyright notice, manufacturing requirement);

   b) it originated in a country that did not have copyright relations with the U.S.; or

   c) it is a sound recording that was fixed in a tangible medium before February 15, 1972.

A "foreign work" is any work that does not fit into any of the following categories:

a) first published in the United States;

b) first published simultaneously in the United States and in a foreign country that has an applicable treaty with the United States, and whose law provides for a copyright term that is at least as long as was U.S. law provides;

c) first published simultaneously in the U.S. and a foreign country that does not have an applicable treaty without a treaty with the U.S.;

d) first published in a foreign country that does not have an applicable treaty with the U.S., but all authors are nationals, domiciliaries, or habitual residents of the U.S. (or in the case of a motion picture, all authors are legal entities headquartered in the United States;

e) unpublished work, and all authors are nationals, domiciliaries, or habitual residents of the U.S. (or in the case of a motion picture, all authors are legal entities headquartered in the United States; or

f) pictorial, graphic, or sculptural work that is incorporated in a building or structure that is located in the United States.

A work that does not fit into any of these categories is a foreign work.

Copyright restoration went into effect on January 1, 1996, for foreign works from countries that were, on that date, members of the World Trade Organization; adherents to the Berne Convention; adherents to the World Intellectual Property Organization (WIPO) Copyright Treaty; adherents to the WIPO Performances and Phonograms Treaty; or the subject of a proclamation under 17 U.S.C. § 104A, subsection (g). Copyright restoration for works from other countries went into effect on the earliest adherence date of the country to one of these treaties or the proclamation date, as applicable.

The duration of a restored copyright is the same as it would have been if it had never entered the public domain.

Pursuant to the Uruguay Round Agreements Act (URAA), copyrights in the described foreign works are automatically restored. No action is required on the part of a copyright owner. An owner of a restored copyright may choose to register the copyright, however.

A person who relied on the public domain status of a foreign work before its copyright was restored (e.g., someone who copied a pre-1972 foreign sound recording before January 1, 1996) is called a reliance party. A reliance party is liable for infringement only if:

a) the foreign copyright owner filed notice with the U.S. Copyright Office within 24 months after the enactment of the Uruguay Round Agreements Act, 17 U.S.C. §104A; or

b) the foreign copyright owner served notice of intent to enforce the copyright directly on the person. In that event, the person so served may continue to exploit the work for twelve months after receiving the notice.

A reliance party may continue to exploit derivative works that are based on a restored copyright, but must pay reasonable compensation for them.

To be eligible for renewal registration, a foreign work that was first published or registered before 1978 must either have been published with the statutory or U.C.C. notice or made the subject of an ad interim registration, on one hand, or registered as an unpublished work, on the other. In addition, it must have met all statutory requirements to maintain copyright through the full original term and into the renewal term. A work that failed to secure copyright in the United States at the time of first publication, or lost it at any time during the original or renewal terms, is not eligible for renewal registration, even if copyright was restored in the United States under the URAA.

UNPUBLISHED WORKS CREATED BEFORE 1978

For unpublished works created before January 1, 1978, copyright protection generally lasts for the life of the author (or the last surviving author, in the case of joint works) plus 70 years, or December 31, 2002, whichever is later. If an unpublished work created before January 1, 1978 is published before December 31, 2002, then the term is extended to December 31, 2047.

The copyright in an unpublished work made for hire, or an anonymous or pseudonymous work, that was created before January 1, 1978, lasts for 120 years from the year of creation or 95 years from date of first publication, whichever expires first, but in no event earlier than December 31, 2002. If it is published before December 31, 2002, then the term is extended to December 31, 2047.

If the author of an anonymous or pseudonymous work is identified, and a statement of identity in proper form is timely and properly filed with the Copyright Office before the end of the term of the copyright in an anonymous or pseudonymous work, then the term of the copyright is governed by the same rules that apply to works created by an identified author.

Before January 1, 1978, distributing copies of a sound recording did not constitute publication of the musical, literary, or dramatic works embodied in it. Accordingly, even though distributing copies of a sound recording during this time period might be considered a publication of the sound recording, it is not considered a publication of the musical, literary, or dramatic works embodied in it. Those works would be deemed "unpublished" despite the publication of the sound recording unless they had been published in some other way (e.g., sheet music.)

PRESUMPTION OF DEATH

There is a rebuttable presumption that at the earlier of 95 years after first publication or 120 years after fixation in tangible form, the author has been dead for 70 years.

STATEMENT OF LIVING STATUS

To avoid premature loss of copyright protection, the copyright owner (or the author's estate) must file a statement of living status, or a date of death, with the Copyright Office. This must be done before the earlier of 95 years after publication or 120 years after fixation in tangible form. If it is not done within that time period, then the copyright expires.

REPOSITORIES OF PUBLIC DOMAIN WORKS

A list of repositories of public domain works is included in Appendix X.

Although extensive, these repositories do not include all public domain works. The fact that a particular work is not included in one of these repositories does not mean that it is not in the public domain.

SUMMARY OF PUBLIC DOMAIN RULES

Here is a distillation of the basic copyright duration rules keyed to specific time periods, excluding works made for hire, anonymous or pseudonymous works, works that been dedicated to the public domain, and works that failed to meet manufacturing or formal requirements.

(I) WORKS FIRST PUBLISHED OR REGISTERED BEFORE JANUARY 1, 1923

Works first published or registered before January 1, 1923 are all in the public domain as of January 1, 2015. The original copyright term was 28 years. If timely renewed, then the total copyright term was 56 years. Many copyrights in works published or registered before January 1, 1923 would have expired before the first statutory extension that occurred on September 19, 1962. Those that were still viable on that date were extended incrementally until the 1976 Act increased the total renewal term to 47 years. To qualify for the additional boost up to 67 years, though, the copyright had to continue to be in its renewal term as of October 27, 1998. If the total copyright term had expired on or before December 31, 1997, then it would not qualify for the additional 20-year extension. Since the total copyright term (original + renewal) under the 1976 Act was 75 years, all copyright secured on or before December 31, 1922 would have expired by December 31, 1997, which was before the effective date of the additional 20-year boost provided in the Sonny Bono Copyright Extension Act of 1998.

(II) WORKS FIRST PUBLISHED OR REGISTERED BEFORE 1964, AND NOT RENEWED

Any work that was first published or registered before 1964, but was not timely renewed, is in the public domain now. The original term was 28 years, and the various extension acts did not eliminate the renewal requirement for works first published or registered before their enactments.

(III) WORKS FIRST PUBLISHED OR REGISTERED AFTER DECEMBER 31, 1922 AND BEFORE 1964, AND TIMELY AND PROPERLY RENEWED

A work published or registered on or after January 1, 1923 would have an original 28-year term expiring on January 1, 1951, at the earliest. If renewed, the 28-year renewal would be scheduled to expire in 1979, at the earliest. Since all such copyrights would still be in existence on January 1, 1978, the 1976 Copyright Act extended the renewal terms of these copyrights to 47 years, and changed the expiration date of the renewal term to the last day of the calendar year in which the renewal term was scheduled to end. The earliest any such copyright could have expired, then, would be December 31, 1998 (1923 + 75 = 1998.) Therefore, they would be in existence on October 27, 1998, the effective date of the additional 20-year extension provided by the Sonny Bono Copyright Extension Act, so they would all get the 95-year copyright term. The earliest a copyright first published or registered after December 31, 1922 could expire, assuming it was properly renewed, would be at the end of the calendar year that is 95 years after January 1, 1923, which would be December 31, 2018. Therefore, the earliest date on which a work in this category can enter the public domain is January 1, 2019.

It was still necessary to renew copyrights in this category. If a copyright in this category was not properly renewed during the last year of the original term, then it would have entered the public domain by January 1, 1992.

(IV) WORKS FIRST PUBLISHED OR REGISTERED IN 1964 TO 1977, INCLUSIVE

The term of a copyright (original + renewal) in works published between 1964 and 1977 is 95 years, whether renewal is registered or not. Renewal became automatic, as to works in this category, in 1992. Works in this category will not begin to enter the public domain until 2060.

(V) WORKS PUBLISHED 1978 TO 2002, INCLUSIVE, BUT CREATED BEFORE 1978

Copyright in works published between 1978 and 2002, inclusive, but which were created before 1978, expires December 31, 2047.

(VI) WORKS PUBLISHED AFTER DECEMBER 31, 2002 BUT CREATED BEFORE 1978

Copyright in works created before January 1, 1978, but not published until after December 31, 2002 lasts for the life of the author plus 70 years, or until December 31, 2002, whichever is later.

(VII) WORKS CREATED AFTER 1977

Copyright in works created on or after January 1, 1978, whether published or not, lasts for the life of the author plus 70 years (subject to exceptions for works made for hire, anonymous and pseudonymous works.)

(VIII) FOREIGN WORKS, SOUND RECORDINGS, AND ARCHITECTURAL WORKS

See the Tables in Appendix II.

EASY REFERENCE CHARTS

Charts showing the durations of copyrights for the various categories of copyright-protected works, and the dates on which they entered or will enter the public domain, are provided in Appendix II.

KEY POINTS:

- ❖ Material may be in the public domain if:
  - It is of a kind that copyright law does not protect;
  - It has been dedicated to the public domain;
  - The copyright has been abandoned; or
  - The copyright term has expired or lapsed.
- ❖ The term of most copyrights is 70 years + the life of the author.
- ❖ The term of copyright in a work made for hire is the earlier of:
  - 95 years after publication; or
  - 120 years after its first fixation in a tangible medium.
- ❖ Special rules for calculating copyright durations exist for:
  - Anonymous or pseudonymous works
  - Certain pre-1978 works

- Foreign works
- Abandoned copyrights.

❖ Sound recordings made in the U.S. before February 15, 1972 are in the public domain, but the musical or literary works performed in them may not be.

❖ Rights in pre-1972 sound recordings may be protected by state or foreign law even if they are not protected by federal copyright law.

❖ Copyrights no longer need to be renewed, but the former renewal requirement has caused some pre-1978 works to enter the public domain.

❖ Noncompliance with pre-1989 formalities has caused some works to enter the public domain.

❖ Certain foreign works may be restored from the public domain.

CHAPTER 14

Fair Use

Fair Use is sometimes a successful defense against a claim of copyright infringement. In essence, it says that although a particular use infringes a copyright, there should be no liability because the particular use in question serves some important public policy interest that outweighs the harm to the copyright owner's interests.

The doctrine has been called "the most troublesome in the whole law of copyright."[13] It unquestionably is the most widely misunderstood, and probably the least unpredictable.

It is an affirmative defense, meaning that a person who is being sued for infringement must assert the defense before a court will consider it, and the person asserting it bears the burden of proof

Although it is not a good idea to rely on the possibility of a "fair use" defense as a justification for copyright infringement, it can be helpful to have a grasp on when it clearly does apply and when it clearly does not apply. If your intended use of copyrighted material is squarely within established parameters of the doctrine, then you may safely proceed to use the material without needing to contact the copyright owner for permission. If it clearly does not come within the meaning of "fair use," then you will need to either obtain the copyright owner's written permission (license) to make such use of it, or refrain from using it. If it is in one of several large gray areas of "fair use" jurisprudence, then you will need to assess whether the risk of liability does or does not outweigh the burden of obtaining the copyright owner's permission. In all cases, of course, the safest route is to obtain a written license from the copyright owner to make the intended use of the work.

---

[13] Dellar v. Samuel Goldwyn, 104 F.2d 661 (2nd Cir. 1939.)

MYTHS

Myths about fair use abound. Here are a few:

- "Copying up to 25 words is fair use"
- "Copying less than 10 percent is fair use"
- "Copying up to 6 bars of a song is fair use"
- "Noncommercial use is fair use"
- "Use for educational purposes is always fair use"
- "It's fair use if you're a nonprofit organization"
- "It's fair use if there's no copyright notice on it"
- "If it's on the Internet, it's fair use"
- "If it's out of print, or if the author is dead, it's fair use"
- "If you give credit to the author, then it's fair use"

Although some of these statements come close, none of them is accurate. In truth, there are not many bright-line tests for determining whether something is fair use. Congress has established certain "safe harbors," though. While these are not exclusive, they are usually the clearest.

STATUTORY EXEMPTIONS

Strictly speaking, statutory exemptions are not precisely the same thing as fair use. 'Fair use' is a term of art. Normally, it requires case-by-case consideration and balancing of four policy-based factors. The exemptions that Congress has established are legislative determinations that certain kinds of activities are fair use. Courts can and have added to them. The difference is that courts must go through a four-part analysis to determine whether a particular use is "fair use" or not. Congress bypasses the necessity for a fair use analysis when it legislates an exemption into existence.

Not all of the statutory exemptions that Congress has established are applicable to websites and blogs. It can be just as important, however, to know which exemptions do not apply as it is to know about the ones that do.

THE DIGITAL MILLENNIUM COPYRIGHT ACT ("DMCA")

The Digital Millennium Copyright Act ("DMCA") is the source of some of the most important statutory exemptions. Among other things, it provides a way for online service providers to avoid contributory liability for infringing content that other people publish or post using their service.

DEFINITIONS OF "SERVICE PROVIDER"

The DMCA contains two different definitions of "service provider." The first is a narrow one: "an entity offering the transmission, routing, or providing of connections for digital online communications, between or among points specified by a user, of material of the user's choosing, without modification to the content of the material as sent or received." This is the original understanding of the meaning of Internet service provider (or "ISP") as a company that provides people with a connection to the Internet.

The second definition is much broader: "a provider of online services or network access, or the operator of facilities therefore, and includes an entity [described by the first definition.]" This definition certainly would include web-hosting services, email services, file-sharing networks, chat rooms, and search engines. It has also been held to apply to online auction services (eBay) and a website that provides commercial real estate listings. In *In re Aimster*, 252 F. Supp. 2d 634 (N.D. Ill. 2003) the court observed that "'service provider' is defined so broadly that we have trouble imagining the existence of an online service that would not fall under the definitions...." It is difficult to argue with this assessment, given that all websites and blogs (other than disabled and empty ones) attempt to provide visitors some kind of entertainment or information. (Whether a particular site is successful or not is an aesthetic question, not a legal one.)

Some DMCA exemptions only apply to service providers that come within the narrower of the two definitions (traditional ISPs.) Others apply to service providers in the broader sense.

COMPLIANCE WITH THE DMCA NOTICE-AND-TAKE-DOWN PROCEDURE

One of the most important sections of the DMCA is 17 U.S.C. § 512(c), "Information residing on systems or networks at direction of users." It applies to service providers in the broadest sense of that term. It clearly applies to web-hosting services, and the language of the statute is broad enough that it could also apply to any website owner or blogger who allows users to upload content to the site (such as a comment on an article or blog post) or to use the site to communicate content to others (e.g., via an email, instant message or a chat feature offered on the site.)

Basically, this section protects a service provider from contributory liability for a user's infringing activity if the service provider does not know or have reason to know about it, provided all the conditions set out in the DMCA are satisfied.

The DMCA also provides a notice-and-take-down-procedure which, if followed by the service provider, will protect it from liability for damages for infringing activity by a user of the service.

To qualify for these protections, the service provider must designate an agent to receive notifications of alleged infringement, and comply with other statutory requirements.

For more information about the DMCA, see Chapter 15.

LINKING TO INFRINGING MATERIAL

A service provider may not be sued for damages, and only injunctive relief may be issued against it, for copyright infringement based on the provider referring or linking of users to a site containing infringing material or activity. The reference could be a directory, index, pointer or mention of the site. A link could be a hypertext link to the site.

This exemption was primarily intended to protect search engine service providers such as Google from liability for displaying a list of search results. In the absence of this exemption, a search engine service's facilitation of access to a website containing infringing content by providing a hypertext link to it might be actionable as contributory infringement.

Although it was primarily intended to protect search engine service providers, the wording of the statute is broad enough that it could apply to any website or blog that has a hypertext link to another website on it.

This exemption applies only if the service provider:

1) does not receive a financial benefit directly attributable to the infringing activity, in a case in which the service provider has the right and ability to control the activity;
2) does not have actual knowledge that the linked website is infringing a copyright, and in the absence of a notification would not be aware of facts or circumstances making infringing activity apparent;
3) promptly removes or disables access to the link, if the service provider acquires such knowledge or awareness;
4) promptly removes or disables access to the link upon receiving notification of claimed infringement;
5) has implemented a policy that provides for the termination of subscribers and account holders who are repeat infringers;
6) informs subscribers and account holders about the policy; and

7)   accommodates and does not interfere with standard technical measures used by copyright owners to identify or protect copyrighted works, and that does not impose substantial costs on service providers or substantial burdens on their systems or networks.

To be effective, the notification must meet the same requirements set out in the notice-and-take-down provisions of the DMCA. (See Chapter 15.) Instead of identifying what is claimed to be infringing content, however, the notice must identify the reference or link, and it must give the service provider information reasonably sufficient to permit the service provider to locate the reference or link.

PHOTOGRAPHS OF ARTWORK ON USEFUL ARTICLES

Copyright law allows you to take a photograph of a useful article even though it may have a copyrighted work incorporated into it, and to use the photograph in advertising or commentary related to the distribution or display of the items, or in news reports.

If, for example, a company lawfully incorporates copyrighted artwork into its logo, and affixes the logo to its products, you may take a photograph of the product and use the photograph in connection with your sales of the product without needing to get permission from the owner of the copyright in the artwork.

Similarly, if you take a photograph of a table on which someone has painted a portrait, you may publish the photograph in conjunction with a news report without needing to get permission from the artist to do so.

STATUTORY LICENSES FOR SOUND RECORDINGS

A person who qualifies for a statutory license to reproduce, distribute or transmit a sound recording is exempt from liability for infringement of the copyright in the sound recording so long as he complies with all the requirements for obtaining and maintaining statutory licenses, including accounting and royalty payment requirements.

Compliance with the terms and conditions of a statutory license, however, only ensures immunity from liability for infringement of the copyright in the sound recording. It does not create any immunity from liability for infringement of the copyright in the underlying musical work.

The qualifications for a statutory license are addressed in Chapter 20.

COMPULSORY LICENSES TO MAKE COVER VERSIONS OF SONGS

A person who qualifies for a compulsory license to make and distribute a cover version of a musical work (i.e., copies of his own performance of a musical work) is exempt from liability for infringement of the copyright in the musical work so long as he complies with all the requirements for obtaining and maintaining compulsory licenses, including accounting and royalty payment requirements.

Compliance with the terms and conditions of a compulsory license, however, only ensures immunity from liability for copying and distributing a cover version of a musical work. It does not create any immunity from liability for publicly performing a musical work. It also does not create any immunity from liability for copying and distributing a sound recording as to which another person owns the copyright.

The qualifications for a compulsory license are addressed in Chapter 20.

EPHEMERAL COPIES

If you have a license (including a statutory license) or a statutory right to publicly display or transmit ("perform") a work, then you may make one copy of it. The copy must be made solely for purposes of archival preservation or security, or solely for use in your own transmissions. No further copies may be made from the copy.

This exemption does not apply to audiovisual works.

If the copy is preserved exclusively for archival purposes, then it may be retained indefinitely. Otherwise, it must be destroyed within six months after it was first transmitted to the public.

If the copyright owner has implemented measures to prevent copying, she must provide a licensee with the means to make a copy if it is technologically and economically feasible to do so. If she doesn't, then the licensee may circumvent the copyright protection measures and make a copy, without liability for violation of the anti-circumvention provision of 17 U.S.C. § 1201(a).

Governmental bodies and nonprofit organizations may make up to thirty copies of a transmission program embodying the performance or display, provided no copies are made from the copies. The governmental body or nonprofit organization may keep one copy indefinitely, for archival purposes. The rest must be destroyed within seven years from the date of the first transmission of the program.

A governmental body or nonprofit organization may make and distribute one copy of a nondramatic musical work of a religious nature (or a sound recording of it) to each transmitting organization that has a right to transmit a performance of the work to the public (pursuant to a license, for example), provided there is no charge for the distribution, and provided the transmitting organization only makes a single transmission of it. The governmental body or nonprofit organization may keep one copy indefinitely, exclusively for archival purposes. All remaining copies must be destroyed within one year after the first transmission.

A governmental body or nonprofit organization that has a right to transmit a performance for deaf or blind persons may make up to ten copies of the performance, and may allow any governmental body or nonprofit organization that is entitled to transmit such performances to blind or deaf persons to use a copy to do so. The copies must be provided at no charge. All copies must used solely for transmissions to blind or deaf persons, or for archival preservation or security. No copies may be made from the copies.

If authorized copies of a sound recording have already been distributed to the public (or if the copyright owner authorizes you to transmit it), and you have acquired a copy of it legally, then you may make a noninteractive digital transmission of it to a business establishment, or transmit it pursuant to a statutory license. If you do so, then you have a statutory license to make one copy ("phonorecord") of the sound recording (unless the terms of an applicable license allow more), provided it is retained and used exclusively by you, and no copies are made of the copy. The copy so made may only be used for your own transmissions, and those transmissions must either be noninteractive digital transmission to a business establishment or made pursuant to a statutory license. The copy may be preserved indefinitely for exclusively archival purposes. Otherwise, it must be destroyed within six months after the first transmission of it. If the copyright owner has implemented measures to prevent copying, she must provide a licensee with the means to make a copy if it is technologically and economically feasible to do so. If she doesn't, then the licensee may circumvent the copy-protection measures and make a copy, without liability for violation of the anti-circumvention provision of 17 U.S.C. § 1201(a).

SYSTEM CACHING

A service provider is exempt from liability for damages for copyright infringement due to the intermediate and temporary storage of material on a system or network controlled or operated by or for the service provider if the material is made available online by another person who transmits it through the system or network to another person at that person's request if:

1) the storage occurs automatically;

2) the material is transmitted to the person without modification to its content;

3) the service provider complies with rules concerning the refreshing, reloading, or other updating of the material when specified by the person making the material available online in accordance with a generally accepted industry standard data communications protocol for the system or network through which that person makes the material available;

4) the service provider does not interfere with the ability of technology associated with the material to return to the person making the transmission the information that would have been available to that person if the material had been obtained by subsequent users directly from that person, except in cases where the technology:

   a) significantly interferes with the performance of the provider's system or network or with the intermediate storage of the material;

   b) is inconsistent with generally accepted industry standard communications protocols; or

   c) extracts information from the provider's system or network other than the information that would have been available to the person transmitting the material if the subsequent users had gained access to it directly from that person;

5) the service provider permits access to the stored material in significant part only to users of its system or network that have met any conditions for access to the material that the person transmitting the material has set, such as payment of a fee or provision of a password, etc.;

6) the service provider promptly removes, or disables access to, material that is claimed to be infringing upon notification of claimed infringement, in cases where:

   a) the material has previously been removed from the originating site or access to it has been disabled, or a court has ordered it removed or access to it disabled; and

   b) the party giving the notification includes in the notification a statement confirming that the material has been removed from the originating site or access to it has been disabled or that a court has ordered that the material be removed from the originating site or that access to the material on the originating site must be disabled;

7) the service provider has implemented a policy that provides for the termination of subscribers and account holders who are repeat infringers;

8) the service provider informs subscribers and account holders about the policy; and

9) the service provider accommodates and does not interfere with standard technical measures that are used by copyright owners to identify or protect copyrighted works, and that do not impose substantial costs on service providers or substantial burdens on their systems or networks.

Damages may not be recovered against a service provider who complies with these requirements, although a court may issue injunctive relief.

FEDERAL GOVERNMENT PUBLICATIONS

Works created by the federal government, or by federal employees within the scope of their employment, do not receive copyright protection. Therefore, they may be freely copied, distributed, displayed, performed, and digitally transmitted. Derivative works may be made from them.

On the other hand, the federal government may own copyrights that have been assigned or transferred to it by others, and it may enforce its rights as a copyright owner with respect to those works.

Works prepared by officers or employees of the U.S. Postal Service, the Corporation for Public Broadcasting, the Public Broadcasting Services, or National Public Radio are not considered works of the U.S. government. Works prepared by officers or employees of the Smithsonian Institution are not considered works of the U.S. government if the author-employee was paid from the Smithsonian trust fund. And the U.S. Secretary of Commerce may secure copyright for a limited term not to exceed five years in any standard reference data prepared or disseminated by the National Technical Information Service pursuant to 15 U.S.C. Chapter 23.

You should not simply take it for granted that you may freely copy and re-publish any publication as to which the federal government owns the copyright. You will need to check to see if the work was created by federal employee(s) for the federal government, on one hand, or assigned or transferred by someone else to the federal government, on the other. If it is the latter, then you may need a license from the federal government to use the work. If the former, then you may freely copy and use it without permission unless it comes within one of the exceptions noted above.

FACULTY AND GRADUATE STUDENT ACTIVITIES

When a public or nonprofit institution of higher education is a service provider (e.g., provides access to the Internet, or maintains an informational or commercial website), it is exempt from liability for damages for the infringing activities of an employee on the basis that it transmitted, routed, or provided connections for, or engaged in system caching with respect to, infringing material transmitted at the employee's direction if:

1) the employee is a faculty member or graduate student at the institution;
2) the employee is performing a teaching or research function;
3) the infringing activities do not involve the provision of online access to instructional materials that are or were required or recommended, within the preceding 3-year period, for a course the employee taught at the institution;
4) the institution has not, within the preceding 3-year period, received more than two notifications of claimed copyright infringement by the employee (excluding notifications involving a known misrepresentation that content infringed a copyright);
5) the institution provides to all users of its system or network materials that accurately describe and promote compliance with copyright laws;
6) the institution has implemented a policy that provides for the termination of subscribers and account holders who are repeat infringers;
7) the institution informs subscribers and account holders about the policy; and
8) the institution accommodates and does not interfere with standard technical measures that are used by copyright owners to identify or protect copyrighted works, and that do not impose substantial costs on service providers or substantial burdens on their systems or networks.

In addition, if all of these conditions are met, then the employee's knowledge or awareness of his own infringing activities will not be imputed to the institution. This means that the institution may avail itself of the notice-and-take-down procedures and exemption with respect to material that one of its teachers or graduate students transmits using the institution's facilities, or uploads to a website (or other online data storage mechanism) maintained by the institution, and also with respect to links to sites with infringing content that the teacher or graduate student posts to a university website.

This exemption only protects the institution from damages. A court may still issue injunctive relief against the institution.

ONLINE COURSES OFFERED BY SCHOOLS AND GOVERNMENT

An accredited nonprofit educational institution or a governmental body may display or perform copyrighted works in web-based instructional programs (i.e., programs digitally transmitted over the Internet), provided all of the following conditions are met:

1) the performance or display is made by, at the direction of, or under the supervision of an instructor as an integral part of a class session offered as a regular part of the systematic mediated instructional activities of a governmental body or an accredited nonprofit educational institution;

2) it is directly related and of material assistance to the teaching content of the transmission;

3) the transmission is made solely for, and, to the extent technologically feasible, the reception of such transmission is limited to students officially enrolled in the course, or officers or employees of governmental bodies as a part of their official duties or employment;

4) the transmitting body or institution has instituted policies regarding copyright; provides materials to faculty, students, and relevant staff members that accurately describe, and promote compliance with, copyright laws; and provides notice to students that materials used in connection with the course may be subject to copyright protection;

5) the transmitting body or institution applies technological measures that reasonably prevent retention of the work in accessible form by recipients of the transmission from the transmitting body or institution for longer than the class session, and unauthorized further dissemination of the work in accessible form by such recipients to others;

6) the transmitting body or institution does not engage in conduct that could reasonably be expected to interfere with technological measures used by copyright owners to prevent such retention or unauthorized further dissemination;

7) the work performed or displayed is not produced or marketed primarily for use in mediated instructional activities that are transmitted digitally;

8) the performance or display is not given by means of a copy or phonorecord that the transmitting body or institution knew or had reason to believe was illegally made or acquired;

9) the work performed or displayed is:

    a) a performance of a musical work;

    b) a performance of a non-dramatic literary work;

    c) a performance of a reasonable and limited portion of a dramatic, audiovisual or other kind of work; or

    d) a display of a work in an amount comparable to that which is typically displayed in the course of a live classroom session; and

10) the work performed or displayed is not a textbook, course pack or other material that is typically purchased or acquired by the students in higher education for their independent use and retention or are typically purchased or acquired for elementary and secondary students for their possession and independent use.

This exemption does not apply to private, for-profit website owners and bloggers. It is limited to government bodies and nonprofit schools.

USE OF MUSIC BY TEACHERS

You do not need the composer's permission to perform a nondramatic musical work in classroom educational activities. This can include Internet transmissions, but only if made by or under the supervision of a teacher as part of a class session offered by a public school or an accredited nonprofit educational institution, and only if it is relevant to the instructional content.

This exception does not apply to works that are specifically made or marketed for classroom instructional purposes, or to copies of works that were not lawfully obtained.

A webcaster invoking this exception must employ technological measures to prevent recipients of the transmission from retaining the work for longer than the class session, and to prevent unauthorized further dissemination of the work. Also, the webcaster must not do anything that interferes with technological measures used by copyright owners to prevent such retention or unauthorized further dissemination.

OTHER EXEMPTIONS

Many statutory exemptions are misunderstood, as evidenced by the fact that people regularly cite them as a basis for a claim of "fair use" when they do not, in fact, apply to their activity. A mistaken belief that something falls within a statutory "fair use" exemption is dangerous. It can expose a person to liability for thousands of dollars in damages and attorney fees for copyright infringement. Accordingly, it is just as important to know which statutory exemptions do *not* apply as it is to know about the ones that do.

The fact that a use does not come within a statutory exemption does not necessarily mean that it is not "fair use." It just means that resort to the less clear-cut, four-prong test will be necessary.

RELIGIOUS SERVICES

Performance of a copyrighted musical work or non-dramatic literary work, or of a dramatico-musical work of a religious nature, or display of a work, in the course of religious services at a place of worship is a permitted "fair use."

This exemption covers performances at the place of worship. It does not apply to broadcasts or transmissions of religious services over the Internet.

MUSICAL PERFORMANCES SPONSORED BY NONPROFIT AGRICULTURAL AND HORTICULTURAL ORGANIZATIONS

A governmental body or nonprofit agricultural or horticultural organization is not liable for performing, and is not subject to vicarious or contributory liability for another person's performance of a non-dramatic musical work at an annual agricultural or horticultural fair or exhibition.

This provision does not exempt all musical performances sponsored by nonprofit agricultural and horticultural organizations. It only applies to performances at an annual fair, not broadcasts or transmissions of them.

FRATERNAL AND VETERANS' ORGANIZATIONS CHARITABLE FUND-RAISING EVENTS

Performance of a non-dramatic literary or musical work in the course of a social function organized and promoted by a nonprofit veterans' organization or a nonprofit fraternal organization to which the general public is not invited is permitted if the proceeds from the performance, after deducting the reasonable costs of producing the performance, are used exclusively for charitable purposes and not for financial gain. This exemption does not apply to the social functions of a college or university fraternity or sorority unless the social function is held solely to raise funds for a specific charitable purpose.

This exemption does not apply to Internet broadcasts or transmissions of the performance.

FACE-TO-FACE EDUCATIONAL ACTIVITIES

Performing or displaying copyrighted works during face-to-face teaching activities at a nonprofit educational institution is permitted.

This exemption does not apply to online educational activities.

FREE, CHARITABLE OR NONPROFIT CONCERTS

Live performances of musical works and non-dramatic literary works are permitted if they are free or if all proceeds are used for charitable, religious or educational purposes.

This exemption does not apply to broadcasts or transmissions of the performance.

PERFORMANCES OF NONDRAMATIC LITERARY WORKS FOR BLIND OR DEAF PERSONS

Performances of non-dramatic literary works for blind or deaf persons (i.e., reading aloud, communicating with sign language, etc.) may be transmitted to blind or deaf persons if the transmission is not made for commercial advantage, provided it is made by:

a)   a governmental body;
b)   a noncommercial educational broadcast station;
c)   a radio subcarrier authorization; or
d)   a cable system.

RECEIVING AND DISPLAYING BROADCASTS AND TRANSMISSIONS

You are permitted to receive and display authorized broadcasts and digital transmissions on a single receiving device such as a television, radio, or networked computer or mobile device, provided you do not charge people to watch or hear it. The purpose of this exemption is to permit a person to watch and listen to television and radio programs, and programs transmitted via the Internet.

This exemption only applies to displaying a received broadcast or transmission. It does not exempt the broadcaster or transmitter from complying with copyright laws. Unauthorized broadcasts and transmissions do not come within the coverage of this exemption.

Also, this exemption does not authorize you to re-transmit a broadcast or transmission that you receive pursuant to the exemption.

HOME TAPING OF TELEVISION BROADCASTS FOR LATER VIEWING

Videotaping a television broadcast for viewing at a later time is permitted, so long as it is not done for financial gain.

The exemption only applies to the rights to copy and display a work at the place where the copy is normally kept. It does not authorize the distribution of copies to others. Nor does it authorize public performance or display of the copy. This exemption does not authorize posting a home-taped television broadcast to your website.

MUSIC IN RESTAURANTS AND BARS

A restaurant or bar may play authorized radio, television, cable and satellite broadcasts or transmissions of non-dramatic musical works if they do not charge people to see or hear them. The exemption is subject to detailed conditions relating to the size of the establishment, and the size and number of screens or speakers that may be employed.

This exemption does not authorize the re-transmission of music beyond the establishment where it is received.

MUSIC IN BUSINESS ESTABLISHMENTS

A retail store or other place of business may play ("perform") authorized radio, television, cable and satellite broadcasts or transmissions of non-dramatic musical works if they do not charge people to see or hear them. The exemption is subject to detailed conditions relating to the size of the establishment, and the size and number of screens or speakers that may be employed.

This exemption does not authorize the re-transmission of music beyond the establishment where it is received.

MUSIC STORES

A retail establishment that is open to the public may "perform" sound recordings of non-dramatic musical works (such as by playing a CD or record album) for the sole purpose of promoting sales of sound recordings or devices used to play them, provided it does not charge people to listen to them.

This exemption does not authorize transmission beyond the establishment.

RADIO BROADCASTS OF SOUND RECORDINGS

The performance of a sound recording publicly by means of a noninteractive digital audio transmission is not an infringement of a copyright in a sound recording if it is part of a nonsubscription broadcast transmission. A "broadcast transmission" has been interpreted to refer only to terrestrial radio stations licensed as such by the FCC. Therefore, the exemption does not apply to Internet radio stations and webcasters.[14] In other words, non-Internet, nonsubscription radio stations that do not broadcast via satellite may freely broadcast sound recordings even if the sound recording itself is in digital format.

This exemption only applies to sound recordings. Unauthorized broadcast of a copyrighted work embodied in a sound recording (such as a musical work) may infringe the copyright in that work.

RADIO SUBCARRIER AUTHORIZATION TRANSMISSIONS TO BLIND OR DEAF PERSONS

A performance of a dramatic literary work may be transmitted to blind or deaf persons if the work was published at least ten years before the performance, provided the transmission is made by a radio subcarrier authorization and is not made for the purpose of commercial advantage.

LIBRARIES AND ARCHIVES

A number of exemptions apply to libraries. Most of these apply to archives, too.

A library may make and distribute one copy of a work in its collection, provided it is not done for commercial gain; a copyright notice or statement is included; and the collection is either open to the public, or open to both library and non-library researchers doing research in a specialized field.

A library may copy and distribute up to three copies of an unpublished work in its collection, if done solely for the purposes of preservation and security or for deposit for research use in another library or archive. The library may copy it to a digital format, but may not distribute it in digital format. The copies may not be made available to the public in digital format outside the library's premises.

A library may make up to three copies of a published work if it is done solely for the purpose of replacing a copy that is damaged, deteriorating, lost,

---

[14] Bonneville International Corp. v. Peters, 153 F.Supp.2d 763 (E.D. Pa. 2001), *aff'd,* 347 F.3d 485 (3d Cir. 2003.)

or stolen, or if the existing format in which the work is stored has become obsolete. This exemption is available only if a replacement cannot be obtained at a fair price. The copies may not be made available to the public in digital format outside the library's premises.

A library may make a copy, for a library patron, of no more than one contribution to a periodical or collective work, or of a small amount of other kinds of works, if the library reasonably believes it will be used for private study, scholarship or research. A copyright warning must be posted where orders are placed.

A library may make a copy, for a library patron, of an entire work in its collection, or a copy of a substantial amount of it, if a copy cannot be purchased at a fair price, and the library reasonably believes it will be used for private study, scholarship or research. A copyright warning must be posted where orders are placed.

Displaying near its photocopy machine a notice that library materials may be subject to copyright protection will protect a library from contributory liability if an unsupervised patron uses the library's photocopy machine (or other equipment) to infringe a copyrighted work.

A library may copy and lend a limited number of copies of an audiovisual news program if it is not done for commercial gain; its collection is either open to the public, or open to both library and non-library researchers doing research in a specialized field; and a copyright notice or a statement that the work may be protected by copyright is included on the copy.

A library may make interlibrary loans of it copies of copyrighted works, so long as the purpose or effect is not to substitute for a subscription to or purchase of the work by the receiving library.

During the last twenty years of any term of copyright of a published work, a library, including a nonprofit educational institution that functions as such, may reproduce, distribute, display, or perform in facsimile or digital form a copy of such work, or portions thereof, for purposes of preservation, scholarship, or research, if the work is not subject to normal commercial exploitation; a copy of the work cannot be obtained at a reasonable price; and the copyright owner has not served notice that it is subject to such exploitation and is available for a reasonable price.

The statutory exemptions are not exclusive. Other kinds of library copying may be permitted under the four-factor fair use standard (See below.)

The statutory exemptions do not override any licensing agreements or contracts under which a library has obtained a copy of a work. Thus, if a library obtains software under a license, and the license prohibits something which an exemption appears to permit, then the library must abide by the terms of the license agreement. Although it may not be liable for copyright infringement if it fails to do so, it may be liable for breach of the license agreement.

Website owners and bloggers are not libraries, so these exemptions do not apply to them.

Transitory Digital Network Communications

An exemption from copyright liability exists for those who provide users with a connection to the Internet, or make the underlying system of network connections operate. In the absence of an exemption, these service providers might otherwise be liable for contributory infringement simply by reason of providing an Internet connection for the infringer.

An Internet service provider is exempt from liability for damages for copyright infringement for transmitting, routing, or providing connections for, material through a system or network controlled or operated by or for the service provider, or the intermediate and transient storage of that material in the course of such transmitting, routing, or providing connections, if:

1) the transmission of the material was initiated by someone else;
2) the transmission, etc. occurs automatically, without selection of material by the service provider;
3) the service provider does not select the recipients of the material;
4) no copy of the material made by the service provider in the course of such intermediate or transient storage is maintained on the system or network in a manner ordinarily accessible to anyone other than anticipated recipients, and no such copy is maintained on the system or network in a manner ordinarily accessible to such anticipated recipients for a longer period than is reasonably necessary for the transmission, routing, or provision of connections;
5) the material is transmitted without modification of its content;
6) the service provider has implemented a policy that provides for the termination of subscribers and account holders who are repeat infringers;
7) the service provider informs subscribers and account holders about the policy; and
8) the service provider accommodates and does not interfere with standard technical measures that are used by copyright owners to identify or protect copyrighted works, and that do not impose substantial costs on service providers or substantial burdens on their systems or networks.

A court may order a service provider to terminate the account(s) of an account holder or subscriber who is using the provider's service to engage in infringing activity. A court may also restrain a service provider from providing access, by taking reasonable steps specified in the order to block access, to a specific, identified, online location outside the United States.

CERTAIN SECONDARY TRANSMISSIONS

A "secondary transmission" is one that further transmits a received transmission. It is different from a simulcast or multicast, in that simulcasts and multicasts are simultaneous transmissions of the primary transmission without first receiving the transmission from another source.

A secondary transmission is exempt from a claim of copyright infringement if it occurs simultaneously with the primary transmission (i.e., it occurs immediately upon receipt of the primary transmission) and any of the following conditions apply:

a) it is transmitted, at no charge, by the manager of a hotel, apartment building or lodging establishment to guests; the primary transmission is by a broadcast station licensed by the FCC (i.e., not Internet transmissions); and the secondary transmission is within the service area of the broadcast station;

b) it is transmitted in connection with an online instructional activity of a governmental body or an accredited nonprofit educational institution that meets all the requirements for exemption (See above);

c) it is transmitted by a carrier that has no control over the content of the primary transmission or the recipients of the secondary transmission, provided the carrier's activities are limited to providing communication channels such as a wires, cables, etc.;

d) the transmission is by a satellite carrier pursuant to a statutory license;

e) the transmission is by a governmental body or nonprofit organization, without charge other than for the actual and reasonable costs of maintaining and operating the secondary transmission service;

f) the transmission is by a cable system with a valid statutory license, provided the transmission is not a violation of FCC rules or regulations; the cable system has complied with accounting and royalty payment requirements; and the primary transmission is not altered in an unauthorized way.

To qualify for any of the above exemptions, the primary transmission must be one that is for reception by the public at large. Even if the primary transmission is only offered to particular people, however, a secondary transmitter may nevertheless be exempt if FCC rules, regulations or authorizations require carriage of the signals comprising the secondary transmission; the primary transmission is by a broadcast station licensed by the FCC; and the secondary transmitter does not alter the primary transmitter's signal.

Some special rules apply to secondary transmissions of the broadcasts of stations located outside the United States.

CERTAIN RETRANSMISSIONS OF RADIO BROADCASTS

Retransmission of a nonsubscription, noninteractive radio broadcast of a sound recording is not an infringement of the copyright in the sound recording in the following situations:

a) the radio station's broadcast transmission is not wilfully or repeatedly retransmitted more than a radius of 150 miles from the site of the radio broadcast transmitter (or, in the case of a subscription retransmission of a nonsubscription broadcast retransmission, 150 miles from the site of the broadcast retransmitter), but the 150-mile limitation does not apply when a nonsubscription broadcast transmission by a radio station is retransmitted on a nonsubscription basis by a terrestrial broadcast station, terrestrial translator, or terrestrial repeater licensed by the FCC;

b) the retransmission is of a radio station broadcast transmission that is obtained by the retransmitter over the air; not electronically processed by the retransmitter to deliver separate and discrete signals; and retransmitted only within the local communities served by the retransmitter;

c) the radio station's broadcast transmission was being retransmitted to cable systems by a satellite carrier on January 1, 1995, and that retransmission was being retransmitted by cable systems as a separate and discrete signal, and the satellite carrier obtains the radio station's broadcast transmission in an analog format, so long as the broadcast transmission being retransmitted embodies the programming of no more than one radio station; or

d) the radio station's broadcast transmission is made by a noncommercial educational broadcast station, consists solely of noncommercial educational and cultural radio programs, and the retransmission is a nonsubscription terrestrial broadcast retransmission

This exemption only applies to sound recordings. Retransmission of a broadcast of a copyrighted work embodied in a sound recording (such as a musical work) may infringe the copyright in that work.

DIGITAL TRANSMISSIONS TO A BUSINESS ESTABLISHMENT NOT IN EXCESS OF THE SOUND RECORDING PERFORMANCE COMPLEMENT

The performance of a sound recording publicly by means of noninteractive digital audio transmission is not an infringement of the copyright in the sound recording if the transmission is to a business establishment for use in the ordinary course of its business, provided the business recipient does not retransmit the transmission outside of its premises or the immediately surrounding vicinity, and that the transmission does not exceed the sound recording performance complement.

The "sound recording performance complement" is the transmission during any 3-hour period, on a particular channel used by a transmitting entity, of no more than:

a) different selections of sound recordings from any one phonorecord lawfully distributed for public performance or sale in the United States, if no more than 2 such selections are transmitted consecutively; or

b) 4 different selections of sound recordings by the same featured recording artist, or from any set or compilation of phonorecords lawfully distributed together as a unit for public performance or sale in the United States, if no more than three such selections are transmitted consecutively.

This exemption only applies to sound recordings. Transmission of a copyrighted work embodied in a sound recording may infringe the copyright in that work.

TRANSMISSIONS WITHIN A BUSINESS ESTABLISHMENT

The performance of a sound recording publicly by means of noninteractive digital audio transmission is not an infringement of the copyright in the sound recording if the transmission is within a business establishment, confined to its premises or the immediately surrounding vicinity.

This exemption only applies to sound recordings. Transmission of a copyrighted work embodied in a sound recording (such as a musical work) may infringe the copyright in that work.

RETRANSMISSIONS AUTHORIZED BY A LICENSED TRANSMITTER

The performance of a sound recording publicly by means of noninteractive digital audio transmission is not an infringement of the copyright in the sound recording if the transmission is a retransmission, including a multichannel video programming distributor, of a transmission by a transmitter licensed to publicly perform the sound recording as part of that transmission, if the retransmission is simultaneous with the licensed transmission and authorized by the transmitter.

This exemption only applies to sound recordings. Retransmission of a copyrighted work embodied in a sound recording (such as a musical work) may infringe the copyright in that work.

RETRANSMISSION SIMULTANEOUS WITH A TRANSMISSION TO AN END USER BY A LICENSED INTERACTIVE SERVICE

A retransmission of a digital audio transmission is not an infringement of the copyright in the sound recording if:

1) the retransmission is of a transmission by an interactive service licensed to publicly perform the sound recording to a particular member of the public as part of that transmission; and

2) the retransmission is simultaneous with the licensed transmission, authorized by the transmitter, and limited to that particular member of the public intended by the interactive service to be the recipient of the transmission.

This exemption only applies to sound recordings. Retransmission of a copyrighted work embodied in a sound recording (such as a musical work) may infringe the copyright in that work.

TRANSMISSIONS INCIDENTAL TO AN EXEMPT TRANSMISSION

A transmission of a sound recording publicly by means of noninteractive digital audio transmission is not an infringement of the copyright in the sound recording if it is a transmission incidental to an exempt transmission occurring either before or simultaneously with the exempt transmission, such as a feed received by and then retransmitted by an exempt transmitter, so long as such incidental transmissions do not include any subscription transmission directly for reception by members of the public.

This exemption only applies to sound recordings. Transmission of a copyrighted work embodied in a sound recording (such as a musical work) may infringe the copyright in that work.

PARENTAL CONTROLS

The making imperceptible, by or at the direction of a member of a private household, of limited portions of audio or video content of a motion picture, during a performance in or transmitted to that household for private home viewing, from an authorized copy of the motion picture, or the creation or provision of a computer program or other technology that enables such making imperceptible and that is designed and marketed to be used, at the direction of a member of a private household, for such making imperceptible, is permitted if no fixed copy of the altered version of the motion picture is created by such computer program or other technology.

ANALOG TRANSMISSIONS

The owner of a copyright in a sound recording has an exclusive right to transmit it digitally, but not an exclusive right to broadcast it by other means, such as analog transmission.

This exemption only applies to sound recordings. Analog transmission of a copyrighted work embodied in a sound recording (such as a musical work) may infringe the copyright in that work.

CERTAIN NON-SIMULTANEOUS SECONDARY TRANSMISSIONS BY CABLE SYSTEMS

The Copyright Act makes certain non-simultaneous secondary transmissions by cable systems exempt from infringement liability, provided the cable system complies with detailed conditions specified in the statute and applicable regulations.

COMPUTER OPERATIONS

Loading a computer program into a computer's memory is permitted, as is decompilation (converting object code to source code.) Distributing copies of it on your website, however, is not covered by this exemption.

REVERSE ENGINEERING

Reverse engineering a computer program is fair use.

FOUR-FACTOR TEST FOR FAIR USE

A use that does not fall within a statutory exemption may nevertheless qualify as fair use if, after considering the four factors set out in 17 U.S.C. § 107, it is determined that the copyright owner's interest in controlling and receiving compensation for the use of the work is outweighed by an important public policy interest in allowing the use.

Section 107 provides:

[T]he fair use of a copyrighted work, including such use by reproduction in copies or phonorecords or by any other means specified by that section, for purposes such as criticism, comment, news reporting, teaching (including multiple copies for classroom use), scholarship, or research, is not an infringement of copyright....

It then directs courts to consider four factors when deciding whether a particular infringing use should be permitted as fair use:

1) the purpose and character of the use;
2) the nature of work;
3) the amount and substantiality of the portion used; and
4) the effect of the use on the market for the work.

There is no rule of decision for cases where some factors support fair use and some do not. Courts make that decision on a case-by-case basis.

PURPOSE AND CHARACTER OF THE USE

The first broad factor that courts are to consider is "the purpose and character of the use."

CRITICISM, COMMENTARY, NEWS REPORTING, EDUCATION OR CHARITABLE USE

Consistent with the language of the statute, the following kinds of uses normally result in a finding that the "purpose and character of the use" factor weighs in favor of a finding of fair use:

- criticism
- commentary
- news reporting
- teaching
- scholarship
- research
- charitable (nonprofit) uses.

The fact that a use falls within one of these categories means that the first factor weighs in favor of a finding of fair use. It does not mean that a use is automatically fair use if it falls into one of these categories, though. The other three factors must still be considered and weighed.

To improve your chances of a judicial finding of "fair use," it is a good idea to quote only so much of another person's work as is necessary; and add your own thoughts about it (criticism or commentary.) Also, attribute the quoted text to the author and include a link to the source of the quoted material.

NON-COMPETITIVE PURPOSES

A use is more likely to be deemed fair use if it does not compete against the copyrighted work in the same market. Conversely, a use is less likely to be deemed fair use if it competes in the same market with the original work.

This is a principal reason that parodies are usually found to be fair use. A parody usually does not compete in the same market with the original work, since fans of the original work are not likely to be in the market for works that poke fun at it.

NONCOMMERCIAL USES

Commercial use is usually less likely to be considered fair use than noncommercial use is. Making copies of a work solely for the purpose of selling them or saving someone the expense of buying a retail copy is highly unlikely to be deemed fair use.

A court may find that a use is "commercial" even if it there was never any intention to make money from it. If your website has advertising on it, and the amount of your advertising revenue is tied to the number of hits your website receives, then your reproduction of a copyrighted work on the site may be considered a commercial use, since its presence can increase the number of visits to your site and thereby increase your advertising revenue.

This is true even if the copyrighted work is informational and educational, and doesn't advertise any product or service.

The fact that only noncommercial use of a work is made does not necessarily assure that it will be deemed fair use. Courts will consider the other three factors, too, when making a final determination whether a particular noncommercial use is "fair use" or not.

PARODY

Parody is usually fair use, even if for a commercial purpose. This is because it is essentially criticism and/or commentary about the original work itself. Criticism and commentary are at the core of the fair use doctrine. Copying more than what is needed is not fair use, however.

Parody may be fair use even if created for a commercial purpose and even if a large amount is copied. Why? Because the two other factors often outweigh these considerations. Parody serves core "fair use" purposes (criticism and commentary.) In addition, it usually has no significant effect on the market for the original work because it doesn't compete in the market for the work itself. The tendency of a parody to depress sales of the original work because of the critical message it expresses about the original work is not what is meant by "effect on the market for the work."

Satire, on the other hand, generally is not likely to qualify as fair use. A parody targets and mimics the original work to make a criticism or comment about the work itself. A satire may mimic the original work, too, but it does not do so for the purpose of criticizing or commenting on the work. A satire may criticize or comment on something else, such as social mores or political institutions, but the purpose of a satire is not to criticize or comment on the work itself. There is a greater need to copy a work, or portions of it, in connection with criticizing or commenting on it than there is to copy a work in connection with criticizing or commenting on something else.

A book using Dr. Seuss characters and style to tell the story of the O. J. Simpson murder trial was held to be satire and therefore not fair use because it merely used elements of the Dr. Seuss series of books; it did not ridicule, criticize or comment on them.[15]

TRANSFORMATIVE USE

A transformative use is any use that alters the purpose, meaning or function of a work, or a portion of it. In other words, it is any use that makes

---

[15] Dr. Seuss Enterprises, L.P. v. Penguin Books USA, Inc., 109 F.3d 1394 (9th Cir. 1997).

the work serve a purpose, express a meaning, or function in a way that is different from the original purpose, meaning or function of the work.

The U.S. Supreme Court has held that the more transformative a new work is, the more likely it is to be fair use.

In *Campbell v. Acuff-Rose Music*, 510 U.S. 569 (1994), the rap group 2 Live Crew case had lifted the opening musical intro and the first line of the Roy Orbison song, "Oh, Pretty Woman" for use in a song they called, "Pretty Woman." The copyright owner sued for infringement. The district court ruled in favor of the band. The court of appeals reversed, rejecting the claim that it was "fair use." The U.S. Supreme Court then reversed the court of appeals' reversal, holding that 2 Live Crew's use of the song without permission was fair use because 2 Live Crew had transformed the song in such a way that the copied portions communicated a different meaning than the original song did. This, the Court ruled, outweighed the other factors, such as the fact that 2 Live Crew had copied "the heart" of the song; and that the group's commercial exploitation of the song negatively impacted the market for the original.

It is not clear how this decision can be squared with cases declaring that the most important consideration is the extent to which an infringing work impairs the market for the original work.

The ruling also seems difficult to square with the Copyright Act's explicit intent to give authors the exclusive right to make derivative works. The Act defines a derivative work as "any form in which a work may be recast, *transformed*, or adapted."[16] According to the U.S. Supreme Court, though, it seems it is fair use to transform a work into something else without the author's permission even if other "fair use" factors do not support it.

Whether the ruling was correct or not, it is now the law of the land that the more transformative a use of a work is, the more likely it is to be a protected "fair use" of the copyrighted work.

Despite the Supreme Court's ruling, it is not always the case that a transformative use is fair use. For example, in *Warner Bros. Entertainment, Inc. v. RDR Books*, 575 F. Supp. 2d 513 (S.D. N.Y. 2008), a case that was decided after Campbell, a court held that an encyclopedia of terms and lexicons used in Harry Potter novels, although transformative, was not "fair use," and that it was instead an infringing derivative work.

Moreover, there are also cases in which the unauthorized use of elements of a pre-existing copyrighted work has been held to be infringement even though the copied elements were put to an entirely different use. For example, although parody is generally held to be fair use, courts have

---

[16] 17 U.S.C. § 101 (*emphasis added.*)

distinguished parody from satire, so that parody is considered fair use but satire is not. Yet satire, by definition, makes use of a work for a purpose entirely different from the original. The purpose of a satire may be to make a reader laugh, or to criticize a social or political institution, person or event, but it is rarely, if ever, used for the same purpose as the original. Nevertheless, some courts exclude satire from "fair use" treatment, at least if the amounts and substantiality of the portions copied are significant.

Since there are many uncertainties and shades of gray in this area, a website owner or blogger would be prudent to avoid relying on "transformative fair use" as a potential defense to infringement. The safest course to follow is to proactively seek a license from the copyright owner.

WORK MANIFESTING AN "ENTIRELY DIFFERENT AESTHETIC"

Although courts have stated that the reason satire does not qualify for fair use is that it does not criticize the work itself but instead uses the work to comment on something else, there are cases where courts, emboldened by the transformative use doctrine announced in Campbell, have held that substantial portions of an artist's work may be copied into a new work even though the new work is not a commentary or criticism of the original work. In *Cariou v. Prince*, 714 F.3d 694 (2d Cir. 2013) the Second Circuit Court of Appeals held that an artist's incorporation of the entirety of another person's photograph into his painting can be a sufficiently transformative use to qualify as fair use even if the use of the photograph was not for purposes of criticism or commentary on the photograph. The court determined that the new work created "a different aesthetic" impression from that imparted by the original work, and therefore was "fair use." In so holding, the court expressly rejected the idea that the new work must either criticize or comment on the original in order to be a protected fair use.[17]

It is difficult to reconcile this decision with those of other courts that have denied fair use status to satire specifically because satire does not criticize or comment on the original work. Most satire certainly does create a different aesthetic from the original. An original work may project a somber, philosophical aesthetic. A satire of it, on the other hand, most likely will create the opposite aesthetic, i.e., humor.

It is also difficult to square the Cariou decision with the exclusive right of the author to make derivative works from his work. The artist in this case

---

[17] The original photograph was taken by Patrick Cariou. A Rastafarian was the subject of the image. Celebrated "appropriation" artist Richard Prince blurred the image a bit and crudely superimposed an electric guitar and violet ovals over the eyes and mouth of the Rastafarian in the photograph.

clearly copied substantial elements of the work and then modified it. That is exactly what it means to make a derivative work. There is nothing in the Copyright Act that requires a derivative work to have the same aesthetic as the original work. The rule now, though, at least in the second circuit, seems to be that an author has an exclusive right to make derivative works only to the extent the derivative work has the same aesthetic as the original work.

The potential significance of this ruling is not yet known. For example, how great a difference will qualify as "entirely different"? Since judges are not art experts, will the testimony of an expert witness qualified to form opinions about aesthetics be necessary in fair use cases? If experts are called in to give opinions about aesthetics, what standard relevant to copyright principles should they employ to determine whether a particular work has an "entirely different" aesthetic or only a "partially different" aesthetic?

"Judges do not share a consensus on the meaning of fair use," the Hon. Pierre Leval, writing in the *Harvard Law Review*, once observed. As a result, it has become what he described as "a disorderly basket of exceptions...."[18]

This is one reason why it is a better idea to get permission from authors, composers, artists, and recording companies before infringing their copyrights, than to take a chance on a court determining that your use of a work is fair use.

LIBRARY COPYING OF BOOKS FOR PRESERVATION OR FOR DISABLED PERSONS

A court has authorized libraries to keep copies of digitized books for preservation purposes and for the use of disabled persons.

COPYING BOOKS FOR USE IN A SEARCHABLE INDEX

Copying books to a digital format for use in a searchable index is considered sufficiently transformative to be fair use. For this reason, a court has authorized Google Books to make copies of over 30 million books without having to pay royalties to the authors.

DISPLAYING THE CONTENTS OF BOOKS IN A SEARCHABLE ONLINE INDEX

An online book search engine that copies the contents of books may publish the contents of the books online for anyone with an Internet connection to access free of charge, without either the service provider or readers having to pay a royalty to authors. A federal circuit court of appeals

---

[18] Pierre N. Leval, *Toward a Fair Use Standard,* 103 HARV. L. REV. 1105 (1990)

has decided that making the actual text of books available to everyone free of charge will not significantly reduce the market for the books. Even if it does, though, the court felt the value to consumers of being able to find and read the portions of books in which they are interested without having to purchase them outweighed the fact that it would result in depriving authors of income.

Although the court justified this ruling on the basis that it is convenient for research purposes, Google Books includes poetry, fiction and other non-informational books in its searchable/readable collection in addition to informational nonfiction books.

The court also concluded that the amount of each book that was actually re-distributed royalty-free to the public in this way was not significant. This conclusion was probably influenced by Google Book's assertions that only "a few snippets," which its website says means only "a few sentences of your search term in context," are displayed in search results. Of course, those who have used Google Books know that entire pages of a book may be displayed, not just a few sentences or "snippets." For example, a search for Allen Ginsberg's multiple-pages-long, book-length poem, Howl, returns the entire poem.

The decision has led to the anomaly that copyright law protects a lyricist's right to prevent others from publishing his lyric online, but it does not necessarily protect a poet's right to prevent others from publishing his poem online if it is in a book -- even though the poem and the song lyric may be exactly the same.

In fairness, Google Books provides a means by which the owner of the copyright in a work may request that a book be removed from the database, if desired.

THUMBNAIL IMAGES IN SEARCH RESULTS

Making and displaying thumbnail images of copyrighted photographs for a search engine's results page is a transformative use, since it transforms the purpose of the photograph from an artistic or other purpose, to serving as a website location identifier. This is considered fair use.

INLINE LINKING

Inline linking – i.e., importing a full-size image, or other content, from another website to a frame on your own website when a user clicks a link -- is not fair use. There is no transformative purpose or meaning when this procedure is used.

HARRY POTTER ENCYCLOPEDIA

Although it might seem to serve just as great a research function to fans of Harry Potter books as Google Books does for readers of fiction and poetry in general, a compendium of terms and lexicons employed in the Harry Potter series of books nevertheless has been held to be insufficiently transformative to qualify as fair use.

BIOGRAPHICAL ANCHORS

A short clip of a portion of a band's performance during a recorded television show, in the context of a biography about the band, is sufficiently transformative to be fair use. This conclusion is buttressed by the fact that such use is not likely to cause financial harm to the copyright owner of the recording of the television show. A clip of the entire performance might not be fair use of the musical work the band performed, though.

COPYING PORTIONS OF TEXTBOOKS FOR STUDENTS

Generally, use for an educational purpose is more likely to be deemed fair use than use for another purpose is. Copying and distributing large amounts of a textbook for use by students, on the other hand, is not likely to be fair use. Students are the principal market for a textbook. Making and distributing large portions of it to students decreases students' need to purchase it, thereby diminishing the market for it.

COPYING AUDIO CD'S TO MP3 FILES

Making MP3 versions of music from an audio CD is not considered transformative enough to qualify as fair use.

TRANSMITTING RADIO BROADCASTS OVER TELEPHONE LINES

Transmitting or retransmitting radio broadcasts over telephone lines is not, in itself, sufficiently transformative to qualify as fair use.

RETRANSMITTING NEWS FOOTAGE OVER TELEPHONE LINES

Retransmitting copyrighted news footage is not, in itself, a sufficiently transformative use to qualify as fair use.

COMPARATIVE ADVERTISING

Although it is a commercial use, use of a work or a portion of it in comparative advertising nevertheless is often deemed a fair use.

THE NATURE OF THE WORK

NONFICTION BOOKS

Academic, scholarly, and other factual or practical works are more likely to be subject to fair use than fiction and other kinds of creative works, but not all infringement of nonfiction works is automatically permitted as fair use. Unauthorized copying and distribution that adversely impacts the market for the work is not likely to be considered "fair use" even if the work is academic, scholarly or other nonfiction.

WORKS THAT AUTHORS SHOULD REASONABLY EXPECT PEOPLE TO COPY

Sometimes the nature of a work implies consent, or permission, to copy it. A form book is an example. Compilers of form books must reasonably expect people to use the forms. Otherwise, there would be little point to publishing them. Accordingly, copying a form from a form book for one's own personal use would probably be considered fair use.

WORKS WITH MINIMAL CREATIVITY OR ORIGINALITY

In general, it may be said that the less creativity or originality there is in the original work, the more likely that use of it is fair use.

WORKS THAT ARE DIFFICULT TO OBTAIN

Difficult or impossible to obtain works are more likely to be subject to fair use than those that are easier to obtain. Of course, this will not be true if an organization is licensed to provide copies at a reasonable cost.

PUBLISHED *VS.* UNPUBLISHED WORKS

Copying a published work is more likely to be deemed fair use than copying an unpublished work is, because the right of first publication is valuable to authors.

AMOUNT AND SUBSTANTIALITY

AMOUNT

Copying an entire work is not likely to be fair use.

A small amount of copying is more likely to be fair use than extensive copying is. On the other hand, courts consider both the quantity and the importance of the portion(s) copied.

Copying only what is needed for a permissible purpose is fair use even if a substantial portion is copied. Copying more than what is needed for a permissible purpose is not fair use.

SUBSTANTIALITY

The significance of the portion copied is as important as the amount copied. Copying the portion of a work that gives it its popular appeal and commercial success – what courts sometimes call the "heart" of the work -- is not as likely to be fair use as copying other elements of the work is.

EFFECT ON THE MARKET

The effect of the use on the market for the original work frequently is the deciding factor in "fair use" cases.

In many cases, this principle is consistent with the Supreme Court's declaration in Campbell that the transformativeness of a new work is the most important factor. The more transformative a new work is, the less likely it is to adversely affect the market for the original work. That did not happen to be the case in Campbell, but it many cases it is.

In a similar vein, the "amount and substantiality" factor often helps support a finding concerning the likely impact on the market for the original work. The smaller the amount of the original work that is copied, and the less substantial the parts copied are, the less likely the new work is to adversely affect the market for the original work.

When thinking about the impact of the new work on the market for the original work, both the actual effect of the defendant's conduct on current markets for the work and the projected effect on the market if the conduct were to become widely engaged in by others should be considered.

The effect on markets of the use of a work that is in direct competition with the copyright owner's work depends on the amount of the work used and whether the defendant's use is commercial or not. The same may be said about making a derivative work in a traditional market (e.g., making a movie based on another person's novel.) Assuming the amount of copied work is substantial and the use is commercial, the effect on the market for the owner's work is likely to be significant. Such uses are not likely to qualify as fair use.

Making a derivative work in a non-traditional market may be more likely to be fair use, but courts are not in agreement about this.

NETWORKED FILE EXCHANGE SERVICES

Because it significantly reduces the market for the original work, using the Internet to exchange copies of copyrighted works with other users is not fair use. For the same reason, providing a service that facilitates such exchanges also is not fair use.

PRESUMPTION THAT NEW WORKS MADE FOR COMMERCIAL GAIN REDUCE THE MARKET FOR THE ORIGINAL WORK

If a use is for commercial gain, then the likelihood of a harmful effect on the market(s) for the author's work is presumed. If the use is for a noncommercial purpose, then the likelihood of a harmful impact on the market(s) for the author's work must be demonstrated.

The absence of a commercial motive or commercial gain, however, does not necessitate a finding of fair use. A finding that an infringing activity adversely affects the market for the original work may prevent a finding of fair use even if the infringer did not profit from the use. For example, making digital downloads available for free on the Internet harms the copyright holders' market for their works, and therefore is not fair use.

The presumption that a commercial use adversely affects the market for the original work is rebuttable. The best way to rebut it is to show that the work competes in a different market, so that sales of the new work do not detract from sales of the original work.

Although the effect on the market for the original work is arguably the most important consideration, it is still only one of four factors that courts are to consider in every case. It is possible that, a court may hold that one or more of the other factors outweighs this consideration in a particular case.

PHOTOCOPYING BY BUSINESSES

Photocopying by a for-profit business usually is not fair use, even if the materials are only distributed internally. Similarly, systematic copying and distribution of journal articles to a business's employees is generally not fair use.

If there is a ready means to pay for the use of a work and the user is a for-profit venture, using the work without paying for it is not likely to be fair use.

For an annual fee, the Copyright Clearance Center provides a license to copy from any work that is registered with it. This can sometimes be an economical solution for businesses that intend to do a fair amount of copying and distribution of copyrighted material.

GUIDELINES FOR CLASSROOM USE

Agreements on guidelines for copying of portions of various kinds of works (e.g., books, magazines, newspapers, poems, artwork, musical works, and sound recordings) have been entered into by organizations representing authors, publishers and educators. They provide detailed guidelines about the amount of a work that may be copied, how often copying may be done, and other matters.

These agreements are probably the source of some of the myths that have grown up around "fair use," such as the notion that copying up to 10% of a work is fair use. These guidelines, though, are not binding on anyone who was not a party to them, nor are they binding on courts. Most importantly, they only apply to teachers in nonprofit educational institutions. They basically attempt to implement the provision of the Copyright Act that specifically describes making multiple copies for classroom use as a fair use of a copyrighted work. They cannot be carried over and applied in other contexts, such as Internet websites. The determination of what amount of copying will be deemed fair use in non-classroom settings depends on different kinds of considerations. It would be a serious mistake to rely on the provisions of these agreements as a basis for deciding how much of the content of another website's content you may copy and paste into yours.

ATTRIBUTION

While attributing a work to its author or creator will not guarantee the success of a "fair use" defense, it can be critical to preservation of the defense. When using copyright protected material pursuant to a claim of "fair use," always be sure to include an attribution of it to its author/creator (and to the copyright owner, if different.) Also provide a link to the source of the material, if one is available.

COPYRIGHT TROLLS

Beware of copyright trolls -- businesses that acquire rights in other people's copyrights and then monitor the Internet to find instances of infringement on the basis of which they can threaten people with lawsuits if they don't pay a state amount of money in settlement of the claim.

Copyright trolls know that even if you have a good "fair use" argument, it will probably don't want to spend a lot of time and money on litigation. The amount of the settlement demand typically less than what you could expect to expend on litigation costs, providing an incentive to pay.

LICENSES AND PERMISSIONS

Given the ambiguity of the fair use doctrine, it will usually be wiser to seek a license than to rely on a possible fair use defense. See Part 3.

KEY POINTS:

- ❖ Federal law allows certain "fair uses" of copyrighted material.
- ❖ "Fair use" is governed by statutory exemptions and a judicially-developed four-factor test.
- ❖ The four factors courts consider are:
  - the purpose and character of the use;
  - the nature of the work;
  - the amount and substantiality of the portion used; and
  - the effect of the use on the market for the work.
- ❖ Things that are usually, but not always, fair use include:
  - criticism and commentary
  - news reporting
  - teaching, scholarship and research
  - charitable nonprofit uses
  - parody
  - some highly transformative works.
- ❖ Attribute all copied works to their authors.
- ❖ When in doubt, get permission.

CHAPTER 15

The Digital Millennium Copyright Act

At common law, a person may be held liable for the wrongful conduct of another person if she aids, abets, or facilitates that conduct in some way – even if she does not personally perform the wrongful act herself. That is to say, courts allow lawsuits for contributory liability against those who hire, encourage, or help another person commit an unlawful act.

The fact that a person may be held liable for another person's communication by "facilitating" it should be a serious concern for anyone who hosts or operates a website or blog that allows users to post comments or other material to it. By providing a forum for users to publish words, images, etc. the host and/or website owner is facilitating the user's publication of those things. That puts any website that allows users to comment or upload content to the site at risk of contributory liability if a user decides to write or upload something that infringes a copyright.

Congress enacted Title II of the Digital Millennium Copyright Act ("DMCA") to ameliorate this risk. This portion of the DMCA sets out rules that are intended to balance the interests of copyright owners, on one hand, and those who provide Internet services -- ISP's, search engine services, email service providers, website hosting services, website owners, and bloggers. It does this by granting immunity from contributory liability to those providers – and only those providers – who comply with the DMCA's provisions.

One of the most important provisions is 17 U.S.C. § 512(c). It establishes a set of rules collectively known as the DMCA's "notice-and-take-down provisions." The Act provides that a service provider may not be sued for damages, and only injunctive relief may be issued against it, for copyright infringement based on the storage, at the direction of a user, of material that resides on a system or network controlled or operated by or for the service provider, if the service provider qualifies for the protections of the Act and complies with the notice-and-take-down provisions.

DMCA REQUIREMENTS

"ONLINE SERVICE PROVIDER"

The DMCA provides this immunity both to Internet Service Providers (ISP's) in the traditional sense, and also to "online service providers." Section 512 defines an online service provider as "a provider of online services or network access, or the operator of facilities therefor." There is no requirement that the service must be a paid one, so those websites and blogs that provide information or entertainment at no charge should come within the definition. A website or blog that facilitates the exchange of ideas and information by its users (sites with chat, instant message, user comments, guest bloggers, for example) arguably is providing a service to its users, whether they pay for those services or not

NO DIRECT FINANCIAL BENEFIT

To receive DMCA protection, the service provider must not receive a financial benefit directly attributable to the infringing activity. This requirement does not apply to service providers (such as companies that provide telephone lines for a transmission) that have neither the right nor the ability to control the content of a site. Because website owners and bloggers do have the ability to control content (such as by removing objectionable content), the "no financial benefit" condition *does* apply to them.

If you are running a truly noncommercial blog or website, this condition usually will not be difficult to meet.

LACK OF INITIAL KNOWLEDGE OF INFRINGING CONTENT

The DMCA will not protect you if you actually know, at the time the user posts the material, that it infringes a copyright, or if you are aware of facts and circumstances making infringing activity apparent.

In most cases, a website owner or blogger will not have foreknowledge of the infringing nature of user-provided content because website users often share material without first informing the owner what it is they plan to post. In the rare case where a user gives advance notice of what he intends to post, however, and either tells you or it is readily apparent that the content intended to be posted infringes a copyright, then the DMCA will not protect you if you then authorize him to post it.

On the other hand, even if you do not have actual advance knowledge that a particular posting will infringe a copyright, you will not be able to invoke the DMCA if you actively encouraged or solicited site visitors to post material to the site that you knew or reasonably should have known were likely to be protected by copyright. (Hint: Don't encourage visitors to your site to upload recordings of other people's music so that other visitors to your site may listen to or download them royalty-free, for example.)

DESIGNATION OF COPYRIGHT NOTIFICATIONS AGENT

To receive the immunity that the DMCA offers, you must designate an agent to receive notifications of claimed infringement. Further, you must let people know who that agent is, and where to send notices of claimed infringement.

To satisfy this requirement, you must:

1) provide the Copyright Office with the name, address, phone number, and email address of the agent, together with any other contact information the Register of Copyrights may deem appropriate; and

2) provide this information to members of the public who visit your website or blog, such as by publishing it to a page on your site that is accessible to the public.

The Register of Copyrights may require payment of a fee to file a designation of a copyright notifications agent. Filing fees are subject to change. Current fees may be found at the Copyright Office website. As of October, 2016, the basic filing fee for a designation of agent is $105. There is an additional fee of $35 for groups of ten or fewer additional name you wish to list as alternative business names or domain names.

Completed forms should be sent, along with the filing fee, to the U.S. Copyright Office.

The Copyright Office maintains a directory of designated agents from the designations filed with the Office. A copyright owner or his agent may use the Office's directory of designated agents to find the designated agent of a service provider that is hosting claimed infringing material, and may use that information to send a notification of claimed infringement to the service provider's designated agent.

There is no required form for the designation, but it must contain all information the Register of Copyright specifies. A sample form meeting those requirements is provided in Appendix IV.

Should you go to all the bother and expense of designating a copyright notifications agent? The answer, as with many things, is: It depends. If you create all the content for your website or blog yourself, and you do not allow user comments, chat, messaging, or the like, then you probably do not need to designate a copyright notifications agent. If other people do or can contribute content to your site or blog (even if it's just user comments or an occasional guest-blog) then you should consider designating a copyright notifications agent. Even if you review user content before it is posted, appointing an agent and complying with DMCA requirements can still be a good idea. It can be very difficult, if not impossible, to know if a user comment or a guest blog contains infringing content or not. If it does, then you may be liable for contributory infringement unless you have appointed a copyright notifications agent and follow all the other required DMCA procedures.

ADOPTION OF REPEAT INFRINGERS POLICY

To qualify for the DMCA immunity, you must also implement a policy of terminating the accounts (or subscriptions, as the case may be) of anyone who uses your service (website or blog) to infringe a copyright more than once.

INFORM PEOPLE OF THE REPEAT INFRINGER POLICY

You must inform subscribers and account holders about the repeat infringer policy.

ACCOMMODATION OF COPYRIGHT-PROTECTION MEASURES

To receive DMCA immunity, you must accommodate, and not interfere with, with standard technical measures that are used by copyright owners to identify or protect copyrighted works, if accommodating them does not impose substantial costs on service providers or substantial burdens your system.

PROMPT REMOVAL UPON LEARNING OF INFRINGEMENT

Even if you did not initially know that a piece of user-provided content infringed a copyright, you must promptly remove or disable access to the material when you learn that it does. If you don't, then the DMCA will not insulate you from contributory liability for publishing the content.

PROMPT REMOVAL UPON NOTIFICATION OF CLAIMED INFRINGEMENT

This condition is different from the preceding one, in that it requires removal of user-provided content that someone *claims* is infringing, irrespective of whether it actually is or not..

NOTICE-AND-TAKE-DOWN PROVISIONS

As indicated above, an online service provider must remove or disable access to material upon receiving notification of claimed infringement. The provider is bound by this requirement, however, only if the notification is valid and properly served.

REQUIREMENTS FOR AN EFFECTIVE NOTIFICATION

To be effective, a notification must:

1) be in writing;
2) be signed (physically or electronically) by a person who is authorized to act on behalf of the copyright owner;
3) identify the work in which copyright is claimed, or set out a representative list if multiple works at a single website are covered in a single notification;
4) identify the material that is claimed to be infringing or to be the subject of infringing activity information reasonably sufficient to permit the service provider to locate the material;
5) state that the complainant has a good faith belief that use of the material in the manner complained of is not authorized by the copyright owner, its agent, or the law;
6) provide the complainant's contact information, such as address, telephone number and/or email address; and
7) state that the information in the notification is accurate, and under penalty of perjury, the complaining party is either the copyright owner or authorized to act on behalf of the copyright owner.

A court is not supposed to consider a substantially defective notice when determining whether a service provider knew about infringing activity or had an awareness of facts or circumstances making infringement apparent.

Service on Website or Hosting Service?

Should DMCA copyright notifications go to the website owner's or the hosting service's notifications agent?

The answer depends on what you are trying to accomplish. If you want to preserve a claim against the website owner based on user-provided content, then serve the website owner's agent. If you want to preserve a claim against the hosting service, then serve the hosting service's agent. If you want to preserve claims against both, then serve them both.

If you want to preserve a claim against the hosting service for content the website owner himself uploaded, then you must serve the hosting service's agent.

You should be able to find contact information for the notification agent on the website or hosting service's website. If not, try searching the Copyright Office's online directory at:

http://copyright.gov/onlinesp/list/a_agents.html.

Go to WhoIs.com to determine who provides the hosting service for a website.

RESPONDING TO A NOTIFICATION

Upon receiving an effective notification, a service provider must promptly remove or disable access to the material that is claimed to be infringing or to be the subject of infringing activity. Failing to do so isn't illegal, but compliance with the requirement is necessary if an online service provider wishes to preserve the kind of immunity from contributory infringement liability that the DMCA offers.

ADDITIONAL STEPS TO AVOID LIABILITY TO CONTENT PROVIDERS

What if a website owner's (or hosting service's) removal of a user's content would violate an obligation owed to the user? For example, what if a blogger has a contract with a guess blogger to publish the guest blogger's piece for a specified period of time, but the blogger is served with a copyright infringement notification? The DMCA addresses the problem by providing that if a service provider wishes to avoid liability to a subscriber/user for removing or disabling access to the subscriber's/user's material, then upon receiving a notification, the service provider must do the following things in addition to removing the material:

1) promptly notify the subscriber that it has removed or disabled access to the subscriber's material; and
2) comply with the requirements pertaining to counter-notifications, if served with one.

DUTY TO HELP CORRECT A DEFECTIVE NOTIFICATION

Generally, a notification that does not contain all of the elements required for an effective notification of claimed copyright infringement does not give rise to any obligation on the part of a service provider to remove or disable access to material that is claimed to be infringing a copyright. And a notice that does not substantially comply with the requirements is not to be considered by a court when determining whether a service provider knew about infringing activity or had an awareness of facts or circumstances making infringement apparent.

Apparently concerned that artists, musicians and other creative types might not dig legal technicalities, Congress imposed an affirmative obligation on service providers such as website owners to help these people out with their notifications, at least when they've gotten them almost right.

Specifically, the DMCA says that if a notification contains each of these four key elements:

1) identification of the copyrighted work claimed to have been infringed (or a representative list);
2) identification of the material claimed to be infringing;
3) sufficient information to permit the service provider to locate the allegedly infringing material; and
4) statement that the complaining party has a good faith belief that use of the material in the manner complained of is not authorized by the copyright owner, its agent, or the law.

then a service provider receiving the notification must promptly try to contact the person or take other reasonable steps to help the person prepare and serve a notification that does substantially comply with the requirements. Otherwise, the attempted notification may be used as evidence against the service provider with respect to the question whether she knew about infringing activity or was aware of facts or circumstances making infringement apparent.

COUNTER-NOTIFICATIONS

Generally, a service provider may safely remove or disable access to material, if it is done in good faith response to a notification of claimed copyright infringement, or is based on facts or circumstances from which infringing activity is apparent. The user who provided the content may file a counter-notification, however, asserting that the material he provided does not, in fact, infringe a copyright.

A service provider is exempt from liability for removing or disabling access to a content provider's material only if:

1) the material was removed or access to it was disabled in good faith;
2) the material was removed or access to it disabled in response to a notification of claimed copyright infringement, or is based on facts or circumstances from which infringing activity is apparent;
3) the service provider takes reasonable steps promptly to notify the content-provider that it has removed or disabled access to it;
4) upon receipt of an effective counter-notification, the service provider promptly provides the person who served the notification of claimed copyright infringement with a copy of the counter-notification;
5) the service provider promptly informs the person who served the notification of infringement that it will replace the removed material or cease disabling access to it in 10 business days; and
6) the service provider replaces the removed material and ceases disabling access to it not less than 10, nor more than 14, business days following receipt of the counter notice, unless its designated agent first receives notice from the person who submitted the notification of claimed copyright infringement that such person has filed an action seeking a court order to restrain the content provider from engaging in infringing activity relating to the material on the service provider's system or network.

If a service provider complies with all DMCA requirements, then he will be protected both from liability to the copyright claimant and from liability to the content provider.

REQUIREMENTS FOR AN EFFECTIVE COUNTER-NOTIFICATION

To be effective, a counter-notification must substantially comply with the following requirements:

1) be in writing;
2) be signed (physically or electronically) by the subscriber;
3) be mailed or transmitted to the service provider's designated agent;
4) identify the material that has been removed or to which access has been disabled;
5) identify the location at which the material appeared before it was removed or access to it was disabled;
6) include a statement under penalty of perjury that the content provider has a good faith belief that the material was removed or disabled as a result of mistake or misidentification of the material to be removed or disabled;
7) provide the content provider's name, address and phone number; and
8) state that the content provider consents to the jurisdiction of federal district court for the judicial district in which the address is located, or if the address is outside of the United States, for any judicial district in which the service provider may be found, and that the content provider will accept service of process from the person who provided notification of claimed copyright infringement or an agent of such person.

MISREPRESENTATIONS

Knowingly making false or misleading statements of fact in a notification or counter-notification may subject you to liability for damages.

17 U.S.C. § 512 provides for a civil cause of action for the recovery of compensatory damages, including attorney fees and costs, against a person who knowingly misrepresents that material or activity is infringing.

The same statute also provides for a civil cause of action for the recovery of compensatory damages, including attorney fees and costs, against a person who knowingly misrepresents that material or activity was removed or disabled by mistake or misidentification.

Making a false statement in a DMCA notice is also perjury, and may be punished accordingly.

WORKS NOT PROTECTED BY COPYRIGHT

The DMCA only applies to works that are protected by federal copyright law. It does not apply to works that are not protected by federal copyright law, such as public domain works and sound recordings made before 1972.

INDEMNIFICATION AGREEMENT

In addition to designating a DMCA copyright notifications agent and complying with other DMCA requirements, you may want to consider requiring guest bloggers, commenters and other content contributors to agree to indemnify you for any damages, attorney fees and litigation costs if you are sued for infringement on account of content they contribute.

TERMS OF USE AND COPYRIGHT POLICY

Your website or blog should include a Terms of Use and a Copyright Policy. These should incorporate the described DMCA notice-and-take-down provisions, describe your policy of terminating the accounts or subscriptions of repeat infringers, and provide contact information for your designated copyright notifications agent. They should also advise users of their rights and responsibilities, describe your rights and responsibilities, and describe the rights and responsibilities of copyright owners, under the DMCA.

The Terms of Service is also where you would want to set out your indemnification requirement as a condition of a person's use of your website or blog.

Finally, it wouldn't be a bad idea to include a clause in your Terms of Service requiring users to post only their own thoughts and words in comments, and to refrain from violating other people's rights in their comments.

OTHER PROVISIONS OF THE DMCA

Although the notice-and-take-down provisions in Title II of the DMCA are likely to be the most relevant to you, it is useful to be aware of what the other five titles of the Act are about.

ANTI-CIRCUMVENTION

Among other things, Title I prohibits circumvention of technological measures that have been taken to prevent access to a copyrighted work. Making or selling devices or services that are marketed or primarily used to circumvent these measures is also prohibited

Exceptions exist for:

- law enforcement and government activities
- nonprofit libraries, archives and schools, but only if done for the sole purpose of determining whether they wish to obtain authorized access
- reverse engineering by a lawful owner of a copy
- .encryption research
- protection of minors
- when necessary to protect a persons' privacy
- security testing.

Tampering with or removing copyright management information is also prohibited, as is distributing copies of products that have been tampered with or had such information improperly removed from them.

Copyright management information means information about the work, the author, the copyright owner, and if applicable, the performer, writer or director of the work, as well as the terms and conditions for use of the work, and any other information as the Register of Copyrights may prescribe.

Both civil remedies and strong criminal penalties are available to enforce this provision.

COMPUTER PROGRAM COPYING DURING COMPUTER USE OR REPAIR

Title III allows the lawful owner of a copy of a program to make reproductions or adaptations during the maintenance or repair of a computer he owns or leases, or when necessary to use the program in conjunction with a computer that is owned or leased by him. The exemption only permits a copy that is made automatically when a computer is activated.

MISCELLANEOUS PROVISIONS

The remaining provisions address a wide variety of things, such as statutory exemption amendments and hull designs.

KEY POINTS:

- ❖ **The DMCA may protect website owners and bloggers from contributory liability for content posted by users and guests.**
- ❖ **The DMCA does not protect those who:**

- know or have reason to know about infringing activity and do nothing to stop it; or
- receive a direct financial benefit from the infringing activity, and have the right and ability to control it.

❖ To get the benefits of the DMCA you must:
  - promptly remove or disable access to infringing material when you learn of it;
  - promptly remove or disable access to material upon receiving notice that it is claimed to infringe a copyright;
  - designate a copyright notifications agent;
  - implement, and inform subscribers and account holders of, a policy of terminating repeat infringers; and
  - accommodate measures that copyright owners use to identify or protect copyrighted works.

❖ Following DMCA procedures also protects you from liability for removing content pursuant to a proper DMCA notice.

❖ Do not make a misrepresentation in a DMCA notice or counter-notification.

❖ Publish DMCA-compliant Terms of Service and Copyright Policy on your site.

❖ Circumventing technological copyright-protection measures is generally prohibited, subject to some exceptions.

❖ Tampering with or removing copyright management information is generally prohibited.

CHAPTER 16

Other copyright defenses

Fair Use and Public Domain are the most commonly invoked defenses to copyright infringement, but they are not the only possibilities.

INDEPENDENT CREATION

The bundle of exclusive rights a copyright owner possesses include: the rights to make and distribute copies; to publicly display it; to publicly perform it; and to make derivative works. (In the case of sound recordings, it generally does not include the right to publicly display or perform the work, but does include the right to publicly perform it digitally.) Independently creating an identical or similar work does not violate any of these rights. If two authors independently write a novel, and neither is aware of the content of the other's work, then neither is guilty of copying the other's work.

Copying does not need to be knowingly, intentionally or even consciously done in order to count as infringement for copyright purposes. The copying may occur on a subconscious level. George Harrison, for example, was successfully sued for copyright infringement on the basis that he subconsciously copied the melody of the Chiffons' song, "He's So Fine" for his song, "My Sweet Lord," without realizing it.

FIRST SALE

The copyright owner's exclusive right to distribute a particular embodiment of a work generally is exhausted upon the first sale or transfer of title to the copy. The owner of a particular copy that has been lawfully made and acquired is entitled to sell, rent or otherwise dispose of its possession without need for permission from the copyright owner. She may also display it, but only at the place where the copy is located.

The first sale doctrine does not mean that purchasing a copy of a work transfers intellectual property rights, though. Owning a copy does not give a person the right to publicly display or perform it by publishing it on a website or blog, or by broadcasting or transmitting it. Nor does it confer authority to make and distribute copies, or to make a derivative work.

The first sale doctrine only applies when ownership of a copy is transferred. It does not apply when only a transfer of possession occurs. Therefore, it does not apply to rentals and licenses.

SOFTWARE LICENSING

Most computer software is distributed through the use of licensing agreements pursuant to which the copyright holder remains the "owner" of all distributed copies. When this is the case, the "buyer" of the software is really only purchasing a license to use the copy, not the copy itself. Accordingly, the first sale doctrine does not apply.

EXCEPTION FOR SOFTWARE AND RECORDED MUSIC

There is one significant exception to the first sale doctrine. Even if he has lawfully acquired it, the owner of a copy of a computer program or a sound recording of a musical work may not rent, lease or lend it to others for commercial advantage without the copyright owner's permission.

EXCEPTIONS AND QUALIFICATIONS

You probably guessed by now that there would be an exception to the exception. You are right. There are a number of qualifications and exceptions to the rule that computer programs and sound recordings of musical works cannot be rented, leased or loaned for commercial advantage without the permission of the copyright owner even after the first sale.

First, nothing in the first sale doctrine or any exception to it prohibits the rental or lending of computer programs and sound recordings of musical works for neither direct nor indirect commercial advantage. For example, you may let a friend borrow your music CD's, so long as you do not charge for it. Remember, though, that computer software is usually only licensed, not sold. When that is the case, the first sale doctrine will not apply at all because a license does not transfer ownership. Instead, a software licensee's rights to rent or loan his copy of the program to others – even for free -- will be governed by the terms of the license agreement.

Next, the exception for sound recordings and computer programs does not apply to copies of audiovisual works. The owner of a copy of a movie on DVD may rent it to others for profit without violating copyright law.

The exception also does not apply to sound recordings of literary or other non-musical works. Accordingly, the owner of a copy of an audiobook may rent it to others for profit without violating copyright law.

Nonprofit libraries and educational institutions may loan or lease copies of sound recordings and computer programs for a noncommercial purpose.

Nonprofit schools may loan a lawfully made copy of a computer program to faculty, staff, and students, or to another nonprofit educational institution.

Nonprofit libraries may loan lawfully made copies of computer programs if a prescribed copyright warning is affixed to them.

A computer program may be rented, leased or loaned if it is embodied in a machine and if it cannot be copied during the ordinary operation or use of the machine. Thus, renting or loaning a car with computerized components to others is not copyright infringement.

Videogames (i.e., computer programs embodied in or used in conjunction with a limited purpose computer that is designed for playing video games) may be rented, leased or loaned. Computer video games, i.e., games that can be played on a general purpose computer, do not fall into this category. You may rent, lease or loan a video game for a PS3 game console, for example, but you generally may not rent, lease or loan a game that can be installed and run on a PC or other computer.

COIN-OPERATED ELECTRONIC GAMES

The owner of a lawfully made and acquired copy of an electronic audiovisual game for use in coin-operated equipment may publicly perform or display the game in coin-operated equipment. A license or permission to display or perform a work of authorship embodied in the game may be required, though, if the copyright in the work of authorship is not owned by the copyright owner of the electronic audiovisual game.

CONSENT OR LICENSE

Consent is a defense to infringement.

Consent may be express or implied. Implied consent may arise from circumstances that would lead a reasonable person to believe the copyright owner has given permission for what would otherwise be an infringing use. A book containing what the cover describes as "easy to use forms" is an example where implied consent to copy for personal use has been given.

Copying permitted by a license, of course, is not infringement.

Consent is not a defense if the use exceeds the scope of the consent given. Distributing copies of the forms in an "easy-to-use" formbook to other people, for example, exceeds the scope of the implied license to copy the forms for one's own use. Consent would not be a defense in that situation.

STATUTE OF LIMITATIONS

A copyright infringement action must be commenced within three years from the date of the last infringement. The statute of limitations is tolled if the claimant had no actual knowledge of the infringing act. Some courts require proof of fraudulent concealment on the defendant's part in order for tolling to apply. Others do not.

The statute of limitations for copyright crimes is five years.

LACHES

Equitable defenses (non-statutory, court-made defenses) are available in infringement proceedings. Laches is one of them.

Laches is similar to a statute of limitations, except it is imposed by a judge, not a legislature. Like a statute of limitations, it may bar a proceeding if the claimant waits too long to commence a legal proceeding. Unlike a statute of limitations, however, the equitable doctrine of laches leaves the question of how much time is "too long" to case-by-case determination.

To raise a laches defense, the defendant must prove three things:

1) unnecessary and unreasonable delay in commencing lawsuit;
2) reliance on the delay by the defendant;
3) causing prejudice to the defendant.

ESTOPPEL

Estoppel is another equitable defense that may be available in some cases. The elements of an estoppel defense are:

1) knowledge of a fact on the part of the claimant;
2) lack of knowledge of the fact by the defendant;
3) claimant intended the defendant to act upon his conduct, or did things that made it reasonable to believe he had that intent;
4) the alleged infringer's reliance on that conduct
5) (v) to his detriment.

ABANDONMENT

Abandonment is a defense that may be raised when a copyright claimant has done things that demonstrate an intention to surrender his rights in the work, and to allow the public to copy it.

Some examples include: placing a notice on a copy of a work that it may be freely copied; knowing failure to take action against widespread infringement; or intentionally destroying the only copy of a videotape of a live broadcast.

Prior to 1989, distributing copies of a work without the copyright notice © affixed was considered an abandonment of the copyright. Since the notice is not required for works published after March, 1989, failing to affix it to a work published after 1989 no longer serves as evidence of abandonment.

MISUSE OF COPYRIGHT

A court may deny relief to a copyright owner who has engaged in misconduct in connection with obtaining or enforcing the copyright.

There are two kinds of copyright misuse:

1) antitrust (where the claimant has violated antitrust laws)
2) use of copyright or copyright law in a way that violates the public policy of copyright law.

Some examples include:

- making false statements or misrepresentations to the Copyright Office
- making spurious threats of infringement litigation
- unfair dealing with an alleged infringer
- including a non-compete clause in a licensing agreement
- including a provision in a licensing agreement that prohibits the licensee from creating its own original creative works.

The defense does not require proof that the plaintiff's conduct caused any particular injury to the defendant. The relevant consideration is whether the plaintiff's conduct has an adverse impact on the public interest.

To be clear, misuse does not invalidate the owner's copyright. It merely precludes its enforcement during the period of misuse. If the plaintiff purges himself of the misuse, then he may once again initiate infringement lawsuits.

SOVEREIGN IMMUNITY

The general rule is that a government may not be sued without its consent. This immunity from suit is known as sovereign immunity.

Congress has specifically waived the immunity of the federal government from liability for copyright infringement. The remedies available are limited, but a copyright infringement lawsuit against the federal government may not be dismissed altogether on the basis of sovereign immunity.

The Copyright Act asserts that states may be sued for copyright infringement, too. This provision seems to be in conflict with the Eleventh Amendment, which says that states may not be sued in federal court.

FIRST AMENDMENT

The First Amendment and copyright law are not an exact fit. The First Amendment protects ideas; copyright does not.

The First Amendment is a potential defense to copyright infringement in cases where the material in question is a matter of public interest. Footage of the JFK assassination would be an example.

The scope of the First Amendment defense is limited. Only that amount of copying that is needed to convey the idea is permitted. Unnecessary copying is not protected by the First Amendment.

The First Amendment does not protect property interests. It cannot be raised as a defense to a charge of dealing in pirated goods, for example.

DEFENSES TO VICARIOUS LIABILITY

Vicarious liability is the doctrine that an employer (or principal) is responsible for the acts of employees (or agents) committed during the course and scope of the employment or agency. Infringement occurs when a person, although not directly committing an infringing act, profits from failing to stop another person's infringing activity. The classic example is where a company assigns an employee the task of establishing a website for the company; the employee publishes infringing content on it; and the employer willfully fails to do anything about it because the website is increasing sales

To establish a claim of vicarious liability against a person, it is necessary to prove that the person had:

1) the right and the ability to supervise the infringer; and
2) a direct financial interest in the infringing activity

The classic example of vicarious infringement is where an employee engages in infringing activity during the course of his employment while performing a function that is within the scope of the employment. If, for example, a company directs ones of its employees to create a website, or write a blog, for the company, then the company may be held liable for any infringing content the employee publishes to it.

Even if an activity is not one which the employer (or principal) specifically told the employee (or agent) to do, the employer (principal) may nevertheless be held vicariously liable for it if the activity is making money for the employer (principal) and the employer (principal) does nothing to stop it. In such cases, a court is likely to find that the activity was conducted during the course and within the scope of the employment (agency.)

It is a defense to vicarious liability that no employment or agency relationship existed. The fact that the employee or agent was engaged in a "frolic of his own," i.e., doing things on his own time and/or not within the scope of employment is another possible defense, if the facts support it.

The absence of any right or ability to supervise an infringer is also a defense to vicarious liability. A person who has no right or ability to supervise an alleged agent or employee does not come within the meaning of an "employer" or "principal."

An employer or principal may assert any defenses that the employee or agent may have to claim of direct infringement, whether it is fair use, the statute of limitations, or some other defense.

DEFENSES TO CONTRIBUTORY LIABILITY

Direct infringement occurs when a person engages in an act of infringement (copying, distribution, etc.) Contributory infringement occurs when a person, although not committing an infringing act, aids, abets, facilitates or encourages another person's infringing activity.

Contributory infringement does not depend on the existence of an employer-employee or principal-agent relationship. The classic example of contributory infringement is a file-sharing service that encourages users of the service to make, upload and download copies of copyrighted music for each other.

To establish a claim of contributory liability, it is necessary to prove:

1) the person knew or should have known about another person's direct infringement; and
2) the person induced or materially contributed to the infringement.

Actual knowledge of a user's infringement is not required for contributory liability if the circumstances are such that the defendant should have known about it. A person who encourages infringing uses of a product or service he is marketing "should know" that purchasers of the product or service will engage in infringing activity even if he is not actually aware of any specific acts of infringement.

On the other hand, mere knowledge of the possibility that a product or service could be used for copyright infringement purposes is not enough to establish that a person should have known it would be used for infringing purposes, if the website, product or service is capable of substantial non-infringing uses. Merely operating a website or blog that allows user comments, for example, should not expose you to contributory liability merely because it is theoretically possible that someone might use the comments section to upload infringing material instead of for making comments. Of course, if an otherwise protected hosting service or website owner learns that infringing material has been or is being published to the site, and fails to do anything about it, then she "knows or should know" about infringing activity, and therefore may be held contributorily liable if she thereafter fails to take appropriate measures to prevent it

When a claim is based on a contributory or vicarious liability theory, the claimant has the burden of proving not only that infringement occurred, but also that the additional elements that are needed to establish contributory or vicarious liability exist. Thus, in addition to any other defenses that may be available, a person's lack of knowledge or of any reason to know about infringing activity would be a defense to a claim based on contributory negligence. The fact that the defendant did nothing to induce, encourage, facilitate or contribute to the infringement would also be a defense to contributory infringement.

If you are interested in learning more about contributory and vicarious liability in the copyright context, have a look at *A & M Records, Inc. v. Napster,*

Inc., 239 F.3d 1004 (9th Cir. 2001) and *Metro-Goldwyn-Mayer Studios, Inc. v. Grokster Ltd.*, 545 U.S. 913 (9th Cir. 2005).

To build a strong defense to contributory liability, you should:

- refrain from knowingly inducing or encouraging infringing uses;
- remove infringing content promptly upon learning of it;
- ensure that your service has a substantial non-infringing purpose; and
- comply with the Digital Millennium Copyright Act. See Chapter 15.

INNOCENT INFRINGEMENT IS NOT A DEFENSE

"Innocent infringement" generally does not absolve a person of liability for infringement. Good faith, ignorance or a lack of intent to infringe, generally are not defenses to copyright infringement.

There is one situation where innocent infringement may be a complete defense to infringement, though. If the person named in the copyright notice appearing on copies of the work is not the copyright owner, then the defendant may assert the defense in an infringement action by proving that he was misled by the notice and that he used the work in good faith based on a purported transfer or license from the person named in that notice. This defense, however, is available only if:

1) the work was not registered in the name of the copyright owner before the infringement began; and
2) no document executed by the person named in the notice and showing the ownership of the copyright was recorded before the infringement began.

In all other cases, innocent infringement is not a defense.

Although it may not be a complete defense, innocent infringement may significantly impact the amount of statutory damages that may be recovered.

Failure to affix a copyright notice substantially reduces the amount of statutory damages that may be recovered – potentially to as little as $200 -- if the defendant did not have actual knowledge of the copyright. And no statutory damages at all may be recovered against an infringer of a work that was distributed without a copyright notice before 1989 unless the infringer had actual knowledge of the copyright.

The copyright notice, like registration, gives constructive notice to the entire world that the work is protected by copyright. Therefore, innocent infringement is not available as a basis for reducing the amount of recovery if the copyright notice is affixed to copies of the work. This is one reason why it is a good idea to include the copyright notice on a published work.

NONCOMMERCIAL USE IS NOT A COMPLETE DEFENSE

The fact that no profit or commercial benefit was gained is not a defense to infringement. It may reduce the amount of damages recovered, and in some situations it may help support a "fair use" defense, but it is not a stand-alone defense.

KEY POINTS:

- ❖ Other possible copyright defenses besides fair use and public domain include:
    - Independent creation (no copying)
    - First sale
    - Consent (license/permission)
    - Statute of limitations
    - Laches
    - Estoppel
    - Abandonment
    - Misuse of copyright
    - Sovereign immunity
    - First Amendment.
- ❖ Innocent (unintentional) infringement is not a defense.
- ❖ Noncommercial use is not defense.
- ❖ Lack of knowledge of another person's infringing activity is a defense to contributory infringement.
- ❖ Lack of a direct financial interest is a defense to vicarious liability.

CHAPTER 17

Strategic lawsuits against public participation

Defamation, invasion of privacy, and other kinds of lawsuits seeking damages or injunctions against people for engaging in speech activity obviously can have a severe chilling effect on the exercise of protected speech and petition rights. In some cases, these kinds of lawsuits are filed for the purpose of inhibiting citizens from exercising their political or legal rights, or to penalize them for doing so.

> The hallmark of a SLAPP suit is that it lacks merit, and is brought with the goals of obtaining an economic advantage over a citizen party by increasing the cost of litigation to the point that the citizen party's case will be weakened or abandoned, and of deterring future litigation.[19]

To deter this kind of lawsuit abuse, a number of states have enacted laws or court rules that provide special procedures and/or remedies for those who are sued for engaging in protected speech or petition activity, such as speech relating to a public official or to a matter of legitimate public concern. These laws are called "anti-SLAPP" laws. (SLAPP stands for "Strategic Lawsuits Against Public Participation.")

Section 425.16 of the California Code of Civil Procedure is an example: It provides

> A cause of action against a person arising from any act of that person in furtherance of the person's right of petition or free speech under the United States or California Constitution in connection with a public issue shall be subject to a special motion to strike, unless the court

---

[19] United States *ex rel.* Newsham v. Lockheed Missiles & Space Co., 190 F.3d 963, 970-71 (9th Cir. 1999) (*citing* Wilcox v. Superior Court, 33 Cal. Rptr. 2d 446, 449-50 (Cal. Ct. App.1994)).

determines that the plaintiff has established that there is a probability that the plaintiff will prevail on the claim.

Some anti-SLAPP statutes or rules provide for an award of attorney fees and costs to the prevailing party.

The applicable statute or court rule typically imposes a very short time frame for invoking anti-SLAPP rights after being served with a SLAPP.

Not all states have enacted anti-SLAPP laws or procedures.

KEY POINTS:

- ❖ **A SLAPP lawsuit is one that is filed for the purpose of deterring exercises of free speech rights.**
- ❖ **Some, but not all, states offer victims of SLAPP lawsuits recourse of some kind.**

PART THREE

Licenses & Contracts

CHAPTER 18

Licensing basics

COPYRIGHTS

Initially, the copyright in a work, including all rights incident to ownership of one, belongs to the creator of the work. There are three mechanisms by which a person other than the creator may acquire rights in it: license, transfer (assignment), and work-for-hire agreements.

WORKS MADE FOR HIRE

A work made for hire is one that is either:

a) created by an employee in the course of his employment; or
b) a specially commissioned work that is created pursuant to an agreement in which the parties expressly agree, in writing, that the work shall be considered a work made for hire.

Works made for hire are an exception to the rule that the copyright in a work originally belongs to the person who creates it. In the case of a work made for hire, the employer, or the person who specially commissioned the work, is considered the "author" of the work.

A work created by an employee within the course and scope of employment is automatically a work made for hire even if there is no written agreement providing for such treatment of the employee's work. In all other situations, a written work-for-hire agreement is necessary.

To be effective, a work-for-hire agreement must be in writing and signed, and it must expressly state that the parties agree the work shall be a work made for hire.

In addition to saying that it will be, the work must actually be created pursuant to the agreement. If the author/artist began creating the work before it was commissioned, then it cannot be a work made for hire. Thus, an author who creates a work before entering into an agreement with a publisher that stipulates that the work is to be classified as a "work for hire" nevertheless continues to retain ownership of the copyright regardless of what the contract says. If you want a work to be a work for hire, then you must enter into a written work-for-hire agreement before the author or artist begins creating the work.

Only certain kinds of commissioned works can be made the subject of a work-for-hire agreement. These are:

- a contribution to a collective work;
- a part of a motion picture or other audiovisual work;
- a translation;
- a supplementary work;
- a compilation;
- an instructional text;
- a test, or answer material for a test; or
- an atlas.

When a work is created pursuant to a work-for-hire agreement, the employer or person who commissioned the work is treated as the author of the work for copyright purposes. As a result, the actual creator of the work will be guilty of infringement if he copies, publicly displays, distributes, publicly performs, or makes derivative works based on it without the permission of the person who hired or commissioned him to create the work. Accordingly, a prudent author or artist who is entering into a work-for-hire agreement may want to include in the agreement a provision giving him a non-exclusive license to use the work in certain ways (such as the right to publish a copy of it on his own website, or the right to include a copy of it in his portfolio.)

Only copyright rights are acquired by virtue of a work-for-hire agreement. Trademark and other intellectual property rights are not. Specific transfers or licenses of those kinds of property need to be made expressly, if at all; they are not implied in the transfer of copyright that occurs in a work-for-hire arrangement. If you hire someone to create a logo or artwork that you want to use in connection with marketing a product or service (which may include your website or blog itself), be sure your contract covers both copyright and trademark rights.

TRANSFERS

A copyright is property. Like any other property, the owner may give or sell it to someone else. A complete transfer of ownership of a copyright during the owner's lifetime is called an "assignment." The assignee of a copyright acquires all the exclusive rights in the work that the copyright owner had.

To be valid, an assignment must be in writing. Before 1978, it could be oral or written. Beginning in 1978, however, it must be in writing or it is not valid.

The writing must be signed by the copyright owner or an authorized agent of the copyright owner.

No particular formality for the writing is required. In some cases, a check endorsement may suffice. Similarly, a written, signed confirmation of an oral assignment may suffice to satisfy the requirement. An oral assignment that is subsequently confirmed in writing is effective as of the date of the oral assignment.

In some cases, a written contract for the sale of a business may suffice even if copyrights are not explicitly mentioned, provided transfer of the copyright is clearly what was intended in the written contract. The better practice, though, is to remove any doubt by addressing the transfer of intellectual property, including copyrights, explicitly in the sales contract.

Recording an assignment is not required. Failing to do so does not affect the validity of the transfer. It is strongly recommended, however. It will help protect you from losing your copyright rights to another person to whom the copyright owner might assign rights in the same work. Recordation provides strong evidentiary support for the existence and date of the assignment.

INVOLUNTARY TRANSFERS

Since a copyright is property, a creditor may be able to seize it for the satisfaction of debts. This kind of transfer is called an involuntary transfer.

A copyright is not subject to seizure by a unit of government.

TRANSFERS BY INHERITANCE

Upon a copyright owner's death, title to the copyright passes to the heirs of her estate or, if she had a will, then to the person designated in the will. A transfer of ownership upon a copyright owner's death is called a transfer by operation of law.

LICENSES

A license is a transfer of one or more of the rights associated with a copyright (reproduction, distribution, public display, public performance, digital public performance, making of derivative works.)

Unlike a transfer of ownership, the grant of a license does not transfer title. A license only grants a person a right to use a specified property in a specified way.

The Copyright Act blurs the distinction between transfers and licenses a bit by defining both assignments and grants of exclusive licenses as "transfers of copyright ownership":

> A "transfer of copyright ownership" is an assignment, mortgage, exclusive license, or any other conveyance, alienation, or hypothecation of a copyright or of any of the exclusive rights comprised in a copyright, whether or not it is limited in time or place of effect, but not including a non-exclusive license.[20]

In copyright law, then, a grant of an exclusive license to exercise one or more of the rights of copyright ownership (distribution, performance, etc.) transfers "ownership" of that right, although it does not necessarily transfer title to the entire copyright.

The explanation for this unusual and confusing language is that Congress wanted to make it possible for exclusive licensees to avail themselves of certain legal benefits of copyright ownership that mere licensees ordinarily do not possess, such as the right to commence a lawsuit against an infringer, and the right to apply for registration of a copyright.

TERMS

The terms of a license agreement are negotiable. Any such agreement, however, should cover at least the following things:

- The specific right(s) transferred
- Exclusive vs. non-exclusive
- Duration
- Geographic scope
- Sublicensing

---

[20] 17 U.S.C. § 101 (2015.)

- Assignments and transfers
- Warranty of ownership of copyright
- Indemnification
- Payment (royalty.)

DIVISIBILITY OF COPYRIGHT RIGHTS

The rights that are bundled in a copyright -- reproduction, distribution, public display, public performance, digital transmission, making derivative works -- may be unbundled and transferred either separately or with other rights. For example, a performance right may be transferred without also transferring a right to make derivative works; reproduction and distribution rights may be transferred without also transferring the right to make derivative works; and so on.

When entering into a license agreement with a copyright owner, take care to ensure that you are acquiring all the necessary rights you need in order to use the copyrighted work in the way you intend. If you want to use copyrighted text or artwork on your website or blog, you will want to be sure the agreement specifically licenses reproduction, distribution and public display rights to you. If you want to be able to make changes to the work, you will need a license to make derivative works. If you want the right to record or broadcast a performance of the work, you will need performance rights. If you want the right to transmit a sound recording over the Internet, you will need digital transmission ("digital public performance") rights.

EXCLUSIVE VS. NON-EXCLUSIVE

A license may be exclusive or non-exclusive. A non-exclusive license is one that gives the licensee permission to use the work but does not give the licensee the right to exclude others from using the work. An exclusive license not only gives the licensee permission to use the work, but also confers the right to exclude everyone else – even the author – from using it.

A licensee of one or more exclusive rights in a copyright is an "owner" of that right, and for this reason has standing to file an infringement claim and apply for registration of the copyright.

WARRANTY AND INDEMNIFICATION

A prudent licensee will want to include a warranty of copyright ownership in the licensing agreement. This is the licensor's promise to the licensee that the licensor has the legal right to license the use of the work to the licensee. It may include an express representation that the uses authorized by the license agreement do not infringe any copyright.

An indemnification clause is one that provides that one party will pay the other for any losses incurred as a result of the indemnifying party's breach of the agreement and/or that party's breach of a warranty contained within the agreement. For example, a licensee may want to require the licensor to indemnify him in the event he is sued for copyright infringement as a result of using the copyright in a way the licensor has authorized.

THE REQUIREMENT OF A WRITING

An exclusive license must be in writing, and it must be signed by the copyright owner. An unsigned or oral exclusive license is not enforceable against the owner.

A non-exclusive license may be written or oral, unless a writing is required under the applicable contract law of a state. Even if state law does not require it, though, a written agreement is a good idea. It can help prevent misunderstandings, and it facilitates enforcement in the event of breach. It is also important in terms of protecting the licensee in the event the copyright owner transfers the copyright to someone else. A written transfer terminates all prior oral licenses. Therefore, a licensee should insist on a written license agreement.

SUBLICENSING AND TRANSFERS OF LICENSES

At common law, ownership of property entailed a right to transfer or license the use of the property to others, but a license did not. If a copyright owner assigned ownership to another person, the new owner could then transfer or license it to others. If, on the other hand, a copyright owner merely licensed a use of the copyright without transferring ownership, the licensee could not transfer or sublicense the use without the copyright owner's permission.

The Copyright Act of 1976 complicated things by defining both licenses and assignments as "transfers of ownership." There are several places in the Act where an exclusive licensee is referred to as the "owner" of the right licensed to him. The addition of this language raises a question whether the Copyright Act changed the common law rule that licenses may not be transferred or sublicensed without the licensor's permission. Some lower courts have interpreted it that way, concluding that an exclusive licensee now has all the rights of an "owner" with respect to the particular right granted to him, including the right to transfer that ownership interest to others.[21] Other courts have come to the opposite conclusion, holding that an exclusive licensee is to be treated as an owner for purposes of the authority granted by the Act to apply for registration and to file infringement suits, but is to be treated as a licensee for purposes of the common law rule that licensees may not transfer or sublicense without the owner/licensor's permission.[22]

Leading authorities and commentators on copyright law are also in disagreement about this issue.[23]

EFFECT ON OTHER RIGHTS

Copyright, trademark, and patent rights are separate and distinct things. A grant of a license to use copyright rights does not confer a license to use a trademark or patent, and vice versa. Accordingly, if a work that is the subject of a copyright license is also a trademark or the subject of a patent (as often happens in the case of computer programs), the copyright licensing agreement should address the question whether and to what extent rights in those properties are also being licensed for use.

Example: Drinking cup seller Homer wants to display Simpsons characters on his website, so he secures a copyright license permitting him to display photographs of Simpsons characters. He then proceeds to display photographs of drinking cups with Simpsons characters on them, offering these cups for sale. Under these circumstances, he might be protected from liability for copyright infringement, but he is not necessarily protected from liability for trademark infringement. Had he wanted to protect himself from both kinds of liability, then he should have secured a license of both copyright and trademark rights in the Simpsons characters.

---

[21] *See, e.g.,* Traicoff v. Digital Media, Inc., 439 F. Supp. 2d 872 (S.D. Ind. 2006)

[22] *See, e.g.,* Gardner v. Nike, Inc., 279 F.3d 774 (9th Cir. 2002); Cincom Sys. v. Novelis Corp., 581 F.3d 431 (6th Cir. 2009)

[23] *See, e.g.,* MELVILLE B. NIMMER & DAVID NIMMER, NIMMER ON COPYRIGHT 10.02[B][4][b]; WILLIAM F. PATRY, PATRY ON COPYRIGHT § 5:103 (Westlaw 2013) (calling *Gardner, supra,* "one of the most baffling copyright opinions ever" and "decision making run amok"); Alice Haemmerli, *Why Doctrine Matters: Patent and Copyright Licensing and the Meaning of Ownership in Federal Context,* 30 COLUM. J.L. & ARTS 1, 14–19 (2006); Peter H. Kang & Jia Ann Yang, Case Note, *Doctrine of Indivisibility Revived?,* 18 SANTA CLARA COMPUTER & HIGH TECH L.J. 365, 371–73 (2002); Aaron Xavier Fellmeth, *Control Without Interest: State Law of Assignment, Federal Preemption, and the Intellectual Property License,* 6 VA. J.L. & TECH. 8, 20–27 (2001); *cf.* Christopher M. Newman, *An Exclusive License Is Not an Assignment: Disentangling Divisibility and Transferability of Ownership in Copyright,* 74 La. L.R. 59-115 (2013)

Copyright is also distinct from the rights of visual artists under the Visual Artists Rights Act (VARA.) Because VARA rights are not transferable, a copyright license or assignment will not be effective to transfer them even if the agreement purports to do so. VARA rights may be waived, however, provided all requirements for a valid waiver of VARA rights are satisfied. (See Chapter 3.)

In every intellectual property licensing agreement, the specific kinds of property and rights that are and are not the subject of the agreement should be spelled out very clearly.

FINDING USAGE RIGHTS INFORMATION ONLINE

Many websites provide information about copyrights, licensing and usage rights, either in the "Terms of Use" or elsewhere on the site. If not, you can usually obtain this information by contacting the website owner.

Do not assume that the website owner owns the copyright in all the material that appears on the website. There is a good chance that she doesn't. Also do not assume that a website owner's assertions about copyright ownership are correct. Not all website owners understand how copyright law works.

USING GOOGLE TO FIND USAGE RIGHTS INFORMATION

The popular Internet search utility available at Google.com allows you to refine your search to limit the results to material with the kind of usage rights you are seeking. Here's how:

1) Go to Advanced Search, www.google.com/advanced_search
2) Enter your search criteria in the spaces provided
3) Click on "Usage Rights" at the bottom of the page.
4) A drop-down menu will offer you the following parameters: Not Filtered by License; Free to Use or Share; Free to Use or Share, Even Commercially; Free to Use Share or Modify; Free to Use Share or Modify, Even Commercially. Select the option that best suits your intended use.
5) Click on the "Advanced Search" button.
6) When the search results list comes up, follow the link to the website that you think will contain what it is you want. Check the website to find specific information about the licensing terms and conditions applicable to whatever it is that you seek to copy.

If you select "Free to Use or Share," your search results will include those works that you are permitted to use or share provided you do not modify them. If you want to be able to modify the work, then you should select "Free to Use Share or Modify."

Unless otherwise specified, a right to use or share a work does not necessarily include the right to use or share it for commercial purposes. If you wish to make commercial use of something, then you should specify "commercially" in your "Usage Rights" criteria.

When Google indicates that something is "free to use," it only means that it is royalty-free if you comply with all the terms and conditions of any applicable license agreement. It does not necessarily mean that the material is in the public domain, or that you do not need to comply with any licensing terms or conditions.

In many cases, the licensing agreement for "free to use" material requires the user to properly attribute the work to its creator and/or the copyright owner. If you fail to comply with this or any other condition set out in the licensing agreement, then you may be liable for copyright infringement. The fact that Google represented it to be "free to use," or that you thought "free to use" meant it was free from any conditions on use is not a defense.

As Google advises on its website, it only displays results based on the usage rights label a website has assigned to a particular work. It does not warrant the accuracy of the label. Whenever you use material from another website, you assume the risk that the website may not actually have a right to it.

TRADEMARKS

A truly noncommercial website owner is not likely to need a trademark license very often. In those situations where one is needed or desired for some reason, however, there are certain things that should be taken into consideration.

TERMS

A trademark agreement should include provisions addressing each of the following things:

- Whether the license is exclusive vs. non-exclusive (in most cases, it will be non-exclusive)
- Duration

- Geographic scope
- Sublicensing
- Assignments and transfers
- Warranty of ownership
- Indemnification
- Payment, which may, usually but not necessarily a royalty
- Quality control
- Genericide prevention
- Termination and enforcement.

Specifically identify the trademark(s) being licensed. If it is a registered trademark, a reference to the registration number should be included.

Unlike a copyright owner, a trademark licensor has a duty to control the quality of the goods or services offered by a licensee under the trademark. If the trademark license does not contain quality control provisions, or if the licensor does not exercise quality control, the arrangement may be deemed a "naked license." Naked licensing can have several adverse consequences, including the possibility that a court may treat the trademark as having been abandoned. On the other hand, if too much control is exercised, then the arrangement may be deemed to be a franchise agreement. This can be an undesirable result for a variety of reasons, including the additional layers of regulations to which franchising is subject.

The "genericide prevention" term is optional. "Genericide" refers to the process by which a trademark loses its distinctiveness as a brand because it comes to be used as a noun rather than as an identifier of the source or origin of goods. "Zipper" is an example. A prudent trademark owner will want to include provisions requiring the licensee to follow certain conventions designed to reduce the risk of the trademark becoming generic. Genericide clauses may require the licensee to always use the mark as an adjective rather than a noun – e.g., "Fritos brand chips" rather than "Fritos." Requiring the use of the ® or ™ symbol is also common.

AUDIOVISUAL WORKS

When using an audiovisual work on your website, you will need to consider each of the individual copyrights contained within it, not just the copyright in the audiovisual work.

In some cases, a copyright owner may have assigned the copyright to the filmmaker, or content may have been created as a work made for hire for the filmmaker. If this is the case, then you may negotiate directly with the filmmaker for a license to use both the audiovisual work and the individual component of it.

In other cases, however, a copyright owner may only have licensed the use of her work to the filmmaker. You might be able to negotiate a sublicense of the work with the filmmaker in a situation like this if his license agreement with the copyright owner permits sublicensing and the agreement is valid in the applicable jurisdiction. Otherwise, you will need to negotiate a license with the copyright owner.

WORKING WITH WEB DESIGNERS AND COPYWRITERS

If someone creates content for your website, then in the absence of an agreement otherwise, he owns the copyright in the content he creates. If he creates a graphic design, then he owns the copyright in the graphic artwork. If he writes text for the page, he owns the copyright in that text. In the absence of a valid agreement otherwise, he owns a copyright in anything he creates for the site. That means that he alone may make derivative works from these things, i.e., modify them. As a website owner, this puts your ownership of the copyright in any content you later add to the site at risk, since a person who creates a derivative work without the copyright owner's permission does not acquire a copyright in the content he contributes In fact, in the absence of an agreement otherwise, a website owner who alters or adds to content created for him by a designer would be infringing the designer's exclusive right to make derivative works from the designer's work.

To protect rights in new content, and to avoid infringement liability to the designer, a website owner should enter into a written agreement with the designer that ensures both that the owner has a right to modify the webpage and that he will be the owner of the copyright in any content he adds to the site and of any derivative works he creates using any element of the designer's work.

WORK MADE FOR HIRE

A better way for a website owner to protect her rights and reduce liability risks is to enter into a work-for-hire agreement with the designer. If the designer's work is a work made for hire for the website owner, then the website owner will automatically be the copyright owner of the content the designer creates. There will be no need for an assignment or license of rights from the designer to the website owner when this is done.

The Copyright Act only allows certain categories of creative contributions to be made the subject of a work-for-hire agreement. Illustrations and graphics a designer creates for your website would come within the "supplementary work" category. The selection and arrangement of website elements could come within the "compilation" category.

If you opt to treat the website as a collective work, then small amounts of text contributed by the designer could be considered contributions to a collective work.

Because contributed text or artwork must be "supplementary," a work-for-hire agreement is not appropriate in cases where the designer creates the entire website including all the text.

You should consider including a clause in the agreement stating that the designer/contributor warrants that the work he creates pursuant to the agreement does not infringe copyright(s) or trademark(s). An indemnification clause also would not be a bad idea.

Only copyright rights are acquired by virtue of a work-for-hire arrangement. Trademark and other intellectual property rights are not. If you hire someone to create a logo or image that you want to use in connection with marketing a product or service (which may include your website or blog itself), your contract should address both copyright and trademark ownership, rights and permissions.

ASSIGNMENT

In cases where a work-for-hire arrangement isn't feasible (such as where the designer creates most of the content for the site, not just the artwork and arrangement of the site), a similar result can be achieved by means of a written assignment of the designer's copyright(s) to the website owner. An assignment is a transfer of ownership of the copyright.

If this approach is taken, make sure that the contract is clear about what this includes – drawings, graphics, text, derivative works, compilations, etc. It would be a good idea to record the assignment with the Copyright Office.

When appropriate, be sure your contract addresses both copyright and trademark rights.

LICENSE

A third alternative would be for the designer to license his work to the webpage owner. If this approach is taken, then you should take care to make sure the agreement is very clear about:

1) the specific works in which the designer claims ownership;
2) the specific works the designer is licensing; and
3) what rights are being licensed to the website owner (reproduction, distribution, public display, public performance, the making of derivative works.)

If the designer claims ownership of elements that you may wish to modify (such as the text of one or more of the pages on the site, for example), then you will want to make sure the agreement explicitly gives you the right to create derivative works, and addresses the following issues: who will own the copyrights in derivative works and derivative works of derivative works; whether the webpage owner has a right to sublicense the right to make derivative works and who will own the copyright in derivative works created pursuant to a sublicense. Keep in mind that courts do not agree about whether sublicenses of an exclusive copyright right are valid;

As always, remember that copyright and trademark are separate and distinct rights. A copyright license is not a grant of permission to use a work, or a portion of a work, as a trademark; and a trademark assignment or license is not a grant of permission to copy, distribute, publicly display or make derivative works based on the copyright-protected elements of the mark. When appropriate, be sure your contract addresses both copyright and trademark rights.

COMBINATION OF LICENSE AND ASSIGNMENT

Ownership of a copyright gives the owner more control over a work than a license does. Accordingly, if a web designer wants to retain control over an element she creates for a website, she should retain ownership of the copyright in that element, and grant the website owner a non-exclusive license. The designer may also want to include a provision in the agreement that the website owner may only use it in connection with the website.

An agreement may provide for the assignment of some elements and the grant of a license for others. For example, a designer who might want to use drawings and graphics in the design of more than one client's website will want to retain ownership of the copyright and agree only to grant a non-exclusive license to a website owner. She may have less concern about any text she has created for the site, and may even expect the website owner to add to, or alter it, over time. The website owner will have an interest in being able to make changes to the text without acquiring special permission, in writing, from the designer each and every time he wishes to make such a change. Accordingly, it would be reasonable for an agreement to provide that the designer retains ownership of the copyrights in the drawings and graphics she creates, granting a non-exclusive license of specified rights to the website owner; and that the designer assigns ownership of the copyright in the text and compilation to the website owner.

Again, copyright and trademark rights are different things. A grant of one is not a grant of the other. If trademarks or logos are part of the deal, make sure your contract covers both copyright and trademark rights.

SAMPLE FORMS

Sample forms for securing licenses and permissions to use copyrighted material and/or a person's name, voice or likeness may be found in Appendices V and IX.

KEY POINTS:

- ❖ A work made for hire is one that is either:
  - created in the course of employment; or
  - specially commissioned.
- ❖ The copyright in a work made for hire belongs to the employer or the person who commissioned the work, not the creator of the work.
- ❖ An assignment is a transfer of ownership; a license is only a grant of the right to use property that somebody else owns.
- ❖ Any of the rights associated with a copyright may be licensed separately or together with other right(s).
- ❖ Licenses may be exclusive or non-exclusive.
- ❖ An exclusive copyright license must be in writing.
- ❖ Several different licenses may be necessary when using an audiovisual work.
- ❖ Put your agreement with any web designer or other content provider for your site in writing.
- ❖ Make sure your agreement with web designers and content providers addresses copyright ownership, both for current content and for content that may be added in the future.

CHAPTER 19

Image licensing

The information and caveats about usage rights information that were discussed in Chapter 18 also apply to images. This chapter addresses additional considerations that arise when using photographs and drawings from other websites.

GOOGLE IMAGE SEARCH

There are two ways to use Google to search for images with the kind of usage rights you are seeking:

I.

1) Go to www.google.com
2) Type in your search term
3) Press Enter or the "Google Search" button. This will bring up a list of search results.
4) Near the top of the page, you will see a list of choices (All, Images, Videos, News, Shopping, More.) If you are looking for a map, click on "More" and select Maps from the drop-down menu. Otherwise, click on one of the other categories. If you click on "All," the search results page will display a list of web pages with the search term(s) you specified. Clicking on "Images" will bring up a page of thumbnails of images that match your search criteria.
5) At the top of the thumbnails page, you will see the list of choices again. This time, click on the "Search Tools" button. This will cause a list of additional choices to be displayed (Size, Color, Type, Time, Usage Rights, and More Tools.)
6) Click on Usage Rights.

7) From the drop-down menu, select which kind of usage rights you are seeking (Reuse, Reuse with Modification, Noncommercial Reuse, Noncommercial Reuse with Modification.) This will cause a list of thumbnail images with the usage rights you specified to be displayed.

8) Click on the image you want to use.

9) Check the website to which the image links to find specific information about the licensing terms and conditions applicable to the image.

II. Alternatively, you can use Google's "Advanced Image Search" feature:

1) Go to www.google.com/advanced_image_search

2) Enter your search criteria in the spaces provided.

3) Click on "Usage Rights" at the bottom of the page.

4) A drop-down menu will offer you the following parameters: Not Filtered by License; Free to Use or Share; Free to Use or Share, Even Commercially; Free to Use Share or Modify; Free to Use Share or Modify, Even Commercially. Select the option that best suits your intended use.

5) Click on the "Advanced Search" button.

6) When the search results list comes up, click on the thumbnail of the image you want to use, and follow the link to the website on which the image appears.

7) Check the website to find specific information about the licensing terms and conditions applicable to image.

When Google indicates that something is "free to use," it only means that it is royalty-free if you comply with all the terms and conditions of any applicable license agreement. It does not necessarily mean that the image is in the public domain, or that you do not need to comply with any licensing terms or conditions. In the case of images, it is not uncommon for the licensing terms to require that you attribute the image to the creator and/or copyright owner whenever you use it. If you fail to comply with this or any other condition set out in the licensing agreement, then you may be liable for copyright infringement.

As Google advises on its website, it only displays results based on the usage rights label a website has assigned to a particular work. It does not warranty the accuracy of the label. When you use an image from another website, you assume the risk that the website may not actually have rights in the image.

IMAGE LICENSING WEBSITES

As a rule of thumb, you should always assume that an image you find online is protected by copyright, and that you will need to get permission or a license if you want to use it on your site. This includes images you locate using Google's search tools, too.

There are several websites that offer images for users to copy and publish on their own web sites. Some require the user to pay a royalty; others do not.

Popular royalty-free image sites include:

- WikiMedia Commons — http://commons.wikimedia.org
- Creative Commons — http://search.creativecommons.org
- Flickr — http://www.flickr.com/creativecommons/
- The Morgue File — http://morguefile.com
- Mashable — http://mashable.com/2009/08/04/free-blog-media/

The fact that an image is offered royalty-free does not mean that it is also free of licensing terms and conditions. Be sure to read the license agreement at such sites carefully. Failure to comply with a term of a license agreement pertaining to a copyright protected work is not merely a breach of the license agreement; it is copyright infringement.

CHOOSING THE RIGHT KIND OF LICENSE

There are many different kinds of image-licensing arrangements. Which kind is best for you depends on the kind of use you intend to make of the image.

Probably the best kind of license is one that allows you to make both commercial and noncommercial use of the image, along with the right to make modifications to the image, all without having to pay a royalty.

A license that permits both commercial and noncommercial use is desirable because it offers greater flexibility than either kind of license alone. With this kind of license, you may use the image on your website whether it is set up to make money or not.

Even if your website or blog is not currently set up to make money, there may come a day when you do want to start making some money from it. If you're using images licensed only for noncommercial use, it will then be necessary for you to replace them with images that are licensed for commercial use. That can be a major inconvenience.

Licenses that allow you to make modifications to the image have some advantages, too. With this kind of license, you will be able to crop the image and change its dimensions to fit into the spaces you've designated for it, and to get it to appear the way you want it to.

CREATIVE COMMONS

Creative Commons offers licenses for thousands of images. Here's how it works: The artist or photographer retains ownership of the copyright but has agreed to grant permission to anyone to use the image for specified purposes and on specified conditions. Most of these licenses require attribution of the image to the artist or photographer who created it. Some only allow noncommercial uses; others allow both commercial and noncommercial uses. Some allow modifications to be made to the work; others do not.

Many Creative Commons licenses contain a "share-alike" provision. This means that if you use the image, then you must offer it to others with the same terms and conditions. For example, if a royalty-free license contains a "share-alike" provision, then no licensee of it may demand the payment of a royalty from others who want to use the image.

PAY SITES

Some image licensing websites require payment for the use of their images. Getty Images, iStock, and Shutter Stock are examples.

Never use an image that you find at a pay-for-use site like Getty Images without fully complying with all payment and other licensing requirements. Some of these sites may embed tracking information in the images they offer, so that copying them without permission or without paying for them can, and often does, result in a cease-and-desist letter accompanied by a demand for payment of damages for copyright infringement. The letter may threaten to sue you unless you agree to pay a sum of money in settlement of the copyright infringement claim. You are just as liable for infringement whether you copy the image directly or you copy the image from another website that has published the image, too. If you receive this kind of letter, you should consult an attorney.

CONTACTING THE COPYRIGHT OWNER DIRECTLY

If an image you want to use is not offered with a license at one of these image banks, you can always contact the copyright owner directly for permission to use it. The fact that the owner of the copyright in an image has not listed licensing information, or has published the statement that "all rights are reserved," does not necessarily mean that she will not agree to give someone permission to use it if asked. Sometimes the artist/photographer will allow royalty-free use of the image subject only to the condition that you attribute it to its creator and provide a link to the original image.

PUBLICITY AND PRIVACY RIGHTS

Whenever an image depicts a person's likeness (a photograph or drawing of a person), you will need to consider not only the photographer's or artist's rights in the photograph or drawing, but also the rights of the subject of the photograph. Photographers' and artists' copyright and VARA rights are not co-extensive with the rights of privacy and publicity belonging to the person depicted in the work.

In many cases, a photographer or artist will secure a license (often called a "model release") from his subject. The release may authorize the photographer to do things with the photograph – copy it, distribute it, display it, edit it, use it in a compilation, etc. That agreement, however, is only between the photographer/artist and the model. A person's grant of a license to one person to use her photograph does not operate as a license of the same rights to other people, as well.

Of course, not every kind of a photograph of a person entails enforceable privacy or publicity rights. The incidental inclusion of a person's image in a newsworthy photograph may not result in liability for invasion of privacy. In general, you are more likely to be at risk of a lawsuit if you use another person's image without permission for commercial or other advantage, or in a misleading or embarrassing way. See Chapters 8 and 9 for more information about publicity and privacy rights.

For a sample model release, see Appendix V.

Trademarks

There should be no need for a trademark license if your photograph or drawing only incidentally depicts a trademark. A photograph of a store window displaying the Coca-Cola logo, for example, will generally be fair use, provided the use you are making is not likely to confuse visitors about the source, sponsorship or endorsement of a particular product or service.

On the other hand, obtaining a license can be a smart proactive measure to protect yourself from potential future claims of dilution or infringement, particularly if you think your website may someday become a commercial one. For more information about trademark licenses, see Chapter 18

KEY POINTS:

- ❖ You may be liable for copyright infringement if you copy and paste an image from another web site without a license or permission.
- ❖ The fact that an image is "free to use" may mean there is no royalty, but you must still comply with licensing terms and conditions.
- ❖ When possible, acquire images with both commercial and noncommercial usage rights.
- ❖ Creative Commons licenses typically contain "share-alike" provisions.
- ❖ You may be liable for copyright infringement if you copy and paste an image without the copyright owner's permission.
- ❖ You are likely to receive a cease-and-desist letter and demand for money damages if you use an image from a pay-site without paying for it.
- ❖ Photographs and drawings of persons may require a license of the person's publicity rights, in addition to a license from the photographer or artist

CHAPTER 20

Music licensing

When seeking a license to use a musical work or sound recording, you will need to think about what kinds of uses you want to make of it, and evaluate whether you will need a trademark license, a copyright license or both.

If you are operating a noncommercial website or blog, and you are not using a portion of a musical work or sound recording that is either identical or confusingly similar to someone's trademark, then you should not have to worry about trademark licensing. Copyright licensing should be your primary concern. The remainder of this chapter deals with copyright licensing.

KINDS OF LICENSES

There are five principal kinds of copyright licenses pertinent to musical works and sound recordings:

- Folio
- Performance
- Mechanical
- Master use
- Synchronization

A mechanical license is a license to make and distribute copies of a musical work. A master use license is a license to make and distribute copies of a sound recording. A performance license is a license to publicly perform a musical work or sound recording. A synchronization license is a license to use music in combination with another work, such as a video. A folio license is a license to publish sheet music or the tablature for a musical work.

The kind of license or licenses you need depends on the kind of use you intend to make of a song and/or a recording of it.

When determining what kinds of licenses you may need, keep in mind that a copyright in a musical work (song) is different from the copyright in a recorded performance of it.

DISPLAYING SHEET MUSIC OR LYRICS

When publishing a musical composition, it is necessary to obtain a license or permission from each person or entity owning a copyright in it.

Songwriters typically assign their copyrights to a publisher. The publisher, in return, agrees to pay a portion (usually 50%) of revenues earned to the songwriter. Alternatively, a songwriter may retain the copyright and enter into a contract under which the publisher has a right to a share of the revenues (again, usually 50 %.)

If the copyright has been assigned to a publisher, then you will need to get a license from the publisher. If the songwriter has retained ownership, then you will need to a license from the songwriter.

FOLIO LICENSE

Once you have determined who owns the copyright(s) in a song, you will need to obtain a license or permission from each copyright owner before you may publish it on your website.

A license to publish music in written form as lyrics and music notation is called a folio license. If you want to publish lyrics, sheet music or music tablature on your website, then you should negotiate with the copyright owner (or his agent) for a folio license.

PERFORMING A MUSICAL WORK

The owner of the copyright in a musical composition has the exclusive right to perform it in public. Broadcasting or streaming a performance of a song – whether it is live or pre-recorded, analog or digital, interactive or noninteractive – is a public performance of it. Therefore, unless you are broadcasting your own performance of a musical work in which you own the copyright, you will need to get permission from the owner of the copyright in the musical composition before you may broadcast or stream it

There are a few limited "fair use" exceptions to this rule. See Chapter 14.

Once you have determined that the musical work copyright owner's permission is necessary, you will need to contact the owner (or his agent) to get a license to perform it.

PERFORMING RIGHTS AGENCIES

Many songwriters and their publishers have designated a rights-management agency to handle licensing of their performance rights for them. The principal ones are:

- ASCAP (the American Society for Composers, Authors and Publishers)
- BMI (Broadcast Music Incorporated)
- SESAC (Society of European Stage Authors and Composers)
- ACMLA (Association of Composers and Publishers of Latin American Music)
- Performing Rights Society (for musical compositions)
- Phonographic Performance Ltd. (for sound recordings.)

The Performing Rights Society and Phonographic Performance Ltd. are UK-based. In the United States, the big three are ASCAP, BMI, and SESAC.

If a particular song is not in the repertory of any agency, then you will need to contact the copyright owner (usually the composer or publisher) directly.

These agencies license the right to publicly perform music, which includes Internet transmissions of performances of songs, as well as more traditional performance venues (live concerts; radio, television and cable television broadcasts; background music for bars, restaurants and retail establishments; and music-on-hold services.) They do not handle mechanical licensing, that is, licenses to make or distribute copies of musical works, or the printing of copies of the lyrics, sheet music or tablature. A performance license does not authorize you to make digital files of the performance available for download on your website, or to sell copies of a CD of the performance on your website.

A performance rights license typically does not include the right to make derivative works. A performance rights license generally does not authorize you to create your own arrangement.

Dramatic performances (such as plays, musical plays, opera and ballet scores) are not usually authorized by a license issued by one of these agencies, but a performing rights license issued by one of these agencies may permit nondramatic performances of musical works that have been used in dramatic performances.

If your website offers interactive streaming (where a user can select when to listen to a particular musical work), then you will need both a performance and a mechanical license. You may be able to get a performance rights license from ASCAP, BMI or SESAC, but they do not handle mechanical licensing.

You will also need both a performance license and a mechanical license if your website features both digital downloading (or sales of hard copies, such as CD's) and streaming (whether interactive, noninteractive, or both) of a performance of a song.

These agencies are usually not an artist's exclusive agent. Accordingly, a person seeking a license to perform a musical work may instead negotiate with the artist directly, if desired (assuming the artist owns the copyright.).

There is no compulsory license for performance rights. (A compulsory license is one that is established by law, when certain conditions are met.) A compulsory license might exist for recording and distributing copies of a musical composition, but not for performing it.

ROYALTY RATES AND TERMS

Each of the performance rights licensing agencies sets its own rates and terms. Usually, the royalty is calculated as a percentage of the licensee's revenue, but an agency may, in the alternative, offer a blanket license for an annual fee.

ASCAP

ASCAP licenses all kinds of public performances of musical works, including radio, television, and cable television broadcasts; live concert performances; public playing of CD's, cassettes, records, or digital recordings of music; and Internet streaming of musical works.

ASCAP has established a variety of different rates and terms, depending on whether performance rights are sought for audio or audiovisual transmissions; live or pre-recorded transmissions; interactive or noninteractive streaming; the size of the establishment and the potential audience; and other considerations.

Different rates apply depending on whether you intend to transmit the work through interactive streaming (where users can select which music, and when, to listen) or noninteractive streams.)

ASCAP offers a blanket license option for Internet transmissions of musical works. With a blanket license, you pay a single fee that allows you to use any song or combinations of songs in the ASCAP repertory. If your site gets less than 30,000 visits and earns revenues of less than $24,000 per year, you may qualify for a reduced annual fee. (Check their website for current rates.) In other cases, use the rate calculator on the ASCAP website to determine the amount of the royalty you will need to pay. Rates for interactive streaming are typically the greater of a percentage-of-revenue royalty calculation and a per-session royalty calculation, subject to a minimum royalty "floor."

More information about this and about rates for noninteractive streaming can be found on the ASCAP website at www.ascap.com.

BMI

BMI also has established a variety of different rates and terms for interactive and noninteractive transmissions and other public performances of musical works, depending on whether performance rights are sought for a music services site; a site that sells other things in addition to music; a business site making only incidental use of music; a nonprofit organization site; or a site that makes audiovisual transmissions of music.

More information can be found at the BMI website at www.bmi.com.

SESAC

SESAC, like the other performance rights agencies, licenses musical works for interactive or noninteractive streaming, and other kinds of public performances. The royalty rate is calculated on the basis of either aggregate tuning hours or a percentage of revenues.

More information can be found at the SESAC website at www.sesac.com.

COPYING AND DISTRIBUTING A MUSICAL WORK

Unauthorized recording and distribution of copies of a performance of a musical composition infringes a right belonging exclusively to the owner of the copyright in the musical composition: the right to make and distribute copies of the musical composition.

There is a distinction between streaming a recording of a performance of a musical work, on one hand, and making a digital file of a recording available for download, on the other. Broadcasting and noninteractive streaming of a performance of a song are considered public performances of the song. Delivering a downloadable digital file (e.g., mp3 file) is not considered a public performance. Offering digital downloads of a performance of a song would not violate the copyright owner's performance right but it may violate the copyright owner's exclusive right to make and distribute copies.

A license to record and distribute copies of a work is called a mechanical license. You usually will need a mechanical license to make and distribute downloadable copies (e.g., mp3 files) of someone else's musical composition, or to make it available on your website through interactive streaming. You will also need a public performance license if, in addition, you also broadcast or stream the recording. If your website features only digital downloading of the song, then you will only need a mechanical license, not a public performance license.

Streaming, whether interactive or noninteractive, is considered a public performance. In the case of noninteractive streaming, no copies are made, so no mechanical license is needed. Only a performance license is needed. Interactive streaming, on the other hand, does require a copy to be made, at least on the transmitter's end. This is why interactive streaming arguably requires both a performance license and a mechanical license.

Of course, if your website offers a combination of interactive and noninteractive streaming, or if it offers a combination of digital downloading and interactive and/or noninteractive streaming, then you will need both a performance license and a mechanical license.

MECHANICAL RIGHTS LICENSING

Mechanical and synchronization rights licensing generally are not handled by performing rights agencies like ASCAP, BMI and SESAC. The Harry Fox Agency is the primary agency for the management of recording rights (the right to record and distribute copies of a musical work. If you are interested in recording and distributing a musical work, you should check with the Harry Fox Agency to see if it is in their repertory.

The Harry Fox Agency can manage the mechanical licensing of a musical work to the extent your plan is to make and distribute physical copies (e.g., CD's), ringtones and/or digital downloads (e.g., mp3 files). It handles both voluntary and compulsory licenses. It does not handle performance rights.

Representative rates as of October 20, 2016:

- $0.091 per CD or permanent digital download of a song up to 5 minutes long;

- $0.0175 per minute (or fraction thereof) for a song that is more than 5 minutes long;

- $0.24 per ringtone download;
- $0.01 per interactive stream.

A small processing fee is also charged.

Licenses for physical copies are for an indefinite term; licenses for downloads, ringtones and interactive streaming are for 1-year terms. Bulk licenses for more than 10,000 streams per year are available.

Rates are subject to frequent change. Check the Harry Fox Agency website, www.harryfox.com, for current rates.

You are not required to go through the Harry Fox Agency. If you prefer, you may either negotiate with the copyright owner (or his agent) directly or invoke and comply with the requirements for a compulsory license.

COMPULSORY LICENSES

A compulsory license is a statutory license to make and distribute copies of a composer's work. It is called a "compulsory" license because it is a license that the Copyright Act automatically grants to someone who wants to record and distribute a song that somebody else has written, provided certain conditions are met. It is "compulsory" because the owner of the copyright in the musical work has no say in the matter. So long as the person desiring to make a recording of the musical work complies with all the statutory conditions, she may proceed to record and distribute her performance of it without the songwriter's (or other copyright owner's) permission.

The compulsory license only applies to the right to record and distribute copies of a recording of a musical work. There is no compulsory license for the public performance of a musical work, such as broadcasting or noninteractive streaming. A compulsory license also does not confer synchronization rights. Having a compulsory license will not give you the right to make a music video of your cover version of someone else's song.

The conditions and limitations on a compulsory license are as follows:

1) It only applies to nondramatic musical works. There is no compulsory license to make and distribute copies of a dramatic work.
2) At least one authorized recording must have been made before the recording for which a compulsory license is sought was. (This is to ensure that the person who writes a song has the first shot at exploiting it commercially.)
3) The new recording must not alter the basic melody or fundamental character of the work.

4)   Notice must be sent to the copyright owner before any copies are distributed, and not later than 30 days after the recording is made.
5)   A royalty must be paid
6)   Periodic accountings are required. (See Appendices VII and VIII.)
7)   Distribution must be to members of the public for private use only.

A compulsory license does not give you the right to make and distribute copies for use in background music systems, jukeboxes, broadcasting, or other public use. In you want to use a musical work in one of these ways, you will need to secure a license from the copyright owner or her agent.

ARRANGEMENTS

The owner of the copyright in a musical work has an exclusive right to make derivative works of his musical composition. This right belongs to the composer initially (or the employer/contractor if it is a work made for hire), but may be transferred to others. An arrangement of a musical composition is a derivative work. If the copyright owner has authorized another person to make an arrangement and retain rights to it, then you will need to obtain the arranger's permission to publish the arrangement, as well permission from the owner of the copyright in the original work.

If you wish to make and publish your own arrangement of a musical composition, you will need to get permission from the composer to make and publish a derivative work. If you wish to protect the copyright in your original arrangement of someone else's song, you will first need to secure a license from the copyright owner to make a derivative work. An unauthorized derivative work does not receive copyright protection.

If, instead of getting the composer's permission, you invoke a compulsory license, the compulsory license includes a license to make a new arrangement of the composition. The new arrangement, however, must not change the basic melody or the fundamental character of the work. A compulsory license for a musical composition does not include any greater right to make derivative works than that.

A compulsory licensee does not acquire a copyright in the arrangement unless the copyright owner expressly agrees.

DIGITAL DOWNLOADS

The Copyright Act specifies that a compulsory licensee has a right to make and distribute "phonorecords" and to make "digital phonorecord deliveries." A "phonorecord" is any physical material object in which sounds (other than audiovisual) are fixed, and from which the sound can be perceived or reproduced either directly or with the aid of a device. Thus, a compulsory license clearly would cover CD's, record albums, cassette tapes, and reel-to-reel tape recordings. The authority to make "digital phonorecord deliveries" means the authority to send recordings to people in digital format, such as mp3 files that may be downloaded from a website.

INTERACTIVE STREAMING

Compulsory licensing is only intended to apply to reproduction and distribution rights, not performance rights. Accordingly, it clearly applies to the distribution of physical copies and computer files that people can download and store on their computers or other data storage devices. And it clearly does not apply to radio and television broadcasts and noninteractive Internet transmissions. Whether it applies to interactive streaming (where a user has the power to select which song to listen to, and when) is less clear.

The compulsory license established in 17 U.S.C. § 115 only authorizes the making and distribution of "phonorecords" and "digital phonorecord deliveries." The statute defines "digital phonorecord deliveries" as:

[E]ach individual delivery of a phonorecord by digital transmission of a sound recording which results in a specifically identifiable reproduction by or for any transmission recipient of a phonorecord of that sound recording, regardless of whether the digital transmission is also a public performance of the sound recording or any nondramatic musical work embodied therein. A digital phonorecord delivery does not result from a real-time, noninteractive subscription transmission of a sound recording where no reproduction of the sound recording or the musical work embodied therein is made from the inception of the transmission through to its receipt by the transmission recipient in order to make the sound recording audible.

The code of federal regulations clarifies that the digital phonorecord may be permanent or it may be made available to the recipient for a limited period of time or for a specified number of performances; and that all phonorecords that are made for the purpose of making a digital phonorecord delivery are themselves digital phonorecord deliveries.

This doesn't really help clear things up very much.

Music industry representatives once asked the copyright board to let them know whether interactive streaming is a "digital phonorecord delivery," and therefore subject to compulsory licensing. The board declined to decide the issue, taking the position that it is a fact question, not a legal question.

Subsequently, industry stakeholders reached a settlement agreement, which was published in the Federal Register. The agreement classifies an interactive stream as an "incidental phonorecord delivery" for purposes of 17 U.S.C. §§ 115(c) (3) (C) and (D). These provisions relate to compulsory licensing of musical works for digital phonorecord delivery. Unless a court someday rules otherwise, then, it would appear that interactive streaming is subject to compulsory licensing, and the royalty rate for it is the rate applicable to "incidental phonorecord deliveries" as determined by the copyright board in a Chapter 8 proceeding.[24]

NOTICE OF INTENTION TO OBTAIN A COMPULSORY LICENSE

If you aren't using an agency, then the first step to getting a compulsory license is to serve written notice of intention to obtain a compulsory license on the owner of the copyright in the musical composition, or the copyright owner's agent. The notice must be served no later than 30 days after recording your performance, and before you distribute any copies.

You may need to conduct a copyright search and do some investigating to ascertain who the owner is. See Chapter 22.

If Copyright Office records do not identify the copyright owner(s), or do not include an address at which notice can be served, then the notice may instead be filed with the Copyright Office.

In the case of co-owners of a copyright, service on one co-owner is deemed to be service on all co-owners.

Unless the copyright owner or agent specifies a different one, the notice must contain the information indicated in the sample form set out in Appendix VI.

A separate notice must be used for each song for which you are seeking a compulsory license.

The notice must be served by mail or a reputable courier service at the last address of the copyright owner that is shown in the Copyright Office records.

If the notice is sent to the address indicated in Copyright Office records, but is returned to sender because the copyright owner is no longer at that address or has refused delivery, then the original notice must be filed with the Licensing Division of the Copyright Office along with a brief statement that

---

[24] A Chapter 8 proceeding is one that is heard and decided by the copyright board pursuant to its authority under 17 U.S.C. §§ 801 *et seq.* to set reasonable royalty rates and other terms for statutory and compulsory licenses.

the notice was sent to the last address for the copyright owner shown by the Copyright Office records but was returned. Appropriate evidence of attempted mailing may be included. No filing fee is required for a notice that is filed under these circumstances.

If the Copyright Office records do not identify the copyright owner or do not provide address information about the copyright owner, then the notice may be served by filing it with the Copyright Office, along with a filing fee. Alternatively, if you happen to know the copyright owner's address by some other means, then the notice may be served by sending it to the copyright owner at that address. If you do it this way, however, then you assume all risk that the address is correct. If you send it to an incorrect address, then the notice will not be deemed to have been properly served.

A Notice of Intention may be served by regular mail. Certified or registered mail is recommended, however, because a mailing receipt is deemed sufficient to establish the date of mailing. This can be critical in the event an issue about the timeliness of your notice is raised at some point. A reputable courier service that provides written documentation showing the first date of attempted delivery will also suffice.

As of October 20, 2016, the filing fee was $75, plus an additional $20 per group of 1 to 10 titles (or $10 per group of 1 to 100 titles, if filing electronically.) Fees are subject to change.

A notice is not deemed filed until both the notice (with all required elements included) and the filing fee(s) are received in the Copyright Office. The Copyright Office does not review notices for legal sufficiency, however.

If your notice identifies more than 50 works, the copyright owner or his agent may demand a copy of the notice and a list of the works be resubmitted in electronic format. The person seeking the license has 30 days after receiving such a demand to provide these things on magnetic disk or another acceptable medium for electronic storage of data. If the copyright owner's demand authorizes it, the list may be sent via email.

Failure to timely and properly serve a Notice of Intention forecloses the possibility of a compulsory license. If you have not obtained either a compulsory license or a voluntary (negotiated) license from the copyright owner, then making and distributing recordings of a musical composition will render you liable to the copyright owner for infringement.

ROYALTY

A royalty must be paid to a copyright owner under a compulsory license only if the copyright owner has registered his copyright in the work or he is identified as the owner in other public records maintained by the Copyright

Office. There is no compulsory license to use music unless the copyright owner is identified in a registration or some other record that has been filed with the Copyright Office.

If the copyright owner is identified in Copyright Office records, then a compulsory licensee must pay a royalty to the copyright owner, but only for any recordings that are made and distributed after Copyright Office records first identified the copyright owner.

Royalty payments must be made by the 20th day of the month following the month in which the royalty was earned,

The amount of the royalty for copies delivered before January 1, 1998 is $0.0275 or $0.005 per minute of playing time (or fraction thereof), whichever is larger.

After December 31, 1997, the royalty may be fixed by negotiated agreement between copyright owner(s) and compulsory licensee(s). The agreement may designate nonexclusive agents to negotiate, agree to, pay or receive royalty payments. The agreement may also specify in what year(s) royalty rates will be determined in a Chapter 8 proceeding. (A Chapter 8 proceeding is commenced by filing a petition with a panel of copyright royalty judges known as the Copyright Royalty Board.)

Instead of specifying that rates and terms will be as provided in a Chapter 8 proceeding, the parties (copyright owner and compulsory licensee) may enter into a voluntary agreement concerning rates and terms of royalties. If they do so, then their agreement, not the rates and terms determined in a Chapter 8 proceeding, governs the rates and terms of royalty payments.

An interested party may commence a Chapter 8 proceeding to determine reasonable royalty rates and terms of royalty payments for compulsory licenses, to go into effect no earlier than January 1 of the second year following the year the petition is filed. Except as noted above, the rates and terms determined by the copyright royalty board are binding on all copyright owners of nondramatic musical works and persons entitled to obtain a compulsory license. Interested parties may submit copies of their voluntary licensing agreements, which the judges may consider when setting reasonable rates for the future. The copyright royalty judges also establish notice and record-keeping requirements.

CURRENT ROYALTY RATE FOR PHYSICAL COPIES & PERMANENT DOWNLOADS

Royalty rates are subject to frequent change. As of October 20, 2016, the royalty rate that has been set by the Copyright Royalty Board for physical copies and permanent digital downloads of nondramatic music is $0.091 per song delivered to a user, or $0.0175 per minute of playing time or fraction thereof, whichever is larger. (A "permanent digital download" is one that may be retained, such as an mp3 file, not subject to the restrictions to which a limited download is subject.) For a ringtone, the rate is $0.24 per ringtone delivered to a user. Accordingly, unless you have entered into a different agreement with the copyright owner or his agent, you must pay a per-song royalty for cover versions of songs that you perform, record and deliver to members of the public on physical copies (e.g., CD's, cassettes, record albums) or permanent digital download files (e.g., mp3 files) as follows:

- $0.091 per song, or $0.0175 per minute (or fraction thereof), whichever is larger, for physical copies (e.g., CD's) and permanent downloads (e.g., mp3 files);
- $0.24 per ringtone.

Check with the Copyright Office for the latest rates.

CURRENT ROYALTY RATE FOR INTERACTIVE STREAMING & LIMITED DOWNLOADS

"Interactive streaming" means that a recording of a musical composition is streamed to an end user's computer or other device at his request so that he may listen to it at the time the request is made. It is also known as on-demand streaming.

A "limited download," as distinguished from a "permanent" download, is a digital transmission of a sound recording of a musical work to an end user, other than a stream, that results in a reproduction of the sound recording that may only be listened to:

a) for a period of less than 1 month, or for periods of up to 1 month if renewed, or in the case of a subscription a period of time following the end of the applicable subscription no longer than a subscription renewal period or 3 months, whichever is shorter; or

b) a specified number of times not to exceed 12 (unless the service, in lieu of retransmitting the same sound recording as another limited download, separately and upon specific request of the end user made through a live network connection, reauthorizes use of another series of 12 or fewer plays, or in the case of a subscription transmission, 12 times after the end of the applicable subscription.)

The royalty for interactive streaming and limited digital downloads involves a different set of calculations than a royalty for physical copies, permanent digital downloads and ringtones does.

Unless you have entered into a different agreement with the copyright owner or his agent, you must pay a per-song royalty for musical works that you record and deliver to members of the public via interactive streaming or limited digital download files (e.g., mp3 files) as follows:

1. Determine the gross annual revenue[25] from sales of interactive streaming and limited downloads of music, minus any revenue from activity to which the promotional royalty rate applies;
2. Apply 10.5% to the amount calculated in Step 1[26]
3. Determine the minimum royalty specified in 37 C.F.R. § 385.13.

   a. Stand-alone nonportable interactive streaming subscription services. For these, the minimum royalty is the lesser of:

   i. the aggregate amount of $0.50 per subscriber per month or

   ii. one of the following, as applicable:

   (I) If a record company is the licensee, and a third-party service has obtained from the record company the rights to make interactive streams and limited downloads of a sound recording together with the right to reproduce and distribute the musical work embodied therein, 18% of the total amount expensed by the service, including the value of any barter or other nonmonetary consideration provided by the service, for such rights, except that for licensed activity occurring on or before January 1, 2008, it is 14.53% of the amount expensed by the service for such rights for the accounting period;

   (II) If the relevant service is the licensee and has obtained from a record company the rights to make interactive streams or limited downloads of a sound recording without the right to reproduce and distribute the musical work embodied therein,

---

[25] "Revenue" includes:
   1) payments from end users for the service;
   2) any revenue received by way of sponsorship and commissions as a result of including third-party "in-stream" or "in-download" advertising as part of the transmission or download, i.e., advertising placed at the start, end, or during the transmission or download; and
   3) any revenue received by way of sponsorship and commissions as a result of placing third-party advertising on a relevant page or on any page that directly follows the page leading up to and including the interactive streaming or limited download page or any page that directly follows it.

[26] For pre-2008 transmissions, the applicable percentage is 8.5%.

22% of the total amount expensed by the service, including the value of any barter or other nonmonetary consideration provided by the service, for such sound recording rights, except that for licensed activity occurring before January 1, 2008, it is 17% of the amount expensed by the service for such sound recording rights for the accounting period.

b. Stand-alone nonportable interactive streaming or limited download subscription services. For these, the minimum royalty is the lesser of:

    i. the aggregate amount of $0.50 per subscriber per month or

    ii. one of the following, as applicable:

        (I) If a record company is the licensee, and a third-party service has obtained from the record company the rights to make interactive streams and limited downloads of a sound recording together with the right to reproduce and distribute the musical work embodied therein, 17.36% of the total amount expensed by the service, including the value of any barter or other nonmonetary consideration provided by the service, for such rights, except that for licensed activity occurring on or before January 1, 2008, it is 14.53% of the amount expensed by the service for such rights for the accounting period;

        (II) If the relevant service is the licensee and has obtained from a record company the rights to make interactive streams or limited downloads of a sound recording without the right to reproduce and distribute the musical work embodied therein, 21% of the total amount expensed by the service, including the value of any barter or other nonmonetary consideration provided by the service, for such sound recording rights, except that for licensed activity occurring January 1, 2008, it is 17% of the amount expensed by the service for such sound recording rights for the accounting period.

c. Stand-alone portable interactive streaming or limited download subscription services. The minimum royalty is the lesser of:

    i. the aggregate amount of $0.80 per subscriber per month or

    ii. one of the following, as applicable:

        (I) If a record company is the licensee, and a third-party service has obtained from the record company the rights to make interactive streams and limited downloads of a sound recording together with the right to reproduce and distribute the musical work embodied therein, 17.36% of the total amount expensed by the service, including the value of any barter or other nonmonetary consideration provided by the service, for such rights, except that for licensed activity occurring on or before January 1, 2008, it is 14.53% of the amount expensed by the service for such rights for the accounting period;

(II) If the relevant service is the licensee and has obtained from a record company the rights to make interactive streams or limited downloads of a sound recording without the right to reproduce and distribute the musical work embodied therein, 21% of the total amount expensed by the service, including the value of any barter or other nonmonetary consideration provided by the service, for such sound recording rights, except that for licensed activity occurring January 1, 2008, it is 17% of the amount expensed by the service for such sound recording rights for the accounting period.

d. Subscription services bundled with other products or services, where the subscription service is not separately priced. For these, the minimum royalty is one of the following, as applicable:

i. If a record company is the licensee, and a third-party service has obtained from the record company the rights to make interactive streams and limited downloads of a sound recording together with the right to reproduce and distribute the musical work embodied therein, 17.36% of the total amount expensed by the service, including the value of any barter or other nonmonetary consideration provided by the service, for such rights, except that for licensed activity occurring on or before January 1, 2008, it is 14.53% of the amount expensed by the service for such rights for the accounting period;

ii. If the relevant service is the licensee and has obtained from a record company the rights to make interactive streams or limited downloads of a sound recording without the right to reproduce and distribute the musical work embodied therein, 21% of the total amount expensed by the service, including the value of any barter or other nonmonetary consideration provided by the service, for such sound recording rights, except that for licensed activity occurring January 1, 2008, it is 17% of the amount expensed by the service for such sound recording rights for the accounting period.

e. Nonsubscription interactive streaming or limited download services. The minimum royalty is one of the following, as applicable:

i. If a record company is the licensee, and a third-party service has obtained from the record company the rights to make interactive streams and limited downloads of a sound recording together with the right to reproduce and distribute the musical work embodied therein, 18% of the total amount expensed by the service, including the value of any barter or other nonmonetary consideration provided by the service, for such rights, except that for licensed activity occurring on or before January 1, 2008, it is 14.53% of the amount expensed by the service for such rights for the accounting period;

ii. If the relevant service is the licensee and has obtained from a record company the rights to make interactive streams or limited downloads of a sound recording without the right to reproduce and distribute the musical work embodied therein, 22% of the total amount expensed by the service, including the value of any barter or other nonmonetary consideration provided by the service, for such sound recording rights, except that for licensed activity occurring January 1, 2008, it is 17% of the amount expensed by the service for such sound recording rights for the accounting period.

4. The greater of (2) or (3) is the "All-In Royalty"

5. Subtract any performance royalties that have been paid through other means for interactive streaming or partial downloads

6. Determine the subscriber-based royalty floor specified in 37 C.F.R. § 385.13

a. For stand-alone nonportable interactive streaming subscription services it is the aggregate amount of $0.15 per subscriber per month

b. For stand-alone nonportable interactive streaming or limited download subscription services, it is the aggregate amount of $.30 per subscriber per month

c. For stand-alone portable interactive streaming or limited download subscription services, it is the aggregate amount of $0.50 per subscriber per month.

d. For subscription services that are bundled with other products or services, where the subscription service is not separately priced, it is the aggregate of $0.25 per month for each end user who has made at least one play of a licensed work during such month

e. There is no subscriber-based royalty floor for nonsubscription interactive streaming or limited download services.

7. The greater of (5) and (6) is the "Payable Royalty Pool"

8. Calculate the per-work royalty allocation of the Payable Royalty Pool for each relevant work. This is done by dividing the Payable Royalty Pool by the total number of non-promotional plays, and then multiplying that fraction by the number of plays a particular song received. Longer songs count as more than one play. Specifically, for transmissions after October 1, 2010, the first five minutes of a song is considered a "play;" each

additional minute is 0.2 "plays." A fraction of a minute is rounded up to the next whole minute. Thus, for example, playing a six-minute song one time would count as 1.2 plays of the song; playing a 10-minute song one time would count as two plays of the song.

When computing subscriber-based royalty rates, a calendar month must be prorated in the case of an end user who was a subscriber for only a portion of the month. Months must be deducted on a prorated basis for end users who were covered by a free trial period that is subject to the promotional royalty rate, except that in the case of a bundled subscription service, subscriber-months are instead determined with respect to active subscribers. The product of the total number of subscriber-months for the accounting period and the specified number of cents per subscriber (or active subscriber, as the case may be) is to be used as the subscriber-based component of the minimum or subscriber-based royalty floor, as applicable, for the accounting period.

When streaming and/or partial downloads are bundled with other products or services, the stand-alone published price for end users of each of the other components of the bundle shall be deducted, when computing gross annual revenue from sales of interactive streaming and limited downloads of music. If there is none, then the average stand-alone published price for end users of the most closely comparable product service in the U.S. is to be used.

The licensee must maintain accounting records showing how the royalty was calculated for each work.

Royalty rates are subject to change. Check with the Copyright Office for the latest rates.

ACCOUNTING STATEMENTS

Monthly royalty payments must be accompanied by a statement of account.

A compulsory licensee must also provide the copyright owner (or his agent) with a CPA-certified annual accounting of royalties earned.

Both the monthly and the annual statements of account should be sent by registered or certified mail.

The accounting statements must contain the information specified by the Register of Copyrights. Sample accounting statements showing the information that must be included are set out in Appendices VII and VIII.

If a licensee fails to provide a monthly or annual accounting statement, the copyright owner may give written notice to the licensee that if the default is not cured within 30 days from the date of notice, the compulsory license will be automatically terminated. Thereafter, any further sale or distribution of copies for which royalties have not been made will be actionable as infringement.

LICENSING FOR INTERACTIVE STREAMS

If you plan to make interactive streams of a musical work available from your website, then you should secure both a performance license and a mechanical license.

LICENSING FOR NONINTERACTIVE STREAMS AND BROADCASTS

If you only plan to broadcast a musical work, or transmit it from your website as a noninteractive stream, then you will only need a performance license, not a mechanical license.

LICENSING FOR DIGITAL JUKEBOX, BACKGROUND MUSIC, AND COPYING AND DISTRIBUTING LYRICS AND TABLATURE

The Harry Fox Agency also handles mechanical licenses for other forms of copying and distribution, such as digital jukeboxes, digital background music, and copying and distribution of lyrics and tablature. The Agency does not handle licensing of Internet radio (noninteractive streaming); print; performance rights; master use; karaoke; or "sampling" rights.

U.S. licensing agencies generally only manage distribution within the U.S. Foreign distribution requires compliance with the laws of the foreign country in which the work is distributed.

LICENSING SOUND RECORDINGS

The preceding sections of this chapter addressed the kinds of licenses that may be needed for various kinds of uses of musical works. The copyright in a musical work and the copyright in a sound recording, however, are separate things. Sometimes the copyright in a musical work and the copyright in a sound recording of it will be held by the same person or company, but that is not always the case. Whenever you plan to make use of a recording of a song, you will need to ensure that you have proper licensing both for the sound recording and for the underlying musical work.

You will also need to consider what kinds of rights (reproduction, distribution, performance, etc.) you need for each.

PERFORMING OR TRANSMITTING SOUND RECORDINGS

The copyright in a sound recording covers the creative contributions of the people who perform on it, as well as the engineers and producers. The composer (or his assignee) has a copyright in the musical composition, but has no copyright interest in the sound recording except to the extent he also performs the song for the recording (or contributes some other creative element to the recording besides the musical composition itself.)

As part of their contract with a record company, recording artists, engineers and other contributors to the recording often agree that their contribution(s) will be work(s) made for hire, or they transfer their copyrights in the sound recording to the record company. That is not always the case, though.

The specific contours of copyright protection for sound recordings are further complicated by reason of the variety of ways Internet technologies have made it possible to share sound recordings.

To understand the rules that are in place today, some familiarity with the history of developments in Internet technology is useful.

No copyright protection for sound recordings existed before 1972. When Congress amended the Copyright Act to provide for it, the copyright in sound recordings initially was limited to an exclusive right to copy, distribute and make derivative works based on them. At first, no exclusive right to publicly perform sound recordings was established at all. This meant that radio and television broadcasters could freely play sound recordings on the air, so long as they paid a licensing fee to the owners of the copyrights in the musical works. Because the owner of a copyright in a sound recording did not have an exclusive right to perform it publicly, no licensing fee had to be paid to the sound recording copyright owner.

At the time, this made sense. Radio broadcasts were all noninteractive, i.e., listeners had to listen to what the radio station played. If they wanted the ability to listen to a particular song at any time they chose, then they had to go to a store and buy a copy of the recording. Recording artists and record companies made their money from sales of physical copies of their recordings in the form of record albums and cassette tapes. Radio broadcasters served the function of advertisers for the records and cassette tapes containing the songs they aired. Essentially, radio stations provided free advertising for record companies. Since they were getting free advertising, it made no sense for record companies and recording artists to expect to be paid a royalty.

The Internet radically changed that model, introducing many new ways of delivering music to listeners. An Internet website could be set up to operate like a traditional radio broadcasting company; or it could be set up to operate like a music store; or it could be set up to operate like a combination radio station/music store; or it could be set up to operate like a block party where everybody brings their own copies of records to play for each other; or it could be set up to operate like a trading club where people exchange copies of their records with each other; or it could be set up to operate like a pirating operation where people make unauthorized copies of records and either sell or give them away to other people.

Streaming creates an especially thorny problem. On one hand, it is like a radio broadcast because it involves the audible playing of a song, usually without leaving the end user with a physical copy that he can play anytime he wants. On the other hand, if the end user has control over the selection and timing of songs to be streamed (i.e., if it is an interactive streaming service), then it operates, in effect, like both a broadcast and a distribution of a copy of a recording.

Making songs available for interactive streaming from a website displaces the need to purchase a copy of the recording. Why buy the cow if you can get the milk for free (or for a small subscription fee)? More to the point, why pay a higher price for something if you can get it cheaper from someone who isn't including the cost of artist and record company royalties in the price?

The Digital Performance Right in Sound Recordings Act (DPRA) was enacted in 1995 in response to the recording industry's concern that Internet music sharing was displacing record sales, depriving recording artists and record companies of a fair return on their performances and investments. The solution was to create an exclusive digital performance right for the owners of copyrights in sound recordings.

The Digital Millennium Copyright Act of 1998 (DMCA) established categories for different kinds of digital transmissions, each with different associated performance rights, statutory licensing requirements, and royalty rates.

Instead of treating Internet radio stations the same as terrestrial radio stations, the DPRA and DMCA require digital transmitters to pay the owners of copyrights in sound recordings a royalty. This is true whether the website operates like a radio broadcaster (e.g., offering only noninteractive, pre-programmed streaming of broadcasts) or gives users control over the selection of music to listen to or download. Some digital transmissions of sound recordings are exempt, but most are not.

An objective of the particularized system of statutory licensing set out in the DMCA is to enable any Internet service to broadcast (perform) sound recordings digitally without needing to get permission from the owner of the copyright in the sound recording, so long as she complies with certain restrictions and pays a reasonable royalty to the owner of the copyright in the sound recording pursuant to a license mandated by statute ("statutory license.")

Congress dealt with interactive streaming a little differently. Interactive streaming tends to function more like a record sale than a radio broadcast. In the case of traditional record sales, the price paid by a record seller to a recording company, and the royalty paid by a record company to the performers, are matters that are negotiated in private contracts. Accordingly, Congress decided to leave the matter of payment for interactive streaming to the recording artists and other parties in interest to negotiate in private contracts amongst themselves, just as record sales contracts are.

Websites that make songs available for interactive streaming or downloading generally are not subject to statutory licensing. That does not mean, however, that they are permitted to infringe the exclusive right of the owner of the copyright in the sound recording to digitally perform it. What it means is that in order to avoid liability for infringement, a website offering interactive streaming or downloading of sound recordings cannot invoke a statutory license, and instead must get permission from the owners of the copyrights in the sound recordings. Unlike the royalty that is required to be paid in the case of a statutory license, the royalty is arrived at by negotiation between the copyright owner and the website owner.

If the owner of the copyright in the sound recording does not give you permission to make it available for interactive streaming or downloading, then you are out of luck. While you might be able to invoke a compulsory license to make a recording of a musical work available in these ways if you own the copyright in the recording, there is no compulsory license to make someone else's sound recording available via interactive streaming or digital downloading.

The only new exclusive right the DPRA established for owners of sound recording copyrights was the right to digitally perform (transmit) the recording. It did not give sound recording copyright owners an exclusive right to publicly perform the recording in other ways. As a result, an Internet simulcast of a terrestrial radio station broadcast of a sound recording could require a license (voluntary or statutory) from the owner of the copyright in the sound recording, even though the terrestrial radio station broadcast does not. (A terrestrial radio station broadcast is not a digital performance.) To address this anomaly, and to achieve a number of other objectives, Congress enacted a number of exemptions from liability for various kinds of things that would otherwise infringe the copyright in a sound recording.

EXCEPTIONS AND EXEMPTIONS

PRE-1972 RECORDINGS

Although copyright protection for musical compositions existed before then, there is no federal copyright protection for sound recordings that were first fixed in a tangible medium before February 15, 1972. As a result, unauthorized reproduction, distribution or transmission of a sound recording that was made before February 15, 1972, although possibly resulting in liability to the owner of the copyright in the musical work, will not result in copyright infringement liability to the owner of the copyright in the sound recording.

Sound recordings fixed in a tangible medium before February 15, 1972 may receive copyright protection under state statutes or common law, however. Federal preemption of state laws granting copyright or copyright-like protection to sound recordings does not begin until February 15, 2067. Consequently, state statutory and common law causes of action for violations of copyright (or copyright-like rights) in pre-February 15, 1972 sound recordings may be pursued against a person who makes an unauthorized use of the sound recording, even though federal copyright remedies are not available.

An example of such a state law is California Civil Code § 980(a) (2). It provides that "[t]he author of an original work of authorship consisting of a sound recording initially fixed prior to February 15, 1972, has an exclusive ownership therein until February 15, 2047, as against all persons except one who independently makes or duplicates another sound recording that does not directly or indirectly recapture the actual sounds fixed in such prior recording, but consists entirely of an independent fixation of other sounds, even though such sounds imitate or simulate the sounds contained in the prior sound recording." New York courts have established a similar rule as part of the common law of that state.

MIMICKING PERFORMANCES

Only digital transmission, the making and/or distribution of copies, and the making of derivative works from the sound recording itself are infringements of a copyright in a sound recording. Imitating a band's performance of a song is not infringement of the sound recording of the band's performance of the song.

A cover band, for example, may perform its own version of a song that it heard being played on a sound recording, and it may even go to great lengths to create a sound that is nearly identical to the sound captured on a previous recording of a song, and this would not be violating the rights of the owner of the copyright in the sound recording. Only actual copying of the sound recording itself (such as by recording the recording itself (or parts of it), or copying and pasting the code from a digital file containing the sound recording) counts as infringement of the copyright in a sound recording.

There might be liability for infringement to the owner of the copyright in the musical work, but new recordings of new performances of a song do not violate the rights of the owner of a sound recording copyright.

LIVE PERFORMANCES

Unrecorded live performances do not receive copyright protection. Only works that are fixed in a tangible medium do.

Congress has established an important exception to this rule, however. If a live performance is being recorded at the same time that it is being transmitted, then the performance is deemed to have been fixed in a tangible medium at the time the transmission was made. This means, for example, that if a band's live performance is being recorded (by you or somebody else) at the time you simulcast it from your website, then you may be guilty of copyright infringement unless a statutory exemption or some other defense is available to you.

Of course, if the musical work that is being performed live has already been fixed in a tangible medium (e.g., sheet music, digital file, recording tape, etc.), then recording or simulcasting a performance of it without permission could infringe the copyright in the musical work. And an unauthorized, non-exempt transmission of someone else's recording of the live performance would infringe the copyright in the sound recording of the performance.

Even if a recording of a live performance does not infringe a copyright, an anti-bootlegging statute imposes both civil and criminal penalties for unauthorized recordings of live musical performances.

ANALOG TRANSMISSIONS

The federal copyright act does not give the owner of the sound recording copyright an exclusive right to broadcast it by means of analog transmission.

RADIO BROADCASTS

An exemption exists for performances of sound recordings by means of noninteractive digital audio transmission as part of a nonsubscription broadcast transmission. A "broadcast transmission" has been interpreted to refer only to terrestrial radio stations licensed as such by the FCC, so this exemption does not apply to Internet radio stations and webcasters. *Bonneville International Corp. v. Peters*, 153 F.Supp.2d 763 (E.D. Pa. 2001), *aff'd*, 347 F.3d 485 (3d Cir. 2003.) The purpose of this exemption is to allow non-Internet, nonsubscription radio stations that do not broadcast via satellite to broadcast sound recordings even if the sound recording they use is in a digital format.

RETRANSMISSIONS OF RADIO BROADCASTS

Retransmission of a nonsubscription, noninteractive radio broadcast of a sound recording is not an infringement of the copyright in the sound recording in any of the following situations:

- the radio station's broadcast is not wilfully or repeatedly retransmitted more than a radius of 150 miles from the site of the radio broadcast transmitter (or, in the case of a subscription retransmission of a nonsubscription broadcast retransmission, 150 miles from the site of the broadcast retransmitter.) The 150-mile limitation does not apply when a nonsubscription broadcast transmission by a radio station is retransmitted on a nonsubscription basis by a terrestrial broadcast station, terrestrial translator, or terrestrial repeater licensed by the FCC. (Note: In 2015, the Copyright Office interpreted this exemption as being inapplicable to retransmissions over the Internet. Therefore, be wary of claims that "geo-fencing" Internet retransmissions of radio broadcasts in a 150-mile radius can be used to avoid exposure to liability for copyright infringement.)
- the retransmission is of radio station broadcast transmissions that are obtained by the retransmitter over the air; not electronically processed by the retransmitter to deliver separate and discrete signals; and retransmitted only within the local communities served by the retransmitter.
- the radio station's broadcast transmission was being retransmitted to cable systems by a satellite carrier on January 1, 1995, and that retransmission was being retransmitted by cable systems as a separate and discrete signal, and the satellite carrier obtains the radio station's broadcast transmission in an analog format, so long as the broadcast transmission being retransmitted embodies the programming of no more than one radio station.

- the radio station's broadcast transmission is made by a noncommercial educational broadcast station, consists solely of noncommercial educational and cultural radio programs, and the retransmission is a nonsubscription terrestrial broadcast retransmission

TRANSMISSIONS TO A BUSINESS ESTABLISHMENT THAT DO NOT EXCEED THE SOUND RECORDING PERFORMANCE COMPLEMENT

The performance of a sound recording by means of noninteractive digital audio transmission is not an infringement of the copyright in the sound recording if the transmission is to a business establishment for use in the ordinary course of its business, provided the business recipient does not retransmit the transmission outside of its premises or the immediately surrounding vicinity, and that the transmission does not exceed the sound recording performance complement.

The "sound recording performance complement" is the transmission during any 3-hour period, on a particular channel used by a transmitting entity, of no more than:

a)   3 different selections of sound recordings from any one phonorecord lawfully distributed for public performance or sale in the United States, if no more than 2 such selections are transmitted consecutively; or

b)   4 different selections of sound recordings by the same featured recording artist, or from any set or compilation of phonorecords lawfully distributed together as a unit for public performance or sale in the United States, if no more than three such selections are transmitted consecutively.

TRANSMISSIONS WITHIN A BUSINESS ESTABLISHMENT

The performance of a sound recording by means of noninteractive digital audio transmission is not an infringement of the copyright in the sound recording if the transmission is within a business establishment, confined to its premises or the immediately surrounding vicinity.

RETRANSMISSIONS AUTHORIZED BY A LICENSED TRANSMITTER

The performance of a sound recording by means of noninteractive digital audio transmission is not an infringement of the copyright in the sound recording if the transmission is a retransmission, including a multichannel video programming distributor, of a transmission by a transmitter licensed to publicly perform the sound recording as part of that transmission, if the retransmission is simultaneous with the licensed transmission and authorized by the transmitter.

SIMULTANEOUS REETRANSMISSIONS TO LICENSED INTERACTIVE SERVICE USERS

A retransmission of a digital audio transmission is not an infringement of the copyright in the sound recording if:

1) the retransmission is of a transmission by an interactive service licensed to transmit the sound recording to a particular member of the public as part of that transmission; and
2) the retransmission is simultaneous with the licensed transmission, authorized by the transmitter, and limited to that particular member of the public intended by the interactive service to be the recipient of the transmission.

TRANSMISSIONS INCIDENTAL TO EXEMPT TRANSMISSIONS

A transmission of a sound recording by means of noninteractive digital audio transmission is not an infringement of the copyright in the sound recording if it is a transmission incidental to an exempt transmission occurring either before or simultaneously with the exempt transmission, such as a feed received by and then retransmitted by an exempt transmitter, so long as such incidental transmission does not include any subscription transmission directly for reception by members of the public.

SOUND RECORDINGS THAT ARE IN THE PUBLIC DOMAIN

Of course, a sound recording that is in the public domain is not protected by copyright. Since the copyrights in musical works and sound recordings of them are separate and distinct things, however, the fact that one is in the public domain does not necessarily mean that the other is. For more information about what is in the public domain, see Chapter 13

NO LESS FAVORABLE TERMS THAN AFFILIATED ENTITIES

When negotiating a licensing contract for noninteractive transmission of a sound recording, check to see if an affiliated entity has a license to digitally transmit the recording. If an affiliated entity has a license to digitally transmit the recording, then the sound recording copyright owner must make a license available to all bona fide entities that offer similar services, on no less favorable terms.

An "affiliated entity" is an entity that engages in noninteractive transmissions and in which the sound recording copyright licensor has a direct or indirect ownership or partnership interest of 5 percent or more of the outstanding voting or non-voting stock.

The "no less favorable terms" requirement does not apply to licenses for interactive streaming.

Also, the sound recording copyright owner is not required to offer "no less favorable terms" for promotional transmissions of up to 45 seconds of the sound recording.

Finally, the sound recording copyright owner may establish different terms and conditions if there are material differences in the scope of the license you are requesting with respect to the type of service, the particular sound recordings licensed, the frequency of use, the number of subscribers served, or the duration.

STATUTORY LICENSES

Congress has provided, in the Copyright Act, licenses to use certain kinds of copyrighted material, under terms and conditions set out in the statute. These are called statutory licenses because they are provided for by statute; they are not dependent upon obtaining the consent of the owner of the copyright in the sound recording.

The public performance of a non-exempt sound recording by means of a noninteractive subscription digital audio transmission that is made by a preexisting satellite digital audio radio service is subject to statutory licensing provided the transmitting service does not automatically and intentionally cause any device receiving the transmission to switch from one program channel to another. If feasible, the transmission must be accompanied by any information encoded in the recording by or under the authority of the copyright owner of the sound recording that identifies the title, the name of the recording artist, and information about the composer.

In the case of a non-exempt subscription transmission that is made by a preexisting subscription service in the same transmission medium that was used by such service on July 31, 1998, or in the case of a non-exempt transmission that is made by a preexisting satellite digital audio radio service, the transmission is subject to statutory licensing if:

1) the transmission does not exceed the sound recording performance complement; and

2) the transmitting entity does not cause to be published by means of an advance program schedule or prior announcement the titles of the specific sound recordings or phonorecords embodying such sound recordings to be transmitted.

The "sound recording performance complement" is the transmission during any 3-hour period, on a particular channel used by a transmitting entity, of no more than:

a) 3 different selections of sound recordings from any one phonorecord lawfully distributed for public performance or sale in the United States, if no more than 2 such selections are transmitted consecutively; or

b) 4 different selections of sound recordings by the same featured recording artist, or from any set or compilation of phonorecords lawfully distributed together as a unit for public performance or sale in the United States, if no more than three such selections are transmitted consecutively.

The transmission of selections in excess of the numerical limits from multiple phonorecords nevertheless qualifies as a sound recording performance complement if the programming of the multiple phonorecords was not willfully intended to avoid the prescribed numerical limits.

In the case of a non-exempt, noninteractive, nonsubscription, digital transmission by a service the primary purpose of which is to sell or promote music-related products, services or events, or in the case of a non-exempt, noninteractive, subscription, digital transmission that is made by a new subscription service, or by a preexisting subscription service other than in the same transmission medium that was used by such service on July 31, 1998, the transmission is subject to statutory licensing if:

1) the transmission does not exceed the sound recording performance complement, except that this requirement does not apply in the case of a retransmission of a broadcast transmission if the retransmission is made by a transmitting entity that does not have the right or ability to control the programming of the broadcast station making the broadcast transmission, unless:

    a) the broadcast station makes broadcast transmissions

        i) in digital format that regularly exceed the sound recording performance complement, or

    ii) in analog format, a substantial portion of which, on a weekly basis, exceed the sound recording performance complement; and

    b) the sound recording copyright owner or its representative has notified the transmitting entity in writing that broadcast transmissions of the copyright owner's sound recordings exceed the sound recording performance complement;

2) the transmitting entity does not cause to be published, or induce or facilitate the publication, by means of an advance program schedule or prior announcement, the titles of the specific sound recordings to be transmitted, the phonorecords embodying such sound recordings, or, other than for illustrative purposes, the names of the featured recording artists, except that a transmitting entity may make a prior announcement that a particular artist will be featured within an unspecified future time period, and in the case of a retransmission of a broadcast transmission by a transmitting entity that does not have the right or ability to control the programming of the broadcast transmission, the requirement of this clause shall not apply to a prior oral announcement by the broadcast station, or to an advance program schedule published, induced, or facilitated by the broadcast station, if the transmitting entity does not have actual knowledge and has not received written notice from the copyright owner or its representative that the broadcast station publishes or induces or facilitates the publication of such advance program schedule, or if such advance program schedule is a schedule of classical music programming published by the broadcast station in the same manner as published by that broadcast station on or before September 30, 1998;

3) the transmission:

    a) is not part of an archived program of less than 5 hours duration;

    b) is not part of an archived program of 5 hours or greater in duration that is made available for a period exceeding 2 weeks;

    c) is not part of a continuous program which is of less than 3 hours duration, or

    d) is not part of an identifiable program in which performances of sound recordings are rendered in a predetermined order, other than an archived or continuous program, that is transmitted at:

        i) more than 3 times in any 2-week period that have been publicly announced in advance, in the case of a program of less than 1 hour in duration, or

        ii) more than 4 times in any 2-week period that have been publicly announced in advance, in the case of a program of 1 hour or more in duration, except that the requirement of this subclause shall not apply in the case of a retransmission of a broadcast transmission by a transmitting entity that does not have the right or ability to control the programming of the broadcast transmission, unless the transmitting entity is given notice in writing by the copyright owner of the sound recording that the broadcast station makes broadcast transmissions that regularly violate such requirement;

4) the transmitting entity does not knowingly perform the sound recording, as part of a service that offers transmissions of visual images contemporaneously with transmissions of sound recordings, in a manner that is likely to cause confusion, to cause mistake, or to deceive, as to the affiliation, connection, or association of the copyright owner or featured recording artist with the transmitting entity or a particular product or service advertised by the transmitting entity, or as to the origin, sponsorship, or approval by the copyright owner or featured recording artist of the activities of the transmitting entity other than the performance of the sound recording itself;

5) the transmitting entity cooperates to prevent, to the extent feasible without imposing substantial costs or burdens, a transmission recipient or any other person or entity from automatically scanning the transmitting entity's transmissions alone or together with transmissions by other transmitting entities in order to select a particular sound recording to be transmitted to the transmission recipient, except that the requirement of this clause shall not apply to a satellite digital audio service that is in operation, or that is licensed by the Federal Communications Commission, on or before July 31, 1998;

6) the transmitting entity takes no affirmative steps to cause or induce the making of a copy by the transmission recipient, and if the technology used by the transmitting entity enables the transmitting entity to limit the making by the transmission recipient of copies of the transmission directly in a digital format, the transmitting entity sets such technology to limit such making of copies to the extent permitted by such technology;

7) phonorecords of the sound recording have been distributed to the public under the authority of the copyright owner or the copyright owner authorizes the transmitting entity to transmit the sound recording, and the transmitting entity makes the transmission from a phonorecord lawfully made under the authority of the copyright owner, except that the requirement of this clause does not apply to a retransmission of a broadcast transmission by a transmitting entity that does not have the right or ability to control the programming of the broadcast transmission, unless the transmitting entity is given notice in writing by the copyright owner of the sound recording that the broadcast station makes broadcast transmissions that regularly violate such requirement;

8) the transmitting entity accommodates and does not interfere with the transmission of technical measures that are widely used by sound recording copyright owners to identify or protect copyrighted works, and that are technically feasible of being transmitted by the transmitting entity without imposing substantial costs on the transmitting entity or resulting in perceptible aural or visual degradation of the digital signal, except that the requirement of this clause does not apply to a satellite digital audio service that is in operation, or that is licensed under the authority of the Federal Communications Commission, on or before July 31, 1998, to the extent that such service has designed, developed, or made commitments to procure equipment or technology that is not compatible with such technical measures before such technical measures are widely adopted by sound recording copyright owners; and

9) the transmitting entity identifies in textual data the sound recording during, but not before, the time it is performed, including the title of the sound recording, the title of the phonorecord embodying such sound recording, if any, and the featured recording artist, in a manner to permit it to be displayed to the transmission recipient by the device or technology intended for receiving the service provided by the transmitting entity, except that the obligation in this clause shall not apply in the case of a retransmission of a broadcast transmission by a transmitting entity that does not have the right or ability to control the programming of the broadcast transmission, or in the case in which devices or technology intended for receiving the service provided by the transmitting entity that have the capability to display such textual data are not common in the marketplace.

17 U.S.C. § 112 also provides a statutory license to make ephemeral copies as needed, in connection with the process of making transmissions that are subject to statutory licensing.

ROYALTIES FOR STATUTORY LICENSES

The Copyright Royalty Board sets rates for performances of sound recordings pursuant to a statutory license. License agreements voluntarily negotiated at any time between copyright owner(s) of sound recordings and entity (ies) performing sound recordings will be given effect in lieu of any decision by the Librarian of Congress or the Board., however.

The copyright royalty also establish requirements by which copyright owners are to receive reasonable notice of the use of their sound recordings, and record-keeping requirements for entities performing sound recordings.

A person wishing to perform a sound recording publicly by means of a transmission that is eligible for statutory licensing may do so without infringing the right of the copyright owner of the sound recording by:

a) complying with notice requirements established by the copyright royalty board, and paying royalties; or

b) if royalty amounts have not been set yet, then by agreeing to pay such royalties as are determined in accordance with federal copyright regulations, or by the copyright royalty judges in furtherance of those regulations.

The receiving agent (person or entity that receives license payments for copyright owners) may enter into agreements for the reproduction and performance of sound recordings by any one or more commercial webcasters or noncommercial webcasters for a period of not more than 11 years. Once published in the Federal Register, the agreement becomes binding on all copyright owners of sound recordings and other persons entitled to payment, in lieu of any determination by the copyright royalty judges. Any such agreement for commercial webcasters may include provisions for payment of royalties on the basis of a percentage of revenue or expenses, or both, and include a minimum fee. The agreement may include other provisions, too, such as requirements by which copyright owners may receive notice of the use of their sound recordings. Thereafter, the terms of such agreement shall be available, as an option, to any commercial webcaster or noncommercial webcaster meeting the eligibility conditions of the agreement.

When a statutory license does not exist, a recording artist who performs on a sound recording must be paid by the copyright owner of the sound recording that has been licensed for transmission, in accordance with the terms of the contract between the recording artist and the owner of the copyright in the sound recording.

An agent designated to distribute receipts from a statutory license must distribute them, after costs, as follows:

- 50% to the copyright owner of the exclusive right to publicly perform a sound recording by means of a digital audio transmission;
- 2.5% to nonfeatured musicians who performed on the sound recording;
- 2.5% to nonfeatured vocalists who performed on the sound recording;
- 45% to the recording artist(s) featured on the sound recording.

Royalties collected under a Section 112 statutory license to make ephemeral copies are distributed directly to the owner of the copyright in the sound recording.

The royalties to be paid pursuant to a statutory license may not be used as a basis for reducing the amount of any royalty payable to the owner of the copyright in the underlying musical work.

SOUNDEXCHANGE

SoundExchange is a sound recording performance rights administrator that collects and disburses statutory license royalty payments from digital transmitters to record companies and recording artists.

SoundExchange only manages licensing of noninteractive streaming of sound recordings. It does not handle licensing for interactive streaming or digital downloads.

SoundExchange also does not manage royalties payable to the owners of copyrights in the musical works.

Performing rights agencies like ASCAP, BMI and SESAC, and mechanical licensing agencies like Harry Fox generally only manage the rights of the owners of copyrights in musical works – usually, songwriters or their publishers. They do not manage rights in sound recordings. For that, you need to work with SoundExchange, provided the recording and the kind of use you wish to make of it is within its coverage. If you want to make a kind of use of a sound recording that is not licensed by SoundExchange, then you will need to contact the owner of the copyright in the sound recording (usually – but not always -- the record company) to negotiate a licensing agreement.

ROYALTY RATES FOR STATUTORY LICENSES

Royalty rates for statutory licensing of copyrights in sound recordings for non-exempt, noninteractive transmissions are adjusted annually: 2016 rates are as follows

Noncommercial webcasters (owned by a governmental or tax-exempt entity)
- Offering both subscription and nonsubscription transmissions (CRB): $0.0023 per performance, for any month in which aggregate listener tuning hours are greater than 159,140. A $500 per station or channel minimum annual royalty must be paid annually; monthly per-performance royalties are credited against the annual royalty.
- Offering only nonsubscription transmissions (WSA): $0.00083 per performance, for any month in which aggregate listener tuning hours

are greater than 159,140. A $500 per station or channel minimum annual royalty must be paid annually; monthly per-performance royalties are credited against the annual royalty.

Microcaster with less than 44,000 aggregate tuning hours per year (about 120 listener-hours per day): A $500 per station or channel royalty must be paid annually. There are no per-performance royalties. For an additional $100, a microcaster can get a waiver of the requirement to make monthly reports of use.

Educational webcaster: $0.0025 per performance, for any month in which aggregate listener tuning hours are greater than 159,140. A $500 per station or channel minimum royalty must be paid annually; monthly per-performance royalties are credited against the annual royalty. For an additional $100, a noncommercial educational webcaster with less than 55,000 aggregate tuning hours per month can get a waiver of the requirement to make monthly reports of use.

Commercial webcasters

Commercial webcaster (CRB): $0.0023 per performance. A $500 per station or channel (up to $50,000) minimum royalty must be paid annually; monthly per-performance royalties are credited against the annual royalty.

Commercial webcaster that is not owned or operated by an entity that also owns or operates a terrestrial radio station, if the webcaster elects this rate (WSA): $0.0023 per performance. A $500 per station or channel (up to $50,000) minimum royalty must be paid annually; monthly per-performance royalties are credited against the annual royalty.

Pureplay webcaster (revenues earned primarily through webcasting): $0.0025 per-performance of subscription/syndicated/ bundled transmissions, plus the greater of $0.0014 per-performance or 25% of gross revenues from nonsubscription transmissions. A $25,000 minimum fee must be paid annually.

Small pureplay webcaster [effective 2015, a service may no longer elect this rate]

Small webcaster nonsubscription service (gross annual revenues less than $1.25 million, including gross revenues of affiliates, third party participation revenues, and revenues from a new subscription service; a webcaster selecting this rate must pay the CRB commercial webcaster rate for any subscription service that he offers): Greater of: (1) 10% of the first $250,000 of gross revenues and 12% of all additional gross revenues, or (2) 7% of expenses. A minimum annual fee of $5,000 must be paid if gross annual revenues are $50,000 or more. Otherwise, the minimum annual fee is $2,000. The "greater of" amount is credited against the minimum annual fee.

Microcaster nonsubscription service (gross annual revenues less than $5,001, including gross revenues of affiliates, third party participation revenues, and revenues from a new subscription service; annual expenses not greater than $10,000; and annual listenership of not more than 18,067 aggregate tuning hours. A webcaster selecting this rate must pay the CRB commercial webcaster rate for any subscription service that he offers): $500 annual fee. There are no per-performance royalties. For an additional $100, a microcaster can get a waiver of the requirement to make monthly reports of use.

Broadcaster nonsubscription webcasts (webcasts by an owner of an AM or FM radio station. Broadcasters must operate subscription-based services under the Commercial Webcaster (CRB) category): $0.0025 per performance. A $500 per station or channel (up to $50,000) minimum royalty must be paid annually; monthly per-performance royalties are credited against the annual royalty.

Small broadcaster nonsubscription webcasts (webcasts with less than 27,777 aggregate tuning hours (about 70 listener-hours per day), by an owner of an AM or FM radio station. Broadcasters must operate subscription-based services under the Commercial Webcaster (CRB) category): $0.0025 per performance. A $500 per station or channel (up to $50,000) minimum royalty must be paid annually; monthly per-performance royalties are credited against the annual royalty. For an additional $100, a small broadcaster can get a waiver of the requirement to make monthly reports of use.

Business background music services

Streaming into retail businesses (bars, restaurants, retail stores, etc.): Royalty of 12% of annual gross proceeds. A $10,000 minimum annual fee is required. Royalty is credited against the minimum annual fee.

Television music services

Stand-alone subscriptions of audio-only digital music programming via residential televisions using cable or satellite television providers: Royalty of $0.0174 per subscriber per month, or 15% of revenue, whichever is greater. A minimum annual fee of $100,000 is required. Royalties are credited against the minimum annual fee.

Bundled subscriptions of audio-only digital music programming via residential televisions using cable or satellite television providers: Royalty of $0.029 per subscriber per month, or 15% of revenue allocated to reflect the objective value of the licensee's service, whichever is greater. A minimum annual fee of $100,000 is required.

Royalties are credited against the minimum annual fee.

Audio-only "music channel" services making transmissions via residential televisions using cable or satellite television providers, which were in existence prior to 1998: See 37 C.F.R. 382, Subpart A; and contact SoundExchange for more information.

SiriusXM Radio

Contact SoundExchange for information.

Rates are subject to change. Check the SoundExchange website, www.soundexchange.com, for current rates.

LIMITATIONS ON EXCLUSIVE LICENSES FOR INTERACTIVE STREAMING

Interactive digital transmission services generally may be subject to compulsory licensing with respect to the musical work, but they are not subject to statutory licensing with respect to the sound recording. There are, however, some statutory limitations on sound recording owners' freedom of contract when licensing interactive streaming rights.

To promote competition and to prevent the monopolization of performance rights in sound recordings, as well as to ensure the existence of more than one outlet for online interactive streaming, Congress has limited the ability of record companies to license recorded performances exclusively to one Internet interactive streaming service for long periods of time. Owners of rights in sound recordings may still grant exclusive licenses to selected interactive streaming services, but the duration of exclusive licenses cannot be longer than 24 months if the licensor holds the copyright to less than 1,001 sound recordings, and cannot be longer than 12 months if the licensor holds the copyright to more than 1,000 sound recordings.

An exclusive licensee is ineligible to receive another exclusive license for the performance of the same sound recording for a period of 13 months from the time the prior license expired.

The 12- and 24- month limitations do not apply if:

a) the licensor has granted and there remain in effect licenses for the public performance of sound recordings by means of interactive digital audio transmission by at least 5 different interactive services, if each such license is for a minimum of 10 percent of the copyrighted sound recordings owned by the licensor that have been licensed to interactive services, but in no event less than 50 sound recordings; or

b) the exclusive license is granted for interactive transmission of up to 45 seconds of a sound recording and the sole purpose of the performance is to promote the distribution or performance of that sound recording.

COPYING & DISTRIBUTING SOUND RECORDINGS

When you make a recording of a song available for downloading and/or purchase from your website, you are making and distributing a copy of both a musical work and a sound recording to the public. The copyright in a sound recording is distinct from the copyright in the work performed on it. Unless you have appropriate permissions or licenses from both, and unless some recognized exception applies, this would be an infringement of either one or both copyrights.

In other words, when making or distributing copies of a sound recording of a musical performance, you will need to ensure that you have the appropriate licensing from the owner of the copyright in the sound recording as well as the owner of the copyright in the musical work performed on it. If they are owned by the same person or company, make sure the license is clear that you are licensing both the musical work and the sound recording.

You will also want to ensure that the agreement is clear about which rights are being licensed. If you are offering CD's or digital downloads, then you will need to license reproduction rights for the musical work and get a master use license (license to use the sound recording master) for the sound recording. You will also want to make sure the agreement covers distribution rights for both the musical work and the sound recording. If you plan to offer interactive streaming, then you will need to make sure the agreement includes, in addition, performance rights for the musical work and digital performance rights for the sound recording.

LICENSING REPRODUCTION & DISTRIBUTION RIGHTS IN SOUND RECORDINGS

The owner of the copyright in a sound recording has exclusive rights to make and distribute copies of it; to make derivative works from the recording (as distinguished from making derivative works from the musical work); and to perform it publicly by means of digital transmission. Accordingly, unless a statutory exemption applies, you will need a license if you want to make and distribute copies of a sound recording.

The compulsory license provided in 17 U.S.C. § 115 to make and distribute copies of a musical work (under some circumstances) does not confer a right to make and distribute copies of the sound recording. The Section 115 compulsory license only creates a right to reproduce and distribute the musical work, not the sound recording. A website operator who wants to make copies of a song recording available for downloading would need to get permission from the owner of the copyright in the sound recording, as well as either a compulsory or voluntary license from the owner of the copyright in the musical work. In some cases, a statutory license may be available with respect to the copyright in the sound recording, under 17 U.S.C. § 114, but most statutory licenses are for noninteractive streaming, and do not apply to interactive streaming or digital downloads.

Moreover, if you digitally transmit a sound recording of a musical work after getting only a license to transmit the sound recording but not a license to distribute the musical work, then you may be liable for infringement to the owner of the copyright in the musical work.

The owner of the sound recording copyright will be liable to the owner of the copyright in the musical work for a third party's transmission of the sound recording with the musical work in it only if the sound recording copyright owner specifically licensed distribution rights in the musical work to the third party.

There are a number of exceptions to the sound recording copyright owner's exclusive rights to make and distribute copies and digitally transmit it.

PRE-1972 RECORDINGS

There is no federal copyright protection for sound recordings that were first fixed in a tangible medium before February 15, 1972. As a result, the unauthorized reproduction or distribution of a sound recording that was made before February 15, 1972, may result in liability for copyright infringement to the composer under the federal Copyright Act, but not to the owner of the copyright in the sound recording.

On the other hand, sound recordings fixed in a tangible medium before February 15, 1972 may receive copyright-like protection under state statutory or common law. Federal preemption of state laws granting copyright or copyright-like protection to sound recordings fixed before February 15, 1972 does not begin until February 15, 2067. As a result, state statutory and common law causes of action for violations of copyright (or copyright-like rights) in pre-February 15, 1972 sound recordings may be pursued against a person who publicly broadcasts the sound recording, even though federal copyright remedies are not available.

California Civil Code § 980(a) (2) is an example. It provides that "[t]he author of an original work of authorship consisting of a sound recording initially fixed prior to February 15, 1972, has an exclusive ownership therein until February 15, 2047, as against all persons except one who independently makes or duplicates another sound recording that does not directly or indirectly recapture the actual sounds fixed in such prior recording, but consists entirely of an independent fixation of other sounds, even though such sounds imitate or simulate the sounds contained in the prior sound recording." New York courts have established a similar rule as part of the common law of that state.

RECORDINGS THAT MIMIC BUT DON'T COPY OTHER RECORDINGS

Only reproduction of the sound recording itself infringes a copyright in a sound recording. Imitating a band's performance of a song on a sound recording does not. A cover band may perform its own version of a song that it heard being played on a sound recording, and this would violate the rights of the owner of the copyright in the sound recording. Only actual copying of the sound recording (such as by recording portions of the recording itself or copying and pasting the code from a digital file containing the sound recording) counts as infringement of the copyright in a sound recording.

There might be liability to the owner of the copyright in the musical work, but new recordings of new performances of a song do not violate any rights of the owner of the copyright in a sound recording.

PUBLIC BROADCASTING COMPANIES

Public broadcasting companies may copy, distribute, and digitally transmit sound recordings as part of educational television and radio programs, so long as they do not distribute the sound recording commercially.

CERTAIN NONINTERACTIVE DIGITAL TRANSMISSIONS

The exclusive performance right of the owner of a copyright in a sound recording means that noninteractive digital transmissions (e.g., Internet radio broadcasts) of a sound recording generally require the transmitter to get permission or a license. The Copyright Act exempts some of these transmissions, and grants a statutory license for many of the rest.

These are discussed in connection with the licensing of performance and transmission rights in sound recordings.

SIMULTANEOUS RETRANSMISSION BY A LICENSED INTERACTIVE SERVICE

A retransmission of a digital audio transmission is not an infringement of the copyright in the sound recording if:

1) the retransmission is of a transmission by an interactive service licensed to transmit the sound recording to a particular member of the public, as part of that transmission; and

2) the retransmission is simultaneous with the licensed transmission, authorized by the transmitter, and limited to the particular member of the public intended by the interactive service to be the recipient of the transmission.

PUBLIC DOMAIN

No copyright protection exists for sound recordings that have entered the public domain. For more information about the public domain, see Chapter 13.

STATUTORY LICENSES

Certain kinds of digital transmissions of sound recordings are subject to statutory licensing. When a statutory license exists, anyone who meets the statutory requirements for it may digitally transmit the sound recording in the manner specified in the statute even if the owner of the copyright in the sound recording has not given permission.

The existence of a statutory license does not prevent the owner of a copyright in a sound recording from entering into a voluntary, negotiated license agreement.

Except for the right to make ephemeral copies in some situations, statutory licenses normally pertain to the transmission of sound recordings, not the distribution of copies of them.

The terms and fees to be paid by a licensee to the owner of the copyright in the sound recording for a license to distribute copies of the sound recording are as established in the contract between the sound recording copyright owner and the licensee.

LIMITATIONS ON EXCLUSIVE LICENSES FOR INTERACTIVE STREAMING

Although interactive streaming services generally are not subject to statutory licensing with respect to the sound recording, there are some limitations on sound recording copyright owners' freedom of contract with respect to licensing interactive streaming rights.

In order to promote competition and prevent the monopolization of digital transmission rights in sound recordings, as well as to ensure the existence of more than one outlet for online interactive streaming, Congress has limited the ability of record companies and other sound recording copyright owners to license recorded performances exclusively to one Internet interactive streaming service for long periods of time. Owners of rights in sound recordings may still grant exclusive licenses to selected interactive streaming services, but the duration of exclusive licenses cannot be longer than 24 months if the licensor holds the copyright to less than 1,001 sound recordings, and cannot be longer than 12 months if the licensor holds the copyright to more than 1,000 sound recordings.

An exclusive licensee is ineligible to receive another exclusive license for the performance of the same sound recording for a period of 13 months from the time the prior license expired.

The 12- and 24- month limitations do not apply if:

a)   the licensor has granted and there remain in effect licenses for the public performance of sound recordings by means of interactive digital audio transmission by at least 5 different interactive services, if each such license is for a minimum of 10 percent of the copyrighted sound recordings owned by the licensor that have been licensed to interactive services, but in no event less than 50 sound recordings; or

b)   the exclusive license is granted for interactive transmission of up to 45 seconds of a sound recording and the sole purpose of the performance is to promote the distribution or performance of that sound recording.

ALBUMS AND COLLABORATIONS

The considerations discussed above with respect to copying, distributing, broadcasting and digitally transmitting musical compositions and sound recordings also apply to compilations of musical works and compilations of sound recordings.

To assess your risk of liability for copyright infringement, and to ascertain what license(s) you may need, you will need to perform the kind of analysis discussed above with respect to each individual recording. First, determine who owns the copyright in the musical composition. Next, determine which sound recordings are protected by federal copyright law, and which ones may only be protected by state law. Once you have done this, then for each song recording in the compilation, analyze what kinds of rights are involved and what kind(s) of license(s) may be needed for the kind of use you intend to make of the songs in the compilation. Then assess whether you need an additional license from the owner of the copyright in the compilation.

LICENSING RIGHTS FROM THE COMPILATION COPYRIGHT OWNER

A person may own a copyright in a compilation even if he does not own a copyright in its individual components. The fact that a musician's copyrighted work and/or a sound recording of a performance of it is included in a compilation does not, in itself, have the effect of transferring the copyrights in the musical composition and the sound recording to the owner of the copyright in the compilation.

A compilation may include matter that is not protected by federal copyright law, such as pre-1972 sound recordings.

Because the copyright in an individual sound recording that is included in a compilation is separate from the copyright in the compilation, digitally transmitting an individual sound recording from the compilation, or making it available for downloading or streaming from your website, may infringe the copyrights in the musical work and in the sound recording even if you have obtained permission from the owner of the copyright in the compilation.

The owner of the copyright in a collective work is presumed to possess the right to reproduce and distribute the works contributed to it only as part of that collective work or a revision of that collective work. Merely owning the copyright in a compilation does not give rise to a right to copy, perform or distribute -- or to authorize others to copy, perform or distribute -- an individual song or recording that is included in the collection.

Copyright protection for a compilation does not confer copyright protection on portions of it that would not otherwise receive copyright protection, such as public domain works. If a sound recording or a musical work would not be protected by copyright before it was compiled, then it will remain unprotected by copyright after the compilation. Only the manner in which the sound recordings are arranged or presented in a compilation is protected by a copyright in the compilation.

If you are only planning to copy, distribute, broadcast or transmit an individual sound recording, then you should not need permission or a license from the owner of the copyright in the compilation. If you plan to use the entire compilation, or a substantial portion of it, then you may need to obtain permission or a license from the owner of the copyright in the compilation, along with whatever licenses and permissions you may need to obtain from the owners of the copyrights in the musical works and sound recordings.

MUSIC VIDEOS

If you want to make a music video by combining a performance of a song with a video, then you will need a synchronization license.

Performing rights agencies normally do not handle synchronization licensing. You will need to negotiate a licensing agreement with the owner of the copyright in the musical composition. You may also need to negotiate license(s) with the owner(s) of the copyright(s) in the video if you are not creating it yourself.

Although licensing agencies do not handle synchronization rights, Songfile.com provides a synchronization licensing service called eSynch. This service is available only if you plan to make noncommercial use of your synchronization. It is ideal for licensing songs that you have combined with visual images or videos for free viewing on your personal or business website, or as background music on your website. It cannot be used to license synchronization rights for music videos that you sell, or that you upload to a third party website such as YouTube, Vimeo, etc. Also, if you use a sound recording in which you do not own the copyright, then you will need a license from the owner of the copyright in the sound recording, in addition to the license you obtain from the owner of the copyright in the musical work.

If you stream the music video you create, then you will need a performance license, a mechanical license, and a synchronization license for the musical composition, in addition to the license(s) that will be needed for the video.

PODCASTS

A podcast is like a webcast or a radio broadcast, except that it is recorded in a downloadable audio file. Unlike a broadcast or a webcast, the user is provided a copy of the broadcast, to which he can listen on-demand.

Because podcasting involves copying, mechanical licenses are required.

There is some disagreement about whether a podcast also requires a performance license. Mechanical licensing agencies take the position that it is a digital phonorecord delivery, so only a mechanical license is needed. Performing rights organizations take the position that it is also a public performance, so a performance license arguably may be necessary, as well. Clearly, it is a copy, so a mechanical license is needed. Whether it is also a "performance" is debatable. The safest course would be to get both a mechanical and a performance license.

If a sound recording is included in the podcast, then you will need a master use license and a digital performance license for the sound recording, in addition to the mechanical (and possibly performance) license(s) for the musical work(s). SoundExchange does not handle licensing of sound recordings for podcasts, because it only licenses recordings to noninteractive services. SoundExchange takes the position that podcasts are interactive transmissions because they are playable-on-demand. Therefore, you will need to negotiate a license with the sound recording copyright owner.

If your podcast includes images, artwork or video along with the musical works and/or sound recordings, then you will need synchronization licenses, too.

SAMPLING

Sampling is the process of reusing a part of an existing sound recording when making a new sound recording. It is very common in the hip-hop and rap genres, and is becoming more common in other genres, too. Dr. Dre reportedly has used over 3,000 "samples" of other artists' recordings in his.

The Copyright Act gives the author (e.g., composer, lyricist, producer) an exclusive right to make and distribute copies of his work. It also gives him an exclusive right to make derivative works from it. A derivative work is one that recasts, transforms or adapts a pre-existing work. Using part of a musical work in a new musical work would be a recasting, and arguably a transformation, of it. Because the owner of the copyright in a musical work (songwriter or publisher) has an exclusive right to make derivative works (as well as the exclusive right to make and distribute copies of it), unauthorized music sampling would seem to infringe the copyright in the musical work.

The Copyright Act also gives the owner of the copyright in a sound recording the exclusive rights to make and distribute copies of the recording; to make derivative works from the sound recording; and to transmit the recording digitally. Music sampling would seem to infringe the copyright in the sound recording, too.

Contrary to popular belief, owing a copy (e.g., a CD) of a sound recording does not transfer the copyright in the sound recording to the person who bought the CD. Nor does it transfer the copyright in the musical work.

Also, there is no "de minimis" rule with respect to sampling of a sound recording. Using even a couple of seconds of a sound recording may be infringement. In one case, it was held that a sampling that involved only three notes constituted copyright infringement of the sound recording, and this was true even though it probably would not have constituted infringement of the copyright in the musical work. (*Bridgeport Music, Inc. v. Dimension Films*, 410 F.3d 792 (6th Cir. 2005). The similarity of the new work and the original work is relevant to the determination whether infringement of a literary or musical work has occurred, but it is not particularly relevant to whether infringement of a sound recording copyright has occurred. A person infringes a copyright in a musical work when he copies it (whether intentionally or subconsciously), and the similarity of the two works can be strong circumstantial evidence of copying. A person who records a new performance of a song, on the other hand, does not violate the copyright in the sound recording unless he copies the actual recording itself. Accordingly, whether the new recording sounds similar, or even identical, to the previous recording is irrelevant. It's the use of the sound recording itself, not the similarity of sounds, that constitutes infringement of a copyright in a sound recording. This is why "sampling" even a de minimis amount of a sound recording is infringement.

Some kinds of sampling may be permitted as "fair use." See Chapter 14.

LICENSING FOR SAMPLING

The fair use doctrine is fraught with gray areas. It is risky to rely on it as a defense to copyright infringement. The more prudent thing to do would be to seek license(s) from the copyright owner(s) to use portions of the musical work and sound recording.

To use a clip from a sound recording in a new sound recording of a new musical work, you will need licenses from the owners of the copyrights in the musical work and the sound recordings to make a derivative work. If you make and distribute copies of it, you will need a mechanical license from the owner of the copyright in the musical work, and a master use license from the sound recording copyright owner. If you broadcast it (or arrange to have it broadcasted), then you will need a performance license from the owner of the copyright in the musical work. If you transmit it digitally, then you will need a license from both the owner of the copyright in the musical work and the sound recording copyright owner. If you plan to include it in another work (e.g., a music video), then you will need synchronization licenses from the copyright owners.

The rights to make and distribute copies, and to perform, musical works usually may be licensed through agencies like ASCAP, BMI, SESAC, and Harry Fox. These agencies, however, normally do not handle licenses to make derivative works. You will need to negotiate derivative work licensing agreements directly with the copyright owner (usually the publisher; sometimes the songwriter.)

The rights to make and distribute copies and to make derivative works of sound recordings must be negotiated with the sound recording copyright owner (usually the record company.) You will not need a performance license for the sound recording if all you plan to do is broadcast it non-digitally (e.g., a terrestrial radio station.) If you plan to transmit it digitally, then the transmitter will probably need a license. Noninteractive statutory digital transmissions may be licensed through SoundExchange. Licenses for interactive digital transmissions must be negotiated with the sound recording license owner (usually the record company.)

If you obtain a master use license from a record company, take care to ensure that the license includes the right to make derivative works, as well as the right to make and distribute copies. A right to reproduce a recording does not necessarily include the right to make derivative works, and vice versa.

Synchronization rights are not handled by licensing agencies. They may be obtained only through negotiation with the copyright owner(s).

A chart of the various kinds of licenses, or combinations of licenses you may need for different kinds of uses you plan to make of musical works and sound recordings appears in Appendix III. The chart also provides guidance about where to begin the process of getting them.

KEY POINTS:

- ❖ **The five kinds of copyright licenses pertinent to music are:**
  - Folio
  - Performance
  - Mechanical
  - Master use
  - Synchronization.
- ❖ **A trademark license may be needed if you intend to use music or sound in connection with marketing a product or service.**
- ❖ **Different uses require different kinds of licenses.**
- ❖ **Anyone who pays the required royalty and complies with statutory conditions has a compulsory license to record and distribute a cover version of any song if the copyright in it has been registered.**
- ❖ **Statutory licenses exist primarily for noninteractive transmissions.**

❖ Usually, but not always, a royalty must be paid for the use of a musical work and/or a sound recording of it.

❖ A single music video or podcast is likely to involve several different works, and may involve several different copyright owners

CHAPTER 21

Software licensing

Incorporating someone else's software into your website, or making it available for use, download or purchase from your website, is advisable only if you have obtained a license to do so from the owner of the intellectual property rights in the software. Computer programs may be protected by copyright, patent, or both.

When people think they are buying computer software they are usually only buying a license to use it in a specified way. The terms of the license may be set out in a document accompanying the software, or they may be incorporated into the software itself.

In some cases, software is programmed in such a way that you will be unable to access it unless you first agree to the terms of use. Clicking on an "I Accept" or "I Agree" button results in a "clickwrap agreement," which can have the same legal effect as signing a written contract.

The terms of use almost always state that you are only being granted a license, and they usually will specify the particular uses you are permitted to make of the software.

Because software vendors normally do not actually "sell" the program itself, but merely license its use, certain kinds of uses to which a user puts a computer program that he has downloaded or copied from an online source may be violations of a license agreement. If a use that exceeds the authority granted by the license also violates one of the exclusive rights of copyright owners (or patent owners, as the case may be), then it may be both a breach of contract and copyright infringement (and/or patent infringement, as the case may be.)

Any of the exclusive rights of a copyright owner (reproduction, distribution, display, performance, making of derivative works) that are not granted by the license remain the exclusive right of the owner. If, as is typically the case, the license agreement specifies the number of copies you are permitted to make (e.g., for backup or personal use), then any additional copies you make that exceed that number breach the licensing contract, and also infringe the copyright. Similarly, if the license expressly prohibits you from distributing the software, then doing so is not just a breach of the license agreement; it is copyright infringement. If there is a patent, then it may also be patent infringement.

If the agreement is silent about distribution, this means the copyright owner has chosen to retain the exclusive right of distribution that copyright law affords him. Therefore, your distribution of the software without permission would infringe the copyright in the computer program. Similarly, if the agreement is silent about public display of the program, then your display of it (such as by posting the source or object code to your website) will be copyright infringement unless you get the copyright owner's permission to do so.

Exploiting a computer program in a way that is not authorized by the license agreement may also expose you to liability for patent infringement, if the program is patented.

KINDS OF SOFTWARE LICENSES

SINGLE-USER LICENSE

A single-user license is one that is intended to give only one person the right to use the software. Some single-user licenses allow the user to install it on a specified number of devices.

CONCURRENT USE LICENSE

A concurrent use license allows more than one person to use the software. The license agreement typically will specify the maximum number of people who are authorized to use it and/or the maximum number of devices on which it may be installed.

VOLUME LICENSE

A volume (or multi-user) licensing arrangement is one in which a number of licenses are sold together, usually at a discount. The individual licenses within the group may or may not be subject to single-user limitations.

SITE LICENSE

A site license is one allowing the use of software on computers at a specific location or within a specific organization.

ACADEMIC LICENSE

This is simply one of the foregoing kinds of licenses, but limited to use by an educational institution and its employees, students, and faculty, or a specified subset thereof. They commonly include restrictions on the purpose for which the software must be used (e.g., nonprofit uses only.)

CLIENT ACCESS LICENSE

These are licenses of server-based programs. Server-based technologies may require additional licensing fees for clients that access the server application. Usually this is charged on a per user basis. Licensing of this sort may require a licensing application or server for the sole purpose of managing the licensing.

END USER LICENSE AGREEMENT (EULA)

An end user license agreement simply means any software licensing agreement in which the licensee is a user of the software (as distinguished from a distributor, for example.)

PREEMPTION

The portions of a licensing agreement that purport to impose an obligation on the user to refrain from infringing the copyright in the computer program are preempted by the federal Copyright Act. 17 U.S.C. § 301 provides:

> [A]ll legal or equitable rights that are equivalent to any of the exclusive rights within the general scope of copyright ... in works of authorship that ... come within the subject matter of copyright ... are governed exclusively by this title. Thereafter, no person is entitled to any such right or equivalent right in any such work under the common law or statutes of any State.

Section 301 goes on to clarify that "[n]othing in this title annuls or limits any rights or remedies under the common law or statutes of any State with respect to ... subject matter that does not come within the subject matter of copyright ...." Nor does it annul or limit state law rights or remedies with respect to "activities violating legal or equitable rights that are not equivalent to any of the exclusive rights within the general scope of copyright...."

What this means is that state or common law claims for breach of a contract to refrain from infringing a copyright are not enforceable. You may still sue someone for infringing a copyright in violation of the contract, but you must file your claim under federal copyright law, not state contract law.

States are permitted to enforce legal and equitable rights that are not the equivalent of any of the exclusive rights protected by copyright law. Therefore, to the extent a right set out in a licensing agreement is not the equivalent of a right protected by copyright law, a state or common law breach of contract claim may be pursued.

BREACH OF AGREEMENT NOT TO COPY UNCOPYRIGHTED MATERIAL

An agreement not to copy matter that is not protected by copyright (such as data) is enforceable under state contract law. This kind of contract does not come within the subject matter of federal copyright law because there is no copyright protection for information, so enforcement of it is not preempted by federal law.

In *ProCD, Inc. v. Zeidenberg*, 86 F. 3d 1447 (7th Cir. 1996), a user of a CD containing a telephone number database made a substantial portion of it available via his website. The vendor of the CD sued for copyright infringement and breach of contract. Because it was merely a list of telephone numbers, it did not meet the originality requirement for copyright protection, so the copyright claims were dismissed. The 7th Circuit Court of Appeals, however, held that the shrink-wrap agreement, which prohibited such use, was not preempted, and therefore breach of the agreement was enforceable under state contract law.

OPEN SOURCE SOFTWARE

Open source software is software the source code of which is made available and may be freely copied, distributed and modified by anyone who agrees to the terms of the license. It differs from proprietary software in that proprietary software licenses normally do not authorize modifications of the source code. Open source software licenses do.

Open source software is intended to promote collaboration and sharing among programmers, the goal being to encourage the development of improvements to software programs. Normally the owner of the copyright in software has the exclusive right to make modifications to the source code, i.e., derivative works. Under an open source license, however, the user may modify the source code and incorporate those changes into projects of his own.

Terms of open source licenses vary. Typically they require any user who makes a derivative work based on, or incorporating, the software to make the source code available to others on the same terms. If you have this kind of license, then you must allow others to make derivative works from the source code of the software you create.

Open source licenses may be classified according to how protective of the open source philosophy they are. A strongly protective license is one that requires any derivative works and any software that dynamically links to the licensed work to be treated as derivative works, and to be distributed under the same open-source terms as the licensed work is. Under this kind of license, merely including a hyperlink to the licensed work results in a requirement that a program must be made open source, too. A weakly protective license requires derivative works to be open source, but does not require software to be open source merely because it links to the open source program.

Permissive licenses do not require copies of the software or derivatives of it to be distributed as open-source software. A permissive license may impose other requirements, though, such as attribution of credit to the original author, a disclaimer of warranties, or the like.

The most common open source license is the GNU General Public License, which falls into the strongly protective category. The Linux operating system is distributed under this license. Examples of weakly protective licenses include the Mozilla Public License and the GNU Lesser Public License. Licenses for Apache versions after 1.0 are examples of permissive licenses, as is the Berkeley Software Distribution License and the MIT License.

Listings and copies of open source licenses may be found at www.opensource.org and www.gnu.org.

If a licensee violates a term of an open source license, the license may automatically terminate if the license agreement so provides. If the license agreement provides for a right to terminate in the event of violation, then it terminates only if the right is exercised. The licensor may also pursue any remedies for copyright infringement and/or breach of contract that may be available.

The Open Source Initiative certifies open source licenses that meet their standards. Among other things, the standards require that the source code must be made available to the licensee; modifications and the making of derivative works must be permitted; distribution of copies and of derivative works must be permitted under the same terms as the original open-source license; and the licensor must treat all end users alike. The standards are published at www.opensource.org/docs/osd.

Contrary to popular belief, there is no requirement that open source software must be made available free of charge. There is no generally applicable prohibition against charging a fee for an open source software license.

If you are planning to incorporate open source software into other programs on your website, or if you plan to include a link to an open source program in proprietary software that you plan to make available on your site, read the licensing agreement very carefully first.

Be aware that the meaning of some of the terms in open source license agreements may not always be clear, and are not always exactly the same meanings as the terms have for the purpose of general copyright law. The term incorporating is an example. Depending on the kind of contract, serious consequences may result from "incorporating" an open source program into a proprietary one, including restrictions on how you may thereafter distribute your proprietary software. Unfortunately, some licenses do not clearly define what it means to "incorporate" an open source program into a proprietary one.

In most cases, offering visitors an option to download and install open source software for use in conjunction with your proprietary software (e.g., an open source plug-in that is to be used in conjunction with your proprietary software) probably will not be deemed an act of "incorporating" the open source software into your program. The line between "incorporating" open source software into proprietary software, on one hand, and using open source software "in conjunction with" proprietary software, on the other, is not always clear, though. Obviously, literally copying lines of source code from an open source file and pasting it into the source code of your proprietary program would be an act of "incorporating" it into your program. But what if, instead of copying and pasting, you simply designed your program in such a way that it is inoperable unless a user downloads and installs a particular open source program? Would this come within the meaning of "incorporating" the open source software? The licensing agreement does not always provide a clear answer to questions like these.

One way to resolve an uncertainty about the meaning of a term in a licensing agreement is to ask the licensor for clarification. If you take this approach, it is probably safe to rely on the answer you are given, provided it is unequivocal and in writing.

Answers to some frequently asked questions about open source licenses are offered on the Open Source Initiative and GNU websites.

Any doubts about whether to use open source software in connection with your website, or about the ramifications of your intended use of it, should be resolved against using it until you have satisfied yourself that doing so will have no unintended adverse consequences.

SHARING YOUR OWN SOFTWARE

Since the expressive elements of a computer program are protected by copyright, the same general copyright considerations apply when you publish a computer program as when you publish text, artwork, and so on.

You will also want to take some additional steps to protect yourself from liability, though, as well as to preserve the commercial value of your invention (the program.)

In all cases, you will want to have an end user license agreement (EULA) in place. Samples of these can be found all over the Internet. In many cases, you can use one of the Open Source templates that can be found online. You will want to tailor it to fit your needs. Unless you are an attorney yourself, it would be a good idea to have an attorney review your draft to make sure that it will accomplish what you want it and that it will be enforceable.

Having written down your terms and conditions somewhere won't do you much good unless you have a way of establishing that someone agreed to them. Subject to only a few limited exceptions, a contract or agreement is not enforceable unless both parties have signaled their acceptance of the terms in some way.

Acceptance of the terms of a contract does not have to be by means of signing a piece of paper. Acceptance may be signaled in other ways, too. Sometimes certain kinds of conduct may implicitly signal acceptance, provided the conduct is widely regarded as an implicit acceptance. For example, when a grocer displays a dollar amount next to an item and a customer brings it to a cash register and tenders the listed amount, the customer is implicitly signaling assent to the price term of an implied sales contract.

An argument might be made that using software that somebody has published online implicitly signals assent to the terms of the license the copyright owner is offering. This might be true, for example, when the licensing agreement is bundled together with the software in a zipped file that the user downloads and then decompresses for use on his computer. It is widely known that a license agreement is normally included when a software program is offered in a zip file. Accordingly, it is possible that a court could find that downloading a decompressing a zip file containing a computer program implicitly signals consent to the license agreement contained within the zip file.

On the other hand, it is also possible that a court might find that a particular user was not familiar with that custom, and had no reason to be, so that acceptance of the license was not implied simply by the act of using the software.

This is why the better practice is to require a user to take some additional affirmative step to signal acceptance of the terms of the license. Examples would be a radio button a user must click on to get access to the software, where the button says, "I agree to the terms of the license." Alternatively, you could set out the license and then require a user to click on a box next to the statement, "I agree to the terms and conditions set out in the licensing agreement." Other variations will work, too, such as a radio button after the license agreement with the words "I accept" on it.

The signaling of acceptance may also be incorporated into the software itself. For example, you could write the code in such a way that the first thing to come up on the screen is a query whether the user accepts the terms and conditions of the licensing agreement, and no further operations can be performed with the program unless and until the user clicks on the "Yes" button.

In all events, you should make the licensing agreement available for the user to read before deciding whether to signal acceptance or not.

TERMS AND CONDITIONS

Standard terms that should be included in any software licensing agreement include:

- Price (or an indication that it is free)
- Duration
- Number of allowed users and/or devices
- Kinds of permitted and unpermitted uses
- Sharing policy and restrictions
- Limitation of liability
- Disclaimer of warranties.

This is not, by any means, an exhaustive list. If you take a look at some sample licensing agreements, such as the ones provided at Open Source, you will see that there are all kinds of additional matters you may want to address –sublicensing; assignments; enforcement; liquidated damages; venue and choice of law for future disputes; arbitration; and others. Carefully consider the terms you want to include in the licensing agreement before publishing it to your website. Users who have signaled assent to your original license terms normally will not be bound by modifications and additions you unilaterally make later.

Even if you want to offer your software for free, you should still take care to impose some restrictions and limitations on use. If you grant users a right to use it and share it an unlimited number of times and for an unlimited period of time, then you will be held to that agreement with any user who signaled assent to it, even if you later modify the agreement. You can't make a modification of the agreement retroactive in a way that will bind people who have not assented to the modification. This can be a very undesirable consequence for you if you decide one day that you would like to market the software commercially, or if you decide for some other reason that you don't want people using and sharing it anymore.

If you include special provisions that the average consumer would not typically encounter in a standard software license, it would be a good idea to design the program or your website in such a way that the user must separately signal assent to that particular term, in addition to signaling assent to the license agreement as a whole. This may help avert future claims that enforcement of that particular contract term would be unfair, unconscionable or the like. Courts do sometimes give credence to claims like that. Not always, but sometimes. Don't give them the opportunity.

CONSULT AN ATTORNEY

Software licensing is an area that is fraught with potential pitfalls and hazards. Although attorneys are not cheap, it would be a very good idea to consult with one if you plan to use computer programs – whether your own or somebody else's – in your website or blog, or if you plan to make a computer program that you have created available to or accessible by visitors to your site.

KEY POINTS:

❖ Computer programs may be the subject of two kinds of intellectual property rights: patent and copyright.

❖ Software buyers normally only buy a license to use a computer program in specified ways, not the program itself.

❖ Federal copyright law does not completely preempt state breach of contract laws.

❖ Open source software is not necessarily free to use.

❖ Open source software licenses often require a licensee to distribute any software created with it on the same terms as those by which the software was acquired.

CHAPTER 22

Copyright research

With any luck, you will never find it necessary to do copyright research. It may become unavoidable, however, when you need to determine whether a particular work is in the public domain or not; or when you want to request a license and need to figure out who the owner of the copyright is.

The copyright notice on a copy of a work is a good place to start, but it is not determinative. Ownership of a copyright in a work may have been assigned to another person after the copy of the work was published. Moreover, not all protected works have copyright notices on them. And a publisher may be mistaken or misled about ownership of the copyright.

CAVEATS

It should be kept in mind that the Copyright Office only maintains records of registrations, yet registration is not a requirement for copyright protection. Therefore, the fact that there is a complete absence of any information about a work in the Copyright Office records does not mean that the work is unprotected.

The absence of a record of a work also does not necessarily mean that it has not been registered. It often can take a long time for the Copyright Office to process and catalog a registration application. Also, a work may have been registered under a different title or as part of a larger work, or collection of works.

Not all foreign works are registered in the United States. A work that is not registered in the U.S. might be registered in another country, and vice versa.

Each country has its own set of laws for determining whether a work is in the public domain or not. A work that is in the public domain in the U.S. is not necessarily in the public domain in a foreign country, and vice versa.

COPYRIGHT CARD CATALOG

The complete copyright card catalog includes all records, including those from before 1978. It is located in the Copyright Public Records Reading Room (lm-404) on the fourth floor of the James Madison Memorial Building of the Library of Congress. The public can use the catalog between 8:30 am and 5:00 pm, Eastern Time, Monday through Friday, except federal holidays.

You can conduct a search yourself, or you may ask the Copyright Office to conduct a search for you, for a fee.

ONLINE COPYRIGHT OFFICE RECORDS

REGISTRATIONS SINCE JANUARY 1, 1978

A trip to Washington, D.C. is not necessary if the work you are researching was registered after January 1, 1978. Copyright registrations from January 1, 1978 to the present can be searched online at www.copyright.gov/records.

WORKS REGISTERED BEFORE JANUARY 1, 1978

Records of registrations from before 1978 are in the process of being archived at http://archive.org/details/copyrightrecords/. The Copyright Office is still working on digitizing this archive. It is not complete.

CATALOG OF COPYRIGHT ENTRIES

The Copyright Office published a Catalog of Copyright Entries (CCE) from 1891 to 1982. It was in print form until 1978. From 1979 through 1982, it was issued in microfiche format. A number of libraries throughout the U.S. maintain copies of the CCE. Many, but not all, of the 660 volumes of the CCE are now online at www.archive.org/details/copyrightrecords/.

The CCE is divided into parts according to the classes of works registered. Each CCE segment covers all registrations made during a particular period of time. Renewal registrations made from 1979 through 1982 are found in Section 8 of the catalog. Renewals prior to that time are generally listed at the end of the volume containing the class of work to which they pertained.

Entries for assignments or other recorded documents are not included. Also, the CCE does not contain a verbatim transcript of registration records. The address of the copyright claimant is not included, for example.

The Copyright Office maintains records of assignments, exclusive licenses, and other documents dealing with copyright ownership.

DERIVATIVE WORKS

When examining a copy of a work in the course of a copyright search, it is important to determine whether that particular version of the work is an original edition of the work or a new version. New versions (derivative works) include, for example, musical arrangements, adaptations, revised or newly edited editions, translations, dramatizations, abridgments, compilations, and works republished with new matter added. The law provides that derivative works, published or unpublished, are independently registrable and that the copyright in such a work does not affect or extend the protection, if any, in the underlying work.

The notice of copyright on a derivative work ordinarily need not include the dates or other information pertaining to the earlier works incorporated in it. Thus, the date in the copyright notice is not necessarily an indication of when copyright in all the material in the work will expire. Some of the material may already be in the public domain, and some parts of the work may expire sooner than others. Even if some of the material in the derivative work is in the public domain and free for use, this does not mean that the "new" material added to it can be used without permission from the owner of copyright in the derivative work. It may be necessary to compare editions to determine what is free to use and what is not.

Ownership of rights in the material included in a derivative work and in the preexisting work upon which it may be based may differ, and permission obtained from the owners of certain parts of the work may not authorize the use of other parts.

SEARCHING THE CATALOG

Entries in the online catalog, and cards in the Card Catalog contain five elements, or categories, of information about a work:

1) the title of the work
2) the author or authors

3) the claimant or claimants, that is, the owner(s) of the copyright, who may be different from the author(s)

4) the date of publication, the day on which copyright protection commenced, or the date of receipt for unpublished works, and

5) the registration number, which is a letter (depending on the classification) followed by from one to seven digits. A renewal registration number consists of the letter R or the letters RE followed by from one to six digits.

In each segment of the catalog, all filing elements are divided into two alphabetized groups: personal names, followed by corporate names and titles.

A researcher should take into account different forms of names and titles. For example, cross-references may not be provided for entries cataloged under Chaikovskii and Tschaikowsky. Entries for Tom James may be cataloged under Tom James, Thomas James, or both. Non-English names such as de Mille and von Franz may appear under the prefix, the surname, or both. A corporate entity such as Walt Disney Productions may appear under that form or under Disney (Walt) Productions.

Online records are particularly sensitive to spacing and punctuation. Bank of America NT&SA; Bank of America N.T. &S.A.; and Bank of America, NT & SA are all different index entries within the electronic files.

Use of the published Catalog of Copyright Entries is recommended when working with pre-1938 indexes. During that period, titles of books, lyricists, and even composers were inadequately entered into the card catalog. The printed volume is therefore invaluable for tracing elements not found on the catalog cards. There is no subject index to the card catalog.

The Copyright Office has divided their records into chronological periods.

1790–1870

During this period, claims to statutory copyright were registered in the office of the clerk of the United States district courts. These records are on microfilm, and are now located in the card catalog area. Entries in these records are arranged first by district court, then alphabetically with chronological entries under each letter. Indexing, which is sporadic, is in the front of some volumes.

The original district court record books are housed in the Rare Book and Special Collections Division of the Library of Congress. The earliest records have been published by the Library of Congress in Federal Copyright Records 1790–1800.

1870–1897

The oldest part of the card catalog, known as the general index, covers registrations from 1870 through 1897. This catalog is used primarily for historical purposes, since any work published or registered before 1923 would not be protected by copyright in the United States. These books may be reviewed in the Copyright Public Records Reading Room.

1898–1937

Beginning with 1898, there is a separate file for each class of copyrighted works or groups of closely related classes. From July 1, 1909, through November 6, 1937, copyright applications were submitted on cards, which were used as the main entries in the individual indexes, filed under the name of the claimant. Books are accessible by separate author and claimant indexes, but not by title, except for composite or anonymous works and certain serials. Periodicals are filed from 1898 to 1909 in a claimant and title index, and from 1909 to 1937 by claimant only. Music can be located through claimant and title indexes. Access by composer is limited; there are no entries under lyricists' names. This file also includes registrations for some musical dramas.

Dramas from 1870 through 1916 are cataloged in the published two-volume work, Dramatic Compositions Copyrighted in the United States, 1870–1916, available in the Copyright Public Records Reading Room (lm-404). Dramas and lectures from 1909 through 1937 are indexed in the card catalog by claimant and, for records after 1917, by title and author as well.

Graphic arts (including photographs, motion pictures, engravings, and maps) are indexed primarily by claimant, with a small working file containing some entries by author and title. Maps are arranged by geographical area under the name of each claimant or by the place name.

Renewals from 1909 through 1937 are indexed by claimant, title, and, depending on the class of work being renewed, author.

1938–1977

The card catalog from 1938 through 1977 is organized by blocks of time. Therefore, the searcher must know the approximate date of publication or registration. Within each segment of this part of the card catalog, all original and renewal registrations are interfiled alphabetically under author's name, claimant's name, and title.

1938–1945

This part of the card catalog, which began in November 1937, is known as the general index. Like the general index of 1870–1897, all classes of registrations are interfiled in one alphabetical sequence. The claimant is the main entry on the original registration card, and added-entry cards exist for the author, title, source author, and source title in the case of a derivative work, and for the name of any other person who had some responsibility in the creation of the work. Similar added-entry cards for related names and titles are interfiled throughout the rest of the card catalog. Also beginning in 1938, the principal access to maps is by claimant, with added entries for place name and author.

1946 –1954

The same consolidated index covering all classes of registrations is in use for works cataloged from 1946 through 1954, but extensive cross-references replace the information formerly given on each added-entry card.

1955–1970

Cards for this period are interfiled alphabetically, but added entry cards provide full information for each registration.

1971–1977

This section of the card catalog, also interfiled alphabetically, covers the period from 1971 through December 31, 1977, the last day on which works were registered under the 1909 copyright law.

1978–PRESENT

Registrations for all works dating from January 1, 1978, to the present, as well as renewals and recorded documents, are available for searching in the online Copyright Office catalog at www.copyright.gov.

ASSIGNMENT AND RELATED DOCUMENTS INDEX AND AUTOMATED DOCUMENTS CATALOG

After establishing the facts of copyright registration, it is necessary to determine whether the ownership of the copyright has been transferred or otherwise altered since the time it was registered. The Assignment and Related Documents Index is the source for tracing documents clarifying the ownership of copyrights that have been officially recorded in the Copyright Office from 1870 through 1977. Legal documents, including wills and contracts transferring copyright from one person or firm to another, are among the kinds of documents indexed. Assignor-transferor and assignee-transferee files are separate until August 15, 1941, and are thereafter interfiled through 1977. A single title file covers the period 1928 through 1977. There is no title file prior to 1928. All recorded assignments and documents from 1870 to the present are on microfilm. Early documents, in various formats, are also bound in books from volume 1 to volume 888.

Access to assignment documents recorded after 1977 is available online at www.copyright.gov. The documents are cataloged and filed by the names of the parties involved and by title.

COMMERCIAL PRINTS

At one time, registrations of commercial prints and labels were filed in the U.S. Patent Office. Two book files, Commercial Prints and Labels Registered in the United States Patent Office, one for 1876–1921 and the other for 1922–40, contain photocopied lists of Patent Office registrations for prints and labels. The lists for 1922–40 are duplicated by a single alphabetical file in the card catalog, arranged by claimant.

Congress gave the Copyright Office responsibility for registering prints and labels in 1940, and they are interfiled in the card catalog after 1940 as a separate registration class.

MOTION PICTURES

From 1894 to 1969 the Copyright Office published Cumulative Catalogs of Motion Picture Entries. A copy for public use is located in the card catalog area of the Library of Congress.

MUSICAL COMPOSITIONS - NOTICES

Under the 1909 copyright law, the own of the copyright in a musical composition had the exclusive right to make the first mechanical recording of the work. After the owner had initially recorded the work, he or she was required to submit to the Copyright Office a notice of use. The work could then be recorded by anyone for a fixed royalty fee or by negotiating a separate contract. Notices of use from 1909 through 1952 are located in separate title and claimant files; from 1953 through 1977 they are interfiled in the card catalog under title and claimant only.

Notices of intention to use, filed by those wishing to record copyrighted music, are filed by title only in a separate index spanning 1909 to 1977.

Under the current law effective in 1978, a copyright owner need only register a claim to copyright to be entitled to receive royalties, so the notice of use file is no longer active. Interested parties can file a notice of intention to obtain a compulsory license in the Licensing Division of the Copyright Office. To inquire about public inspection of this file, call (202) 707-8150 or send email to licensing@loc.gov.

GETTING COPIES & HELP FROM THE COPYRIGHT OFFICE

If you wish to obtain certified copies of the original applications or copies of the works themselves, you may request them from the Copyright Office for a fee. The Office will also initiate in-process searches as well as searches in the correspondence and unfinished business files of the Copyright Office for material that may contain original letters from authors and publishers, deposit copies (possibly unique examples) on which no cataloging action has been undertaken, and similar information. The researcher can also inspect any of the original record books and applications stored in the Copyright Office.

You may hire the Copyright Office to search copyright records if you wish. As of October 20, 2016, the fee is $200 per hour, with a two-hour minimum. Accordingly, it is a good idea to request an estimate first.

In addition to searches, the Copyright Office's Records Research and Certification Service ("RRCS") also provides copies of copyright records for use in litigation or other authorized purposes; prepares copies of certificates of registration or renewal; certifies copyright records facilitates requests to inspect deposits and other records; and provides access to catalogs, indexes and other records. For information, email to copysearch@loc.gov, or fax a request to (202) 252-3485, or call (202) 707-6787.

Requests for searches, search estimates, copies of public records, or other RRCS services also may be submitted by mail to the address shown in Appendix X.

The Copyright Office does not give legal advice; does not enforce copyrights; and does not issue ISSN, ISBN or ISRC numbers.

CONTENTS OF A SEARCH REQUEST

When making a search request about a work, include the names of:

- the work (i.e., the title of the work);
- the author(s); and
- the copyright claimant(s).

You should also include as much additional information as you can, including: variations on the title of the work; pseudonyms for the author of the work; name of the probable copyright owner; year when the work was created, published, registered (or a guess); type of work (e.g., book, motion picture, musical work, etc.); copyright registration number(s); year of registration, if any; and any other information you have about the registration.

When requesting a document, you should include the document recordation number; title of the work; any registration numbers listed in the document; and the name(s) of the person(s) who executed the document.

LIMITATIONS OF COPYRIGHT OFFICE SEARCHES

A Copyright Office search is not conclusive. Information about a work may be incomplete or nonexistent for various reasons.

An unpublished work created before January 1, 1978 may or may not be registered as of the date that the search is conducted, because unpublished works were enforceable under state common law without the need for registration prior to January 1, 1978. A work may be registered under a different title or as a part of a larger work. A registration for a pre-1978 work may or may not be renewed as of the date that the search is conducted The Copyright Office's Public Catalog does not include recent registrations or recordations that have not yet been added to the database. Recording transfer documents is optional, so documents concerning ownership of a work may or may not be recorded with the Office. The Copyright Office's records do not contain a separate title for a contribution to a collective work or a contribution to a database, but only the title of the collective work or database as a whole.

The Copyright Office does not maintain a list of works that are in the public domain. Nor does it maintain records of trademarks and patents.

Finally, and probably most important of all, a copyright may exist even though it is not registered. The fact that no copyright is registered does not mean that a work is in the public domain.

KEY POINTS:

- ❖ Resources for copyright research include:
  - Copyright Card Catalog;
  - Online Copyright Office records;
  - Catalog of Copyright Entries;
  - Assignment and Related Documents Index;
  - Commercial Prints and Labels Registered in the United States Patent Office;
  - Cumulative Catalogs of Motion Picture Entries;
  - Dramatic Compositions Copyrighted in the U.S., 1870–1916.
- ❖ Not all copyrighted works are registered.
- ❖ A work that is not registered in the U.S. might be registered in another country, and vice versa.
- ❖ Works that are in the public domain in the U.S. are not necessarily in the public domain in foreign countries, and vice versa.
- ❖ The copyright in a derivative work is different from the copyright in the original work; it does not extend the term of the original work.
- ❖ You can ask the Copyright Office to conduct a search, for a fee.

Copyright-Free Materials

Note: Although these things do not receive copyright protection, the words and symbols used to express them may be protected. Also, a particular selection and arrangement of these things may be protected even if the thing itself isn't. The fact a particular use is not prohibited by copyright law does not mean that it is permitted by trademark, patent, trade secret or other laws.

This is not an exhaustive list.

algorithms

alphabetization

animal-generated output

architectural designs published before December 1, 1990

architecture of a building constructed before December 1, 1990

athletic or sports movements such as football plays, cheerleading routines, etc. (but depictions, photographs or descriptions of them might be protected)

blank forms

bridge or dam designs

character that is not unique or distinctive (in a fictional work)

computer-generated output (no human judgment involved)

concepts

contest rules

copy of another work (e.g., a photograph of a photograph; or a photocopy of text written by someone else)

digitization

extemporaneous speech (unrecorded)

facts

fair use of material that would otherwise be protected by copyright

federally protected emblems, names, slogans and insignia such as Smokey Bear, etc. (but other federal laws may prohibit the use of these things; see 18 U.S.C. ch. 33)

federal government publications (with some exceptions)

fonts

forms

functional aspects of a design

functional movements (for example, walking is not copyrightable as choreography)

geometric shapes (unless arranged in a creative way)

ideas

improvisation (unrecorded)

information

insights

instructional manuals

inventions

jokes and gags

judicial decisions

laws or other edicts issued by a governmental entity (but United Nations and O.A.S. edicts may be protected by copyright)

lists of ingredients or contents

live broadcast or performance that is not recorded

medical imaging used as such (X-rays, ultrasounds, MRI images, etc.)

methods

names, whether real or fictional

nonliteral components of a computer program

numbers

owner's manuals

page numbering

plot of a story

process or procedure

public domain material

published in the U.S. before March 1, 1989 without a copyright notice (subject to some exceptions)

recipe ingredients

road designs

scene or subject depicted in a photograph

scènes à faire

sequence

short phrases

slogans

social dances that are commonly performed (e.g., square dance, line dance)

sound recording made before February 15, 1972 (but may be protected by state law)

stage directions

standard architectural features and configurations
stock scenes
structure
symbols, icons or designs that are well known
systems
themes
theories
titles
typeface designs
unrecorded performances
useful items (but nonfunctional elements may be protected by copyright)
user interface
utilitarian aspects of works
White Pages directory
word (i.e., no one can own a copyright in a single word)
Yoga positions.

APPENDIX II

Dates of entry into the public domain

Unpublished works		
Type of work	Copyright term	Public domain as of 1/1/2017
Author's work	Author 's life + 70 years	Authors who died before 1947
Author's work, date of death unknown	120 years from date of creation	Works created before 1897
Anonymous & pseudonymous works	120 years from date of creation	Works created before 1897
Works made for hire	120 years from date of creation	Works created before 1897

Published works		
Date of publication	Copyright term	Works in the public domain as of 1/1/2017
Before 1923	None (expired)	All.
1923-1977--pub'd w/o notice	None (lapsed)	All.
1978 to 2/28/1989 – pub'd w/o notice; not registered w/i 5 years of publication	None (lapsed)	All.
1978 to 2/28/1989 – pub'd w/o notice; registered w/i 5 yrs of publication	Life of author + 70 years	Authors who died before 1947
1978 to 2/28/1989 – work-for-hire published w/o notice; registered w/i 5 yrs of publication	earlier of 95 years after publication or 120 years after creation	Created before 1897
1923 to 1963 – published w/notice; not renewed	28 years	All.
1923 to 1963 – published with notice and renewed	95 years after publication	None until 2019
1964 to 1967 – published with notice	95 years after publication	None until 2060
1978 to 2/28/1989 – created after 1977 and published with notice	Life of author + 70 years	None until 70 years after author dies
1978 to 2/28/1989 – work-for-hire created after 1977 and published with notice	earlier of 95 years after publication or 120 years after creation	None until 2074.
1978 to 2/28/1989 – created before 1978 and published with notice	Later of: Life of author + 70 years, or December 31, 2047	None, until 2048.
March 1, 1989 to 2002 – created after 1977	Life of author + 70 years	None, until 70 years after author dies.
March 1, 1989 to 2002 – work-for-hire created after 1977	earlier of 95 years after publication or 120 years after creation	None, until 2085.
March 1, 1989 to 2002 – created before 1978	Later of 12/31/2047, or author's life + 70 yrs	None, until 2048.

After 2002	Life of author + 70 yrs	None, until 70 years after author dies.
After 2002 – work made for hire	Earlier of 95 years after publication or 120 years after creation	All that were created before 1897

Foreign Publications
(Note: Works published in the U.S. simultaneously or within 30 days of the foreign publication are not "foreign publications" for purposes of this chart.)

Date of publication	Copyright term	Works in the public domain as of 1/1/2017
Before 1923	None (expired)	All.
1923 to 1977—published in U.S. w/o notice &/or not timely renewed; in the public domain in the foreign country	None	All.
1923 to 1977 – published in the U.S. with notice, and with renewals	95 years after publication	None.
1923 to 1977 – published abroad w/o notice &/or renewal; not published in U.S.; not in the public domain in its home country as of 1/1/1996	95 years after publication	None.
1923 to 1977 - published in the US more than 30 days after publication abroad, w/o notice and/or w/o renewal; not in the public domain in its home country as of 1/1/1996	95 years after publication	None.
1923 to 1977 – published in the U.S. less than 30 days after publication abroad	(Treat as an American publication)	(Treat as an American publication)
1978 to 2/28/1989 - published w/o notice; in the public domain in its source country as of 1/1/1996	None (lapsed)	All.
1978 to 2/28/1989 - published w/o notice in a Berne Convention country & not in the public domain in its source country as of 1/1/1996	Life of author + 70 years	None.

1978 to 2/28/1989– work--for-hire published w/o notice in Berne Convention country; not in the public domain in its source country as of 1/1/1996	95 years after publication	None.
1978 to 2/28/1989 - published with notice by a non-US citizen in a U.C.C. country	Author's life + 70 years	None.
1978 to 2/28/1989 – work-for-hire published with notice by a non-US citizen in a U.C.C. country	95 years after publication	None.
On or after 3/1/1989 – published in a Berne Convention country	Author's life + 70 years	None.
On or after 3/1/1989 – work-for-hire published in a Berne Convention country	95 years after publication	None.
On or after 3/1/1989 – published in a country w/o copyright treaty with U.S.	None.	All.
1/1/1909 to 12/31/1977 – published in non-English language; not republished w/notice; & published exclusively in Alaska, Arizona, California, Hawaii, Idaho, Montana, Nevada, Oregon, Washington, Guam, or the Northern Mariana Islands	(Treat as an unpublished work until the date of the first U.S.-law-compliant publication)	(Treat as an unpublished work until the date of first legally-compliant U.S. publication)
Before 5/27/1973 - published in Turkmenistan or Uzbekistan by a citizen thereof	None.	All.
After 5/26/1973 – published in Turkmenistan or Uzbekistan by a citizen thereof	May be protected under the U.C.C.	May be protected under the U.C.C.
Created by a resident of & published in Afghanistan, Eritrea, Ethiopia, Iran, Iraq or San Marino	None.	All.

Copyrights once owned or administered by the Alien Property Custodian, and if restored, would be owned by a government, as of 1/1/1996 (or the date of the country's membership in the Berne Convention or the WTO, whichever is earlier, if the country is Andorra, Angola, Armenia, Bhutan, Cambodia, Comoros, Jordan, Democratic People's Republic of Korea, Laos, Malaysia, Micronesia, Montenegro, Nepal, Oman, Papua New Guinea, Qatar, Samoa, Saudi Arabia, Solomon Islands, Sudan, Syria, Tajikistan, Tonga, United Arab Emirates, Uzbekistan, Vanuatu, Vietnam, or Yemen.)	None.	All.

Sound Recordings (Note: the copyright in the musical or literary work performed on it may have a different term)		
Date of Fixation or Publication	**Copyright term**	**Works in the public domain as of 1/1/2017**
Before February 15, 1972 - unpublished	State protection only	State protection ends 2067
After February 14, 1972 - unpublished	Life of author + 70 years	None until 2067.
After February 14, 1972 – unpublished work-for-hire, or anonymous or pseudonymous	120 years from date of fixation.	None until 2067.
Fixed before February 15, 1972 – published in the U.S.	State protection only	State protection ends 2067
2/15/1972 to 12/31/1977 published w/o notice in US	None (lapsed)	All.
2/15/1972 to 12/31/1977 published with notice in US	Later of 95 years after publication or 2068	None until 2068

1978 to 2/28/1989- published in U.S. w/o notice & w/o subsequent registration	None (lapsed)	All.
1978 to 2/28/1989- published in US with notice	Later of 2049 or life of author + 70 years	None until 2050.
1978 to 2/28/1989 – work-for-hire published in the U.S. with notice	Earlier of 120 yrs after creation or 95 yrs after publ'n, but after 2049	None until 2050.
On or after March 1, 1989, in the U.S.	Later of 2049 or Life of author + 70 years	None until 2050.
On or after March 1, 1989 – work made for hire, in the U.S.	Earlier of 120 yrs after creation or 95 yrs after publ'n, but after 2049	None until 2050.
Before 1923 - in a foreign country	State protection only	State protection ends 2067.
1923 to 2/28/1989 – in a foreign country -- in public domain in its home country as of 1/1/1996, or published in U.S. w/i 30 days of foreign publication	State protection only	State protection ends 2067.
1923 to 2/14/1972 – in a foreign country, not in public domain in home country as of 1/1/1996; at least one author was not US citizen or was living abroad; not published in U.S. w/i 30 days of foreign publication	Enters public domain on February 15, 2067	2067
2/16/1972 to 12/31/1977 – in a foreign country; not in the public domain in home country as of 1/1/1996; at least one author was not a U.S. citizen or was living abroad; no U.S. publication w/i 30 days of foreign publication	Later of 95 years after publication or 2068	None until 2068.

1978 to 2/28/1989 – in a foreign country, not in the public domain in home country as of 1/1/1996; at least one author not a U.S. citizen or was living abroad; not published in U.S. w/i 30 days of foreign pub.	Life of author + 70 years	None.
1978 to 2/28/1989– in a foreign country, work-for-hire; not in the public domain in home country as of 1/1/1996; at least one author was not U.S. citizen or was living abroad, not published in U.S. w/i 30 days of the foreign publication	Earlier of 95 years from publication or 120 years from creation	None.
On or after March 1, 1989 – in a foreign country	Life of author + 70 years	None.
On or after March 1, 1989 – in a foreign country, work made for hire	Earlier of 95 years from publication or 120 years from creation	None.
Created by a resident & published in Afghanistan, Eritrea, Ethiopia, Iraq, Iran, or San Marino	None.	All.
Works fixed in tangible form before 1996, published in a foreign country, copyright was once owned or administered by the Alien Property Custodian, and if restored, would be owned by a government, as of 1/1/1996 (or the date of the country's membership in the Berne Convention or the WTO, whichever is earlier, if the country is Andorra, Angola,	None.	All.

Armenia, Bhutan, Cambodia, Comoros, Jordan, Democratic People's Republic of Korea, Laos, Malaysia, Micronesia, Montenegro, Nepal, Oman, Papua New Guinea, Qatar, Samoa, Saudi Arabia, Solomon Islands, Sudan, Syria, Tajikistan, Tonga, United Arab Emirates, Uzbekistan, Vanuatu, Vietnam, or Yemen.)		

Architectural Works		
Date of Design	**Date of construction**	**Duration of copyright**
Before December 1, 1990	Constructed or published before December 1, 1990	Not protected. (Blueprints might be protected as drawings)
Before December 1, 1990	Not published before 12/1/1990; building not completed as of 12/31/2002	Not protected. (Blueprints might be protected as drawings).
Before December 1, 1990	Not published before 12/1/1990; building completed between 12/1/1990 and 12/31/2002	Life of author + 70 years
Before December 1, 1990, work made for hire	Not published before 12/1/1990; building completed between 12/1/1990 and 12/31/2002	Earlier of 95 years from publication or 120 years from creation
After November 30, 1990	Anytime	Life of author + 70 years
After November 30, 1990, work made for hire	Anytime	Earlier of 95 years from publication or 120 years from creation

APPENDIX III

Music Licenses & Where to Get Them

Use:	Licenses Needed From:	
	Music Publisher (musical work)	**Record Company (sound recording)**
Noninteractive streaming of a recording artist	Performance	Performance
Noninteractive streaming of cover version	Performance	---
Interactive streaming of a recording artist	Mechanical Performance	Master Use Performance
Interactive streaming of cover version	Mechanical Performance	---
Downloads of recording artists	Mechanical	Master Use
Downloads of cover version	Mechanical	---
Ringtone; limited downloads	Mechanical	Master Use
Music videos or website background music	Mechanical Synchronization Performance	Master Use Synchronization Performance
Podcasting	Mechanical Performance? Synchronization?	Master Use Performance? Synchronization?
Display lyrics, sheet music or tablature	Folio	---

	How to get it	
Kind of license:	Music Publisher (musical work)	Record Company (sound recording)
Performance by means of noninteractive streaming of a sound recording of a recording artist	ASCAP, BMI, SESAC, or negotiation	SoundExchange; statutory license; or negotiation
Performance other than noninteractive streaming of a sound recording of a recording artist	ASCAP, BMI, SESAC, or negotiation	Negotiation
Mechanical license for use in music video or as website background music	Negotiation	N/A
Mechanical license for uses other than music video or website background music	Harry Fox Agency; compulsory license; or negotiation	N/A
Master use	N/A	Negotiation
Synchronization	Negotiation	Negotiation
Folio	Negotiation	N/A

APPENDIX IV

Interim Designation of Agent to Receive Notification of Claimed Infringement

Full Legal Name of Service Provider:

_____

Alternative Name(s) of Service Provider (including all number under which the service provider is doing business):

_____

Address of Service Provider:

_____

Name of Agent Designated to Receive Notification of Claimed Infringement:

_____

Full Address of Designated Agent to which Notification Should be Sent (a P.O Box or similar designation is not acceptable except where it is the only address that can be used in the geographic location):

_____

Telephone Number of Designated Agent: _____

Facsimile Number of Designated Agent: _____

Email Address of Designated Agent: _____

Signature of Officer or Representation of the Designating Service Provider:

_____ **Date** _____

Typed or Printed Name and Title:

_____

Note: This Interim Designation Must be Accompanied by a Filing Fee*Made Payable to the Register of Copyrights.
*Note: Current and adjusted fees are available on the Copyright website at www.copyright.gov/docs/fees.html
Mail to: U.S. Copyright Office, Designated Agents, P.O. Box 71537, Washington, DC 20024-1537

Sample Model Release

Here is a sample model release form. The reader is cautioned, however, that no single form is suitable for every situation in which a permission to publish a person's likeness may be needed. You should consult with an attorney for advice and assistance with drafting a form that will best protect your interests and suit your needs. Also note that a separate form, with different language, is needed to get permission from the copyright owner to use a photograph that is protected by copyright.

[Language appearing in brackets is for your information and guidance only. It should be removed before actually using the form.]

Model Release

For valuable consideration received, I hereby grant to [insert your name or the name of your company here] the absolute and irrevocable right and unrestricted permission concerning any photographs that he/she has taken or may take of me or in which I may be included, to use, reuse, publish, and republish the photographs in whole or in part, individually or in connection with other material, in any and all media now or hereafter known, including the Internet and any digital storage medium, and for any purpose whatsoever, specifically including [list here any specific uses you want to make of the photograph(s), such as advertising, illustration, promotion, art, commentary] without restriction as to alteration; and to use my name in connection with any use if he/she chooses to do so. I hereby release and discharge [your name or the name of your company] from any and all claims and demands that may arise out of or in connection with the use of the photograph(s), including without limitation any and all claims for defamation, misappropriation of name or likeness, invasion of privacy, or violation of any right of publicity or privacy. I further release and discharge [your name or name of your company] from any and all liability that may arise by virtue of any modification, blurring, distortion, alteration, optical illusion, or use in composite form, whether intentional or otherwise, of the photograph(s). This authorization and release shall also inure to the benefit of the heirs, legal representatives, assignees and licensees of [your name or the name of your company.] I am a legally competent adult and have the right to contract in my own name. I have read this document and fully understand its contents. This release shall be binding upon me and my heirs, legal representatives, and assigns.

Dated: _____

Signature of Model:

_____

Printed Name of Model:

_____

Address:

_____

_____

Other contact information [telephone number; email address]:

_____

Date of birth: _____

[If you want to use a person's likeness in a way that someone might consider controversial, offensive or embarrassing, or that might create a misimpression, then you should include in the release a specific description of how the photograph will be used, and a statement that the model understands that the photograph will be used that way and, if applicable, that it may create that impression, and consents anyway.]

APPENDIX VI

Notice of Intention to Obtain a Compulsory License for Making & Distributing Phonorecords

[Note: Write "Not Applicable" if a question does not apply.]

1. Full legal name of the person or entity intending to obtain the compulsory license:

_____

Fictitious or assumed names used when conducting the business of making and distributing phonorecords. If none, so indicate.

_____

2. Full street address and telephone number. [Note: A post office box address is not acceptable unless it is the only address that can be used in that geographic location]:

_____

_____

3. Email address, if any: _____

4. Kind of business organization seeking the compulsory license (corporation, partnership, limited liability company, sole proprietor, etc.)

_____

a. Is this a corporation registered with the SEC? ___Yes ___No
b. If this is a corporation that is not registered with the SEC, then list the names of all officers and all owners of 25% or more of securities

_____

c. In all other cases, list the names of all owners of 25% or more interests

_____

5. Name and title of the chief executive officer, managing partner, sole proprietor, or other similar person with equivalent managerial responsibility (if this is a business that is seeking the license):

_____

6. If the entity seeking the license is a holding company, trust or other entity that is not expected to be actively engaged in the business of making and distributing copies under the license, then all of the above information must be provided with respect to the business entity that is expected to be actively engaged in such business.

_____

_____

_____

7. Fiscal year, which may be a calendar year: _____

8. With respect to the musical work you seek to license, state:
Title of the musical work:

_____

Name of its author(s), if known:

_____

Name of copyright owner(s), if known:

_____

The kind of phonorecords for which the license is sought (e.g., single disk, long-playing disk, cassette tape, cartridge, reel-to-reel tape, digital phonorecord delivery, or a combination):

_____

Expected date of initial distribution: _____
Name of the principal recording artist or group engaged or expected to be engaged to perform the music on a recording under the license:

_____

Catalog number(s) and label name(s) on phonorecords made or to be made under the compulsory license:

_____

If a recording and/or copies of a recording have already been made, then state the date(s) of such manufacture: _____

9. Copyright Office records have been searched for the name and address of the copyright owner, and the results of that search are as follows:

_____

_____

[If Copyright Office records do not identify the copyright owner(s), or do not include an address at which notice can be served, then state that with respect to the nondramatic musical work named in the Notice of Intention, the registration records or other public records of the Copyright Office have been searched and found not to identify the name and address of the copyright owner of the work.]

Signature: _____   Date: _____
  [Printed Name]

[If signed by an agent, include a statement that the agent is authorized to execute the Notice of Intention on behalf of the person or entity intending to obtain the compulsory license. If the notice is filed with the Copyright Office electronically, then rather than signing the Notice, the person or entity, or an authorized agent, shall attest that he or she has the appropriate authority of the licensee, including any related entities listed, if applicable, to submit the electronically filed Notice on behalf of the licensee.]

APPENDIX VII

Monthly Statement of Account under Compulsory License for Making & Distributing Phonorecords

Period of time covered by the statement: _____

Full legal name of licensee:

_____

Fictitious names, if any (band name, stage name, pseudonym, etc.).

_____

Full street address and telephone number. [Note: A post office box address is not acceptable unless it is the only address that can be used in that geographic location]:

_____

_____

Names of every person who owns at least a 25% interest in the distribution of the song:

_____

_____

Song title (prepare a separate statement for each song)

_____

Name of the author(s) of the song: _____

Name of the performer or band performing the cover version:

_____

Length of your recording of the song (in minutes and seconds);

_____

Catalog number(s) and label name(s) used in the phonorecords:

_____

Types of phonorecords and digital phonorecord deliveries (single disk, long-playing disk, phonorecord (e.g., digital download), cassette, reel-to-reel tape):

_____

Number of phonorecords and digital phonorecord deliveries made:

_____

Number of digital phonorecord deliveries that were not successfully delivered due to a failed transmission: _____

Number of digital phonorecord deliveries that were retransmitted in order to complete or replace a failed delivery: _____

Total royalty payable (total number of digital phonorecord deliveries made, excluding failed deliveries, multiplied by the statutory royalty rate:

_____

I certify that I have examined this Monthly Statement of Account and that all statements of fact contained herein are true, complete, and correct to the best of my knowledge, information, and belief, and are made in good faith"

Signature: _____ Date: _____
                  [Printed Name]

APPENDIX VIII

Annual Statement of Account under Compulsory License for Making & Distributing Phonorecords

Period of time covered by the statement [fiscal year, which may be a calendar year]:

_____

Full legal name of licensee:

_____

Fictitious names, if any (band name, stage name, pseudonym, etc.).

_____

Compulsory licensee's business address. [Note: A post office box address is not acceptable unless it is the only address that can be used in that geographic location]:

_____

_____

Nature of the business organization used by the compulsory licensee in connection with the making and distribution of phonorecords (for example, a corporation, a partnership, a limited liability company, or an individual proprietorship):

_____

Is the compulsory licensee a corporation registered with the SEC?
_____Yes   _____No
Is the compulsory licensee a corporation that is not registered with the SEC?
_____Yes   _____No
If the compulsory licensee is not a corporation, provide the names of each entity or individual owning an interest of 25% or more in the entity exercising the compulsory license:

_____

Song title (prepare a separate statement for each song):

_____

Name of the author(s) of the song:

_____

Length of your recording of the song (in minutes and seconds):

_____

Total royalty payable (total number of digital phonorecord deliveries made, excluding failed deliveries, multiplied by the statutory royalty rate):

_____

Total sum paid under the Monthly Statements of Account: _____
Royalty payment calculation:

_____

_____

Signature: _____ Date: _____
                    [Printed Name]

Certification by a certified public accountant:

_____

APPENDIX IX

Request for Permission to Use Copyrighted Material

Dear [Address to the copyright owner. If you cannot deter-mine whether the material is owned by the author or the publisher, then send to both and ask for a response from that the authorized holder of the copyright]:

[Briefly describe site and your interest in the material you want to copy.]

I request permission to include the excerpt(s) outlined below in my website [blog], [Name and url of your website/blog.] Because I would like to keep it posted there without bothering you with successive requests for permission every time the website is updated, I also ask permission to include it/them in any future editions, derivative or subsidiary works of the website/blog. [If desired, you may also include a request for permission to use the work in other ways, too, such as "in any language" or "in the advertisement and promotion" of your website or blog. Be as specific as possible.]

I am looking forward to receiving your permission and giving your material greater exposure. Let me know the acknowledgement you wish to be given.

Thank you.

Sincerely,
[Signature]
[Printed name]

MATERIAL TO BE REPRINTED:
Title: _____
Author: _____
Copyright date & holder: _____
Page ____ to page ____, the portion beginning "[first words of excerpt]..." and ending "... [last words of excerpt."
Acknowledgment to read as follows: _____

APPENDIX X

Resources

Advocacy and Information

Berkman Center for Internet and Society
cyber.law.harvard.edu

Educause
www.educause.edu

Electronic Frontier Foundation
www.eff.org

First Amendment Center
http://www.newseuminstitute.org/first-amendment-center/

Internet Society
www.internetsociety.org

Tech Law Forum
https://santaclaralawtechlawforum.wordpress.com/

Stanford Center for Internet and Society
http://cyberlaw.stanford.edu

Legal Research

Fair Use Index
www.copyright.gov/fair-use/

Justia.com
www.justia.com

Leagle, Inc.
www.leagle.com

Lexis-Nexis
http://www.lexisnexis.com/en-us/home.page

Westlaw
www.thomsonreuters.com

World Intellectual Property Organization (WIPO)
http://www.wipo.int/amc/en/domains/search/index.html

World Legal Information Institute
www.worldlii.org

Copyright

Library of Congress
www.loc.gov

U.S. Copyright Office
101 Independence Ave. S.E.
Washington, D.C. 20559-6000
(202) 707-3000
(877) 476-0778 (toll-free)
www.copyright.gov

Records Research and Certification Service
P.O. Box 70400
Washington D.C. 20559-0400
copysearch@loc.gov
(202) 707-6787

Compendium of U.S. Copyright Practices
www.copyright.gov/comp3/

World Intellectual Property Organization
http://www.wipo.int

Public domain repositories

Creative Commons
www.creativecommons.org

Librivox (audiobooks)
http://librivox.org

Prelinger Archives (motion pictures)
https://archive.org/detail/prelinger

Project Gutenberg (books)
www.gutenberg.org/wiki/Main_Page

Smithsonian Institution Public Domain Images
https://www.flickr.com/photos/smithsonian

Wikimedia Commons
https://commons.wikimedia.org

Trademarks and domain names

Internet Corporation for Assigned Names and Numbers
www.icann.org

Trademark ID Manual (searchable)
https://tmidm.uspto.gov/id-master-list-public.html

Trademark Manual of Examining Procedure
https://tmep.uspto.gov/RDMS/TMEP/current

U.S. Patent and Trademark Office (USPTO)
www.uspto.gov

World Intellectual Property Organization
http://www.wipo.int

Patents

Google Patent Search
www.google.com/patents

U.S. Patent and Trademark Office (USPTO)
www.uspto.gov

World Intellectual Property Organization
http://www.wipo.int

Trade Secrets

National Conference of Commissioners on Uniform State Laws
www.nccusl.org

Privacy

Electronic Privacy Information Center
www.epic.org

International Association of Privacy Professionals
www.privacyassociation.org

Privacy Rights Clearinghouse
www.privacyrights.org

U.S. Federal Trade Commission (FTC)
www.ftc.gov

U.S. Department of Health and Human Services
www.hhs.gov

Computer Crimes

Computer World
www.computerworld.com

Federal Bureau of Investigation (FBI)
www.fbi.gov

Internet Crime Complaint Center
www.ic3.gov

National Cyber Security Alliance
www.staysafeoknline.org

U.S. Federal Trade Commission (FTC)
www.ftc.gov

U.S. Department of Justice
Computer Crime & Intellectual Property Section
https://www.justice.gov/criminal-ccips

Licensing

American Society for Composers, Authors and Publishers (ASCAP)
www.ascap.com
Association of University Technology Managers
www.autm.net

Broadcast Music Incorporated (BMI)
www.bmi.com

Copyright Clearance Center
http://www.copyright.com/
(978) 646-2600
or (855) 239-3415
info@copyright.com

Creative Commons
http://search.creativecommons.org

Flickr
www.flickr.com/creativecommons/

Google Image Search
www.google.com/advanced_image_search

Harry Fox Agency
www.harryfox.com

MIT Technology Licensing Office
http://tlo.mit.edu/

Open Source Initiative
www.opensource.org/docs/osd

Society of European Stage Authors and Composers (SESAC)
www.sesac.com

SoundExchange
http://www.soundexchange.com/

Technology Transfer Center
(e-newsletters)
http://techtransfercentral.com/signup/

WikiMedia Commons
http://commons.wikimedia.org

SELECTED BIBLIOGRAPHY

Bargfrede, Allen and Cecily Mak. *Music Law in the Digital Age*. Berklee Press, 2009.

Bettinger, Torsten, ed. *Domain Name Law and Practice, An International Handbook*. Oxford University Press, 2005.

Boyle, J. Shamans. *Software and Spleens:: Law and the Construction of the Information Society*. Harvard University Press, 1996.

Boyle, James. *The Public Domain: Enclosing the Commons of the Mind*. Yale University Press, 2008.

Browning, John G. *The Lawyers Guide to Social Networking: Understanding Social Media's Impact on the Law*. Aspatore, 2010.

Cavazos, E. A. and Morin G. *Cyberspace and the Law: Your Rights and Duties in the On-line World* MIT Press, 1994.

Cairns, R. "Opportunities, Risks and Some Intellectual Property Constraints Surrounding the provision and Use of On-line Services" (1996) 4 International Journal of Law and Information Technology 19.

Reed, C. & Walden I. "Legal Problems of Electronic Bulletin Board Operators" " (1994) 2 International Journal of Law and Information Technology 287.

Citron, Danielle K. *Hate Crimes in Cyberspace*. Harvard University Press, 2014.

Collins, Matthew. *The Law of Defamation and the Internet, 3rd Edition*. Oxford University Press, 2010.

Darrell, Keith B. *Issues in Internet Law: Society, Technology and the Law, 9th Edition*. Amber Book Company, 2014.

Darrow, Jonathan J. and Gerald R. Ferrera. "Social Networking Websites and the Digital Millennium Copyright Act: A Safe Harbor from Copyright Infringement Liability or the Perfect Storm?" *Northwestern Journal of Technology & Intellectual Property*, 2007, p. 1.

Dolan, William F. and Marc D. Levi. "Striking a Balance Between Linking and Infringing." *National Law Journal*, October 16, 2000, p. C6.

Eaglesham, Jean. "How Far Does Copyright Extend in Cyberspace?" *Financial Times (London)*, January 15, 2001, p. 18.

Edwards, Lilian and Charlotte Waelde, editors. *Law and the Internet, 3rd Edition*. Hart Publishing, 2010.

Fellmeth, Aaron Xavier. "Control Without Interest: State Law of Assignment, Federal Preemption, and the Intellectual Property License." *Virginia Journal of Law and Technology*, 2001, pp. 8-27.

Ferrera. Gerald R., et al. *Cyberlaw: Text and Cases, 3rd Edition.* South-Western, Cengage Learning, 2012.

Ficsor, M. *The Law of Copyright and the Internet: The 1996 WIPO Treaties, Their Interpretation and Implementation.* Oxford University Press, 2002.

Fried, Joseph P. "Internet Complaints Are Climbing." *New York Times*, November 2, 2000, p. B8.

Gant, Scott. *We're All Journalists Now: The Transformation of the Press and Reshaping of the Law in the Internet Age.* Free Press, 2007.

Goldberg, David, Gavin Sutter and Ian Walden. *Media Law and Practice.* Oxford University Press, 2009.

Grimmelmann, James. *Internet Law: Cases and Problems.* Semaphore, 2016.

Grossman, Mark. "Staying Out of Trouble Online." *Miami Herald*, Techlaw, October 30, 2000.

_____. "Legal Tips for Website Owners." *Miami Herald*, Techlaw, February 12, 2001.

Haemmerli, Alice. "Why Doctrine Matters: Patent and Copyright Licensing and the Meaning of Ownership in Federal Context." *Columbia Journal of Law and the Arts*, 2006, p. 1.

Hayes, Arthur S. *Mass Media Law: The Printing Press to the Internet.* Peter Lang Publishing, 2013.

Hill, Joshua B. and Nancy E. Marion. *Introduction to cybercrime: computer crimes, laws, and policing in the 21st century* Praeger, 2016.

Kang, Peter H. and Jia Ann Yang. Case Note, "Doctrine of Indivisibility Revived?" *Santa Clara Computer and High Tech Law* Journal, 2002, pp. 365-73.

Kehoe, Louise. "Trespass Ruling Adds Tangles to the Web." *Financial Times* (London), May 31, 2000, p. 17.

Kohn, Al and Bob Kohn. *Kohn on Music Licensing, 2d Edition.* Aspen Law & Business, 2005.

Legal Guide for Bloggers. Electronic Frontier Foundation, www.eff.org/issues/bloggers/legal. Accessed September 30, 2016.

Lessig, Lawrence. *Code and Other Laws of Cyberspace, Version 2.0, 2nd Edition.* Basic Books, 2006.

_____. Free Culture: *The Nature and Future of Creativity.* Penguin, 2004.

MacKinnon, Rebecca. *Consent of the Networked: The Worldwide Struggle for Internet Freedom.* Basic Books, 2012.

McCarthy, J. Thomas. *McCarthy on Trademarks and Unfair Competition.* West, 2002.

McLeod, Kembrew and Peter DiCola. *Creative License: The Law and Culture of Digital Sampling*. Duke University Press, 2011.

Monseau, Susanna. "Balancing Trademark Rights on the Internet: The Case of Domain Name Disputes." *Journal of Legal Studies in Business*, Winter 2000, pp. 91-110.

Newman, Christopher M. "An Exclusive License Is Not an Assignment: Disentangling Divisibility and Transferability of Ownership in Copyright." *Louisiana Law Review*, 2013, pp. 59-115.

Nimmer, Melville D and David Nimmer. *Nimmer on Copyright, rev. ed.* Matthew Bender, 2013.

Nunziato, Dawn C. *Virtual Freedom: Net Neutrality and Free Speech in the Internet Age*. Stanford Law Books, 2009.

Packard, Ashley. *Digital Media Law*. Wiley-Blackwell, 2010.

Patry, William. *Patry on Copyright*. Westlaw, 2013.

Pearson, Mark. *Blogging & Tweeting Without Getting Sued*. Allen & Unwin, 2012.

Pearson, Mark and Mark Polden. *The Journalist's Guide to Media Law, 4th Edition*. Allen & Unwin, 2011.

Pember, Don R. and Clay Calvert. *Mass Media Law, 17th Edition*. McGraw-Hill, 2011.

Radin, Margaret, John A. Rothchild and Gregory M Silverman. *Intellectual Property and the Internet*. Foundation Press, 2004.

Reich, Pauline C., editor. *Cybercrime and Security*. Oceana, 1998.

Risch, Michael. "Why Do We Have Trade Secrets?" *Marquette Intellectual Property Law Review*, 2007, p. 1.

Rustad, Michael L. *Internet Law in a Nutshell*. West, 2009.

————. *Software licensing, cloud computing agreements, open source, and internet terms of use: a practical approach to information age contracts in a global setting*. LexisNexis, 2016.

Schechter, Roger E. and John R. Thomas. *Intellectual Property: The Law of Copyrights, Patents and Trademarks*. West Group, 2003.

Smartt, Ursula. *Media and Entertainment Law*. Routledge, 2011.

Solove, Daniel J. *The Future of Reputation: Gossip, Rumor and Privacy on the Internet*. Yale University Press, 2007.

Sparrow, Andrew P. *The Law of Virtual Worlds and Internet Social Networks*. Gower, 2010.

Spinello, Richard. *Cyberethics: Morality and Law in Cyberspace, 6th Edition*. Jones & Bartlett Learning, 2016.

Stankova, Desislava. *E-Law Guide for Bloggers (Part One): How to Use Other People's Creative Works*. http://www.chicoverdose.com/e-law-guide-for-bloggers-how-to-use-other-peoples-creative-works/, April 9, 2015.

Street, F. Lawrence and Mark P. Grant. *Law of the Internet*. Lexis, 2003.

Tham, Yang-Ming. "Honest to Blog: Balancing the Interests of Public Figures and Anonymous Bloggers in Defamation Lawsuits." *Villanova Sports & Entertainment Law Journal*, 2010, p. 229.

Thurmon, Mark A. "New Developments in Trademark Law." *Wake Forest Intellectual Property Law Journal*, 2009, p. 1.

Towers-Romero, Sandi. *Media and Entertainment Law*. Delmar Cengage Learning, 2009.

U.S. Copyright Office. *Compendium of U.S. Copyright Office Practices, 3rd Edition*. http://www.copyright.gov/comp3/docs/compendium.pdf, 2014.

Vogele, Collette et al. *Podcasting Legal Guide: Rules for the Revolution*. http://mirrors.creativecommons.org/Podcasting_Legal_Guide.pdf, 2006.

Wang, Faye F. *Internet Jurisdiction and Choice of Law: Legal Practices in the EU, US and China*. Cambridge University Press, 2010.

INDEX

ABOUT THE AUTHOR

Tom James is an attorney in private practice with over 20 years of experience, ranging from vindicating First Amendment rights in appellate courts to advising and representing web hosting services, small businesses, nonprofits and individuals. The principal focus of his practice is trademark and copyright law.

He is a magna cum laude graduate of the University of California at Berkeley and Southwestern University, and a past recipient of the American Jurisprudence Award for legal scholarship. A long-time member of the Minnesota bar association, he is licensed to practice before the United States Trademark Trials and Appeals Board, the Federal Circuit Court of Appeals, the Eighth Circuit Court of Appeals, and the state and federal courts of Minnesota.

Mr. James has published articles in a variety of bar journals, consumer periodicals, and online publications.

When not busy practicing law or writing, he likes to hike, run marathons, and travel. You can contact him at tom@tomjameslaw.com.

If you found this book useful, please leave a review on Amazon.com.